Progress to Proficiency
Student's Book

Progress to Proficiency

Student's Book

Leo Jones

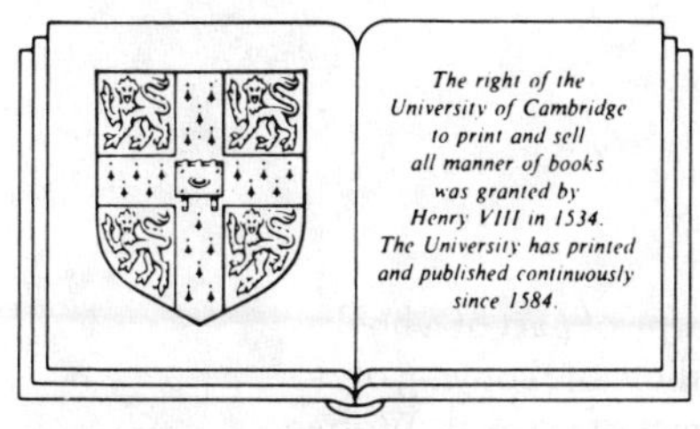
The right of the
University of Cambridge
to print and sell
all manner of books
was granted by
Henry VIII in 1534.
The University has printed
and published continuously
since 1584.

Cambridge University Press
Cambridge
New York Port Chester
Melbourne Sydney

Published by the Press Syndicate of the University of Cambridge
The Pitt Building, Trumpington Street, Cambridge CB2 1RP
40 West 20th Street, New York, NY 10011, USA
10 Stamford Road, Oakleigh, Melbourne 3166, Australia

First published 1986
Sixth printing 1990

Printed in Great Britain
at The Bath Press, Avon

ISBN 0 521 31342 2 Student's Book
ISBN 0 521 31343 0 Teacher's Book
ISBN 0 521 30850 X Set of 2 cassettes

WV

Contents

Thanks

My special thanks to Christine Cairns and Alison Silver for all their hard work, friendly encouragement and editorial expertise.

Thanks also to all the teachers and students at the following schools and institutes who used the pilot edition of this book and made so many helpful comments and suggestions: The Bell School in Cambridge, the British Council Institute in Barcelona, The British School in Florence, the College of Arts and Technology in Newcastle upon Tyne, the Eurocentre in Cambridge, Godmer House in Oxford, the Hampstead Garden Suburb Institute in London, Inlingua Brighton & Hove, International House in Arezzo, Klubschule Migros in St Gallen, The Moraitis School in Athens, the Moustakis School of English in Athens, the Newnham Language Centre in Cambridge, VHS Aachen, VHS Heidelberg, VHS Karlsruhe, Wimbledon School of English in London and Ray Thomson in Switzerland. Without their help and reassurance this book could not have taken shape.

Introduction

This book is for students preparing for the University of Cambridge Certificate of Proficiency in English examination. Its 18 units, each based on a different topic, will help you to develop and improve your English up to the standard required in the Proficiency exam. The exercises are designed to help you to improve the specific language skills tested in the different papers of the exam. In addition, you will discover that these exercises are often entertaining, sometimes challenging, frequently informative and occasionally provocative or even surprising.

A Proficiency course should be: (a) enjoyable, (b) intellectually stimulating and (c) geared to the exam. These three requirements are kept in mind throughout this book. Each unit contains a variety of exercises and activities, focussing on the knowledge and the various sets of skills you require for the Proficiency exam: vocabulary, reading, use of English, listening, oral communication and composition. As you work through these exercises, you will progressively build up your proficiency in these language skills.

You will notice a gradual change in the nature and style of the exercises and activities from unit to unit. At the beginning they help you to improve your English by giving you guidance and enjoyment; towards the end you will be acquiring some of the special skills needed for the Proficiency exam, where your knowledge of English is going to be tested objectively.

Many of the exercises and activities are designed to be done in co-operation with other students, working in pairs or small groups. This is to encourage each of you to consider and then discuss all the answers to the questions. If exercises are done round the class, someone else usually answers first or someone gets the teacher to answer the difficult questions, and this tends to discourage the others from thinking for themselves. Working in pairs or small groups usually takes longer, but it really does help you learn more effectively and to remember better – and it's enjoyable too.

Although working through this book will help you to maintain your progress in English, don't forget that it is your teacher who can help you to improve the specific aspects of English that you are weakest in and guide you towards exercises that seem most valuable for you and your class. But most important of all is *you*! By asking questions, seeking advice, continuing to expand your vocabulary, reading as much English as you can, talking and listening to English whenever you can both in class and outside, you are the one who is most responsible for your own progress. To do well in the Proficiency exam you need to be confident and flexible in your use of English. And to develop confidence and flexibility needs time, practice and some hard work. Good luck!

1 Adventure

1.1 Vocabulary

A Look at this photograph.
Would you encourage a young brother or sister (or your own child) to do this?
Have you any personal experience of this kind of sport?
What kinds of adventures or dangerous sports would you avoid at all costs? Why?
What kind of a person does an adventurer or an explorer need to be?

B Work in pairs. Take a look at these words and phrases, often used when talking about adventures – do you understand them all? Which of them will fit best into each gap in the sentences on the next page?

achievement determination companionship hardships
modesty hair-raising foolhardy safe and sound tempting fate
going round in circles jeopardised lose heart

1 Some people admire the bravery of mountaineers, but I can't help feeling that many of them are simply ....
2 Going round the world in a hot-air balloon was a fantastic ....
3 The odds against their reaching the Pole were phenomenal, but they pressed on and didn't ....
4 Facing dangers and difficulties together is supposed to give the members of an expedition an amazing feeling of ....
5 Setting off on an expedition without thorough preparation and with inadequate equipment is ....
6 By taking such unnecessary risks the success of the entire expedition was ....
7 The intrepid explorer had accomplished a phenomenal feat of endurance and courage, but still he spoke about it with great ....
8 To sail single-handed across the ocean takes both skill and ....
9 They were lost alone in the desert and suffered from hunger, thirst and numerous other ....
10 They had been attacked by alligators, waded across piranha-infested rivers and had countless other .... adventures.
11 They lost their bearings in the depths of the jungle and spent days just ....
12 Everyone thought they had no chance of escaping but some weeks later they emerged from the jungle ....

C Can you supply a suitable word to complete each of the following sentences? The initial letters are given as a clue.

13 The members of an expedition have to accept the authority of their l.............................. unquestioningly.
14 The team of climbers attempted to reach the s.............................. of the mountain.
15 One of the climbers fell down a crevasse while attempting to cross the g..............................
16 The avalanche came down seconds after they had crossed the slope – they really did have a n.............................. escape.
17 The view from the peak was absolutely b..............................
18 He was the first man to cross the English Channel by h.............................. g..............................
19 The only way to get supplies to the expedition was to drop them by p..............................
20 Lost in the desert, they were hundreds of miles from the nearest o..............................
21 They paddled their canoes down a fearsome gorge, but then they came to the worst r.............................. they had yet encountered.
22 After the storm the captain discovered that two members of his crew had been swept o..............................
23 Many of the famous European explorers in Africa were either missionaries or sent to establish c..............................s.
24 I'm fascinated by other people's adventures but, being a coward myself, I'm best suited to being an a.............................. traveller.

1.2 Brazilian Adventure

Reading

CHAPTER IV

OUTLOOK UNSETTLED

THERE are, I suppose, expeditions and expeditions. I must say that during those six weeks in London it looked as if ours was not going to qualify for either category. Our official leader (hereinafter referred to as Bob) had just the right air of intrepidity. Our Organizer, on the other hand, appeared to have been miscast, in spite of his professional-looking beard. A man of great charm, he was nevertheless a little imprecise. He had once done some shooting in Brazil, and we used to gaze with respect at his photographs of unimaginable fish and the corpses (or, as it turned out later, corpse) of the jaguars he had killed. But when pressed for details of our own itinerary he could only refer us to a huge, brightly-coloured, and obsolete map of South America, on which the railway line between Rio and São Paulo had been heavily marked in ink. 'From São Paulo,' he would say, 'we shall go up-country by lorry. It is cheaper and quicker than the train.' Or, alternatively: 'The railway will take us right into the interior. It costs less than going by road, and we shall save time, too.' It was clear that Bob, for all his intrepidity, viewed our Organizer's vagueness with apprehension.

At the other end — in Brazil, that is to say — the expedition's interests were said to be in capable hands. Captain John Holman, a British resident of São Paulo whose knowledge of the interior is equalled by few Europeans, had expressed his willingness to do all in his power to assist us. On our arrival in Brazil, as you will hear, this gentleman proved a powerful, indeed an indispensable ally; but at this early stage of the expedition's history our Organizer hardly made the most of him, and Captain Holman was handicapped by the scanty information which he received with regard to our intentions. In London we were given to understand that the man who really mattered was a Major Pingle — George Lewy Pingle. (That is not his name. You can regard him as an imaginary character, if you like. He is no longer quite real to me.)

Major Pingle is an American citizen, holding — or claiming to hold — a commission in the Peruvian army. He has had an active and a varied career. According to his own story, he ran away from his home in Kentucky at the age of 15; joined a circus which was touring the Southern States: found his way across the Mexican border: worked for some time on a ranch near Monterey:

accompanied an archaeological expedition into Yucatan, where he nearly died of fever: went north to convalesce in California: joined the ground staff of an aerodrome there and became (of all things) a professional parachutist: went into partnership with a German, whose ambition it was to start an air-line in South America: and since then had travelled widely in Colombia, Peru, Chile, and Brazil. All this, of course, we found out later. All we knew, or thought we knew, in London was that Major Pingle was a man of wide experience and sterling worth who had once accompanied our Organizer on a sporting expedition in Brazil, and who was even now preparing for our arrival in Brazil — buying stores, hiring guides, and doing everything possible to facilitate our journey. A great deal, obviously, was going to depend on Major Pingle. 'This Major Pingle,' I used to tell people, 'is going to be the Key Man.'

It was difficult to visualize Major Pingle, all those miles away. The only thing we knew for certain about him was that he was not very good at answering cables. This, we were told, was because he must have gone up-country already, to get things ready. Whatever the cause, however, very imperfect liaison existed between his headquarters in São Paulo and ours in London; and when a letter did at last reach London from Brazil, our Organizer lost it. So it was impossible to find out definitely whether Major Pingle's preparations were being made in the light of our plans, or whether our plans were being made to fit his preparations, or neither, or both. It was all rather uncertain.

(from *Brazilian Adventure* by Peter Fleming)

A Work with a partner. When you've read the passage, answer the questions below. Each gap can be filled with one word or a short phrase. The first is done for you as an example.

1 There was a strong chance that the expedition would never leave London.
2 Bob, the leader, looked ....
3 'Miscast' (line 8) is a word normally used when talking about .... not explorers.
4 'A little imprecise' (line 9) is an example of ....
5 The Organiser had shot .... jaguar(s) on a previous trip to Brazil.
6 The Organiser's travel plans were not only vague but also ....
7 Bob was .... about the Organiser's vagueness.
8 Captain Holman in Brazil knew .... about the expedition's plans.
9 Major Pingle seems to be a man who ....
10 Whilst still in London, the writer was sure their most valuable contact in Brazil was ....
11 The party were told by .... that Major Pingle had gone up-country.
12 Major Pingle had been sent .... telegram(s) from London.

13 The members of the party were shown .... letter(s) from Major Pingle.
14 It was quite possible that Major Pingle was making no .... at all for the expedition.
15 Judging by what the writer tells us, the expedition is likely to be a ....

B How would you describe the *tone* of the writing?
Does it make you want to read more about the adventure? Why (not)?
If you had been leader of the expedition, what steps would you have taken to ensure that all the necessary preparations were made?
What do you think the expedition found when they actually did arrive in Brazil?

1.3 Everest in Winter *Reading*

Gales hit Everest team at 23,500 ft

from JOE TASKER on Everest

DESPITE almost continuous gales and heavy snowfalls, the eight-man British Everest Winter Expedition has managed to establish its Camp III at a height of 23,500 ft. In a cable sent last week Joe Tasker describes how the team is coping with the severe conditions:

Winter has really taken hold on Everest. We have had bad weather ever since Christmas and our Camp II proved unusable as winds threatened to tear the tents from the mountain side. One was slashed open by a gust at six o'clock one morning and John Porter only saved his hands from frostbite by holding them in a pan of hot tea.

Frostbite is never far away and we have to watch for signs of numbness in the fingers and toes and keep our faces covered or turned away from the wind. Metal objects can only be handled with gloves to prevent the flesh sticking and burning from the cold.

The Japanese expedition camped nearby has suffered badly. One team member was lost in a spell of severe weather and several others have frostbite. [The Japanese are since reported to have given up their attempt.]

During a short improvement in the weather Peter Thexton and I managed to move 1,000 ft above Camp II and dig through into a crevasse to make a snow cave. This now forms Camp III and is a secure haven against the worst weather.

From here Adrian Burgess and I managed to reach 24,000 ft on the West Shoulder, giving us our first sight of the rest of the route and magnificent views of Nuptse, Lhotse and Everest's South-West Face. The site where we plan to set up Camp IV could be seen along an easy but windswept ridge.

The secret of success seems to lie in establishing another snow cave as Camp IV at 25,000 ft.

Climbing in winter has

proved every bit as harsh as we expected and progress is agonisingly slow. However, we have been allowed an extension of our Nepalese Government climbing permit to 15 February and a short spell of good weather should allow a summit attempt.

At present John Porter and Peter Thexton are occupying Camp III, Alan Burgess and Brian Hall are at Camp I, pinned down by hurricane force winds, and the rest of us are stuck at base camp waiting for a break in the weather.

Work with a partner. After you've read the article, see if you can answer these questions – they can all be answered in one word or a short phrase.

1 Why was Camp II abandoned?
2 Who nearly got frostbite?
3 How does frostbite first manifest itself?
4 Who did get frostbite?
5 Why is the information about the Japanese expedition's withdrawal given in parenthesis?
6 Where was Camp III established?
7 Where is the proposed site of Camp IV?
8 Why can't the team stay on Everest until the spring?
9 How many men are at base camp at the time of writing?
10 What has been the worst aspect of the weather?

How would you describe the *tone* of the passage?
Does the writing make you keen to read Joe Tasker's next report? Why (not)?

1.4 Prepositions

Take a look at this description of Judith Chisholm's record-breaking round-the-world solo flight. You'll see that there are 30 numbered gaps. Fill each of them with one of these prepositions:

around around at at by during during for for for
in in in in in including into like of on on over
over through to unlike with within without without

(In cases where more than one preposition seems appropriate, choose the one you think makes best sense.)

1.5 Idioms with TAKE *Use of English*

Rewrite each of the sentences so that it still means the same, using the words on the left together with the correct form of the verb TAKE. Look at the example first.

1 The explorers disregarded the mosquitoes, flies and snakes.
NOTICE The explorers . . . took no notice of the mosquitoes, flies and snakes.

2 First one of the party steered the boat, then the other steered it.
TURNS The members of the party . . .

3 They had to dismantle their vehicles to get them across the gorge.
PIECES They had to . . .

4 A sudden thunderstorm surprised the climbers and they got very wet.
SURPRISE The climbers were . . .

5 Bob agreed to undertake the leadership of the expedition.
ON Bob agreed . . .

6 The world believed his fantastic story of having got to the Pole alone.
IN The world was . . .

7 After a pause for questions and refreshments he continued his story.
UP He . . .

8 That reminds me of the time I climbed to the top of Mount Fuji.
BACK That . . .

9 He couldn't stop looking at the crocodile's jaws.
EYES He . . .

10 They assumed that someone would pick up their signals and come to their aid.
GRANTED They . . .

1.6 The white man in Africa *Questions and summary*

Read this passage through and then decide with a partner how you would answer the questions below. Then write down your answers.

The transition from the slave trade to the colonial invasions was a complex one. But an African trade unionist, J.H. Mphemba, looking back in 1929, believed that the essentials of the story, from an African standpoint, could be comparatively simply stated:

> First, the white man brought the Bible. Then he brought guns, then chains, then he built a jail, then he made the native pay tax.

The saying passed into African folklore. When the whites first came, it was said, "They had the Bible and we had the land. After a while, we found that things changed round. Now they have the land and we have the Bible." The Ethiopian emperor Theodore made much the same point when, facing British invasion, he said: "I know their game. First, it's traders and missionaries. Then it's ambassadors. After that, they bring the guns. We shall do better to go straight to the guns."

The missionaries may have begun the process, but scientific inquiry came first. One June evening of 1788, at a meeting of the Saturday's Club – a scientific society that was also interested in geographical questions – the members decided to form an Association for Promoting the Discovery of the Interior Parts of Africa. The task proved long, but by the 1870s the Association's successor, the Royal Geographical Society, knew a great deal about the principal topography of Africa, even if much detail had still to be explained.

The explorers followed African trails, and the missionaries came after them or, like Livingstone, took part in the work of geographical research. Great numbers of missionary societies were founded in France between 1816 and 1870, while Portugal and Spain, as well as Italy, Germany and the Scandinavian countries, launched many others. Saving the Africans from themselves became something of a popular craze in those high evangelical times.

The driving inspiration, as we can now see, came from a perverse interpretation of the history of the slave trade. Europeans had initiated and promoted the Atlantic slave trade, but this was forgotten. Following the line of pro-slaving apologists of earlier times, it was held that the trade was only an extension of what was mistakenly believed to be the ever-present practice of slavery inside Africa itself. Europeans must therefore help Africans to liberate themselves. And by now, of course, the argument had some colour of truth, for the slave trade had indeed extended the condition of slavery inside Africa.

Geographical exploration and missionary zeal combined in the work of "liberation". Financing an expedition up the Niger from the sea in 1832, the British government ordered it "to make treaties with the native chiefs for the suppression of this horrible traffic; and to point out to them the advantages they will derive, if, instead of the wars and aggressions to which it gives rise, they will substitute an innocent and legitimate commerce."

But soon it appeared that exploration and missionary zeal were not the only forces at work, for now the European coastal traders came in with loud demands. They were particularly active along the coastland of the Niger Delta, where an "innocent and legitimate commerce" in palm oil – much needed in nineteenth-century Europe for soap and lubricants – had taken the place of slaving. The Europeans had obtained a monopoly on the sea, and were now determined to achieve a monopoly on land as well, which meant that firm action would have to be taken against African producers and traders. In 1861 the British seized Lagos Island and proclaimed it a colony. Step-by-step invasion of the mainland duly followed.

(from *The Story of Africa* by Basil Davidson)

1 Explain what each of these words and phrases mean in the context of the passage:
standpoint (line 3) missionaries (line 14) successor (line 18)
popular craze (line 26) slave (line 28)
(Now that you've read the passage once through, it's a good idea to underline these words in the passage.)

2 What is the writer's attitude to the 19th century European missionaries?
3 What was 'perverse' about the European interpretation of the history of the slave trade?
4 Why does the word 'liberation' have inverted commas in the passage in line 36?
5 Why is 'innocent and legitimate commerce' in inverted commas in line 44?
6 What is meant by 'this horrible traffic' in line 38?
7 What were the reasons for Britain proclaiming Lagos Island a colony?

1.7 Safety in the hills *Listening*

1 Before you hear the recording can you guess or deduce what the missing information in the chart below might be?
2 Listen to the recording, filling in the missing information below.
3 Compare your answers with a partner's before listening to the recording again to clear up any doubts you may still have and to add any points you missed first time.
4 From your own experience and common sense what other advice would you give to someone who was setting off for a walk in the hills or mountains? Do you agree with all the pieces of advice given in the programme?

SAFETY PRECAUTIONS FOR HILL-WALKERS

1 DO go as a party of at least ....
and DON'T walk alone.
2 DO expect ....
and DON'T rely on ....
3 DO allow enough .... and DON'T get caught by ....
4 DO walk at the pace of the ....
and DON'T continue walking in ....
5 DO carry a .... and a ....
and DON'T rely on your own sense of ....
6 DO take warm .... clothes.
7 DO wear proper ....
and DON'T wear .... or ....
8 DO let others know before you ....:
.... you're going and .... you'll be ....
and DON'T forget to report your ....

1.8 A Japanese adventurer *Listening*

1 You'll hear part of a radio broadcast about Naomi Uemura. As you listen to the recording for the first time, fill in the *dates* missing from the chart below.
2 As you listen to the recording for the second time, fill in the other missing details below and put a cross (✘) beside any feats that Uemura has *not* achieved, according to the interview.
3 Compare your answers carefully with a partner's. If necessary, listen to the recording again to sort out any discrepancies.

Year	Ascent	Year	Solo journey
....	Mont Blanc (highest mountain in Europe – 4,807 m)	....	Down the Amazon by .... (6,000 km)
....	Mt Everest (highest mountain in Asia – 8,848 m)	....	Across Greenland ice cap by dog sled (......... km)
....	Mt McKinley (highest mountain in .... – 6,193 m)	....	From Atlantic to Pacific by dog sled (......... km)
....	Mt Aconcagua (highest mountain in .... – 6,960 m)	....	To the North Pole by dog sled (750 km)
....	Mt Kilimanjaro (highest mountain in .... – 5,895 m)	....	Across the Pacific by rowing boat (9,000 km)
....	Mt Jaja (highest mountain in Australasia – 5,029 m)	....	Across Antarctica by dog sled (3,500 km)

1.9 Dangerous pursuits *Picture conversation*

Work in pairs. One of you should look at communication activity 1 on page 256 while the other looks at activity 37 on page 280. Each of you will see a different photograph there – so **do not** look at your partner's picture. Use these questions to find out as much as possible about each other's pictures:

How many people are there in the photo?
What is happening?
What has just happened and what's going to happen next?
Where do you think the picture was taken?
Where was the photographer standing to take it?
How do you think the people are feeling?
Why do you think they decided to do what they're doing?
What is your attitude to people like that?

1.10 Around the world *Communication activity*

Work in pairs. One of you should look at activity 7 on page 261 while the other looks at activity 39 on page 281. You will be finding out about the record-breaking solo voyage of Naomi James. Do not look at each other's information, just at your own.

Naomi James

1.11 Writing a narrative *Composition*

'Describe an exciting or frightening experience you have had.'

1 Look at the composition below. What do you like about it? And what do you dislike about it? Working with a partner, can you suggest how it could be improved?

It had been a long, tiring journey to S________. The ferry, which should have taken at most five hours, had had engine trouble and didn't arrive till 2 a.m. As the harbour itself was several miles from the main town - the only place where accommodation was available - and much too far to walk even by daylight, we hoped against hope that the local bus service would still be running. Sure enough one tiny, ancient blue bus was waiting on the quayside but imagine our dismay when we saw that about 98 other passengers were also disembarking with the same destination! We fought our way onto the bus and waited for the driver to appear. A man staggered out of the bar nearby and groped his way into the driving seat - presumably he'd been drinking since early evening when the ship was supposed to arrive.

We were very frightened. Most of the passengers hadn't seen the driver come out of the bar. The bus went very slowly up the steep road. On one side the cliffs dropped vertically down to the sea hundreds of feet below. We arrived in the town at 3 a.m. but there was no accommodation. We found a taxi to take us to the other side of the island. We slept on the beach.

As it began to get light and the sun rose over the sea, waking us from our dreams, we realised that it had all really happened and that we were lucky to be alive.

2 Write about an exciting or frightening experience of your own.
3 Show your completed story to another student and ask for his or her comments before you hand it in to your teacher.

2 Language

2.1 Vocabulary

A Working with a partner, can you supply the missing words to complete each of the first ten sentences? Take a look at the example first.

1 If you don't know the meaning of a word in a text, try to work out its meaning from the c*ontext*.
2 Two words that have the same meaning (eg *sad* and *unhappy*) are known as s..............................
3 Two words that have opposite meanings (eg *nice* and *nasty*) are known as a..............................
4 Many professions have their own dialect, known as j..............................
5 Although it's fine to be able to use colloquial English in conversation, it's probably best to avoid using s..............................
6 The accent of British English which has become the standard for teaching and learning is known as R.............................. P..............................
7 Saying 'It's a lovely day' when the weather's bad is an example of i..............................
8 Telling someone who's done something stupid that he's 'absolutely brilliant' is an example of s..............................
9 Some well-known sayings (eg 'Look before you leap') are known as p..............................
10 An expression that has been over-used and no longer sounds fresh and original (eg 'To coin a phrase') is known as a c..............................

B Can you write down the names of the following punctuation marks? The first is done for you as an example.

; *semi-colon*   :   !   -   —   " "   *   ( )   /   's

C In the next ten sentences *three* of the alternatives can be used to complete the sentence correctly and *two* are incorrect. Take a look at the example first.

11 He's going to .... about English as the language of international communications.
say   speak ✓   talk ✓   tell   lecture ✓

12 If you keep .... I won't be able to understand what you're trying to say.
grumbling   mumbling   murmuring   muttering   rambling

13 During a lecture I try to .... down the main points that are made.
doodle jot note scribble sketch

14 I'm afraid I've only had time to .... the articles you recommended.
glance at scan skim study peruse

15 When he told me about his misadventures I couldn't help ....
chuckling grinning sniggering shrugging stammering

16 He looked at me with a .... on his face and began to tell me off.
frown gasp gulp scowl sneer

17 On seeing the body hanging from the apple tree she started to ....
scream shriek squeak squeal yell

18 He went on to .... that I wasn't working hard enough . . .
implicate imply infer intimate suggest

19 . . . and his .... made me feel quite guilty even though I was innocent.
attitude dialect expression idiom tone

20 He used a(n) .... which I couldn't quite follow.
expression clause phrase idiom speech

D If you're reading a non-fiction book you'll come across the following abbreviations, which are often found in a footnote or the index, as well as in reports and articles. Can you rewrite each one using a complete word or phrase? Look at the examples first.

eg *for example/for instance*	etc *and so on/and so forth*	
ie	cf	ff
pp	qv	ibid
NB	©	

2.2 Attitudes to language *Reading*

Decide whether the following statements are true (T) or false (F), according to the text.

1 The writer is amused by his own prejudices about language.
2 It is wrong to use American expressions in British English.
3 The 'popular lady columnist' writes a column about language.
4 'I guess' is an expression imported from the USA into Britain.
5 The writer uses capital letters in 'the British Way of Life' because he considers it to be superior to other cultures.
6 The writer ridicules people who despise foreign languages.
7 The writer believes that German is an ugly language.
8 Although a rural accent may sound attractive, it may also be looked down on.
9 The writer believes that a Cockney (London) accent doesn't sound any more ugly than a BBC announcer's accent.
10 Languages shouldn't be described as either 'beautiful' or 'ugly'.
11 Prunes are associated with death in English poetry.
12 British people's accents may not just tell a listener what region they come from, but also the social class they belong to.
13 East Midland English was at one time a regional dialect used by the élite in England.
14 People who use Standard English may have more power than people who use regional dialects.

To what extent do the author's comments on British people's attitudes to foreign languages and to each other's accents and dialects seem comparable to the attitudes of people in your own country?

A language is a system of communication used within a particular social group. Inevitably, the emotions created by group loyalty get in the way of objective judgements about language. When we think we are making such a judgement, we are often merely making a statement about our prejudices. It is highly instructive to examine these occasionally. I myself have very powerful prejudices about what I call Americanisms. I see red whenever I read a certain popular woman columnist in a certain popular daily paper. I wait with a kind of fascinated horror for her to use the locution 'I guess', as in 'I guess he really loves you after all' or 'I guess you'd better get yourself a new boy-friend'. I see in this form the essence of Americanism, a threat to the British Way of Life. But this is obviously nonsense, and I know it. I know that 'I guess' is at least as old as Chaucer, pure British English, something sent over in the *Mayflower*. But, like most of us, I do not really like submitting to reason; I much prefer blind prejudice. And so I stoutly condemn 'I guess' as an American importation and its use by a British writer as a betrayal of the traditions of my national group.

Such condemnation can seem virtuous, because patriotism – which means loyalty to the national group – is a noble word. While virtue burns in the mind, adrenalin courses round the body and makes us feel good. Reason never has this exhilarating chemical effect. And so patriotic euphoria justifies our contempt of foreign languages and makes us unwilling to learn them properly. Chinese is still regarded in the West as a huge joke – despite what T.S. Eliot calls its 'great intellectual dignity' – and radio comedians can even raise a snigger by speaking mock-Chinese of the 'Hoo Flung Dung' variety. Russian is, of course, nothing more than a deep vodka-rich rumble bristling with 'vitch' and 'ski'. As for German – that is an ugly language, aggressively guttural. We rarely admit that it seems ugly because of two painful wars, that it is all a matter of association. Sometimes our automatic sneers at foreign languages are mitigated by pleasant memories – warm holidays abroad, trips to the opera. Italian can then seem beautiful, full of blue skies, *vino*, sexy tenors. Trippers to Paris, on the other hand, furtively visiting the *Folies Bergère*, project their own guilt on to the French language and see it as 'naughty', even 'immoral'.

Within the national group, our prejudices tend to be very mixed and, because they operate mainly on an unconscious level, not easily recognizable. We can be natives of great cities and still find a town dialect less pleasant than a country one. And yet, hearing prettiness and quaintness in a Dorset or Devon twang, we can also despise it, because we associate it with rural stupidity or backwardness. The ugly tones of Manchester or Birmingham will, because of their great civic associations, be at the same time somehow admirable. The whole business of ugliness and beauty works strangely. A BBC announcer says 'pay day'; a Cockney says 'pie die'. The former is thought to be beautiful, the latter ugly, and yet the announcer can use the Cockney sounds in a statement like 'Eat that pie and you will die' without anybody's face turning sour. In fact, terms like 'ugly' and 'beautiful' cannot really apply to languages at all. Poets can make beautiful patterns out of words, but there are no standards we can use to formulate aesthetic judgements on the words themselves. We all have our pet hates and loves among words, but these always have to be referred to associations. A person who dislikes beetroot as a vegetable is not likely to love 'beetroot' as a word. A poet who, in childhood, had a panful of hot stewed prunes spilled on him is, if he is a rather stupid poet, quite capable of writing 'And death, terrible as prunes'. We have to watch associations carefully, remembering that language is a public, not a private, medium, and that questions of word-hatred and word-love had best be tackled very coldly and rationally.

We are normally quick to observe regional variations in the use of the national language, but we feel less strongly about these than we do about class divisions in speech. If we speak with a Lancashire accent,[1] we will often be good-humoured and only slightly derisive when we hear the accent of Wolverhampton or Tyneside. Sometimes we will even express a strong admiration of alien forms of English – the speech of the Scottish Highlands, for instance, or Canadian as opposed to American. But we feel very differently about English speech when it seems to be a badge or banner of class. The dialect known variously as the Queen's English or BBC English or Standard English was, originally, a pure regional form – so-called East Midland English, with no claim to any special intrinsic merit. But it was spoken in an area that was, and still is, socially and economically pre-eminent – the area which contains London, Oxford, and Cambridge. Thus it gained a special glamour as the language of the Court and the language of learning. It has ever since – often falsely – been associated with wealth, position, and education – the supra-regional dialect of the masters, while the regional dialects remain the property of the men. In certain industrial areas it can still excite resentment, despite the fact that it no longer necessarily goes along with power or privilege.

[1] An *accent* is a set of sounds peculiar to a region, as opposed to a *dialect*, which covers, in addition to peculiarities of sound, peculiarities of grammar and vocabulary.

(from *Language Made Plain* by Anthony Burgess)

2.3 This book . . . *Reading*

Here are the opening lines of the forewords / prefaces / introductions to three different books.

1 Read them through and decide, with a partner, what each extract tells you about:
   a) the writer himself
   b) the purpose of the book
   c) the presumed readers of the book

A This book might be described as an exercise in applied stylistic analysis. Its principal aim can be stated quite briefly: to present a discussion of an approach to the *study* of literature and a demonstration of its possible relevance to the *teaching* of literature. The approach with which I shall be concerned draws a good deal from linguistics and this discipline will provide the general perspective adopted in the discussion. This does not mean, however, that I shall exclude those considerations of interpretation and artistic effect which are the immediate concern of literary criticism. I do not believe

B If this book doesn't change you
give it no house space;
if having read it you
are the same person you

were before picking it up,
then throw it away.

Not enough for me
that my poems shine in your eye;
not enough for me
that they look from your walls
or lurk on your shelves;
I want my poems to be in your mind
so you can say them when you are in love
so you can say them when the plane takes off
and death comes near;
I want my poems to come between
the raised stick and the cowering back,
I want my poems to become
a weapon in your trembling hands,
a sword whose blade both makes and mirrors change;
but most of all I want my poems sung
unthinkingly between your lips like air.

C This book is for students preparing for the University of Cambridge Certificate of Proficiency in English examination. Its 18 units, each based on a different topic, will help you to develop and improve your English up to the standard required in the Proficiency exam. The exercises are designed to help you to improve the specific language skills tested in the different papers of the exam. In addition, you will discover that these exercises are often entertaining, sometimes challenging, frequently informative and occasionally provocative or even surprising.

A Proficiency course should be: (a) enjoyable, (b) intellectually stimulating and (c) geared to the exam. These three requirements are kept in mind throughout this book. Each unit contains a variety of exercises and activities, focussing on

2 Look again at extract A (from *Stylistics and the Teaching of Literature* by Henry Widdowson). Which phrases strike you as being 'academic'? Look for examples of complex structures or very formal style and for 'learned' vocabulary.

3 Look again at extract B (from *New Numbers* by Christopher Logue). Which phrases strike you as being 'poetic'? Look for examples of imagery or personification.
Try reading it aloud – does it sound the same as it looks? What if it were in prose – would it still have the same effect?

4 Look again at extract C (familiar?). Which phrases strike you as being 'down to earth' or 'pragmatic'? Look for examples of language that appeals to the reader – a student of English like yourself.

5 Which piece of writing impresses you or pleases you most? Explain why.

2.4 Reporting speech *Use of English*

A Look at the utterances in section B and imagine the circumstances in which each might have been spoken. Then choose a suitable reporting verb from this list that could be used to report each of the utterances, as in the example.

accuse advise allow apologise dissuade forgive
persuade promise suggest warn

B Now change each sentence into reported speech, using a suitable verb. Imagine that each was spoken to you by a friend. Look at the example first.

1 'I'll certainly give you some help tomorrow afternoon.'

PROMISE *He promised to help me the next afternoon.*
or He promised that he would help me the next afternoon.

2 'Make sure that you don't start giggling during the interview.'
3 'There's no point in writing it all out in longhand if you can use a typewriter, is there? It'd just be a waste of time.'
4 'I don't think you ought to boast about your command of English, you know.'
5 'Why don't you spend a little time listening to recordings of different English accents?'
6 'If you type this letter out for me, I'll buy you a drink, OK? Thanks!'
7 'You're the person who stole my dictionary, aren't you?'
8 'Look, I know you were very rude to me but I don't really mind because I know you were in a bit of a state.'
9 'I'm most awfully sorry, but I seem to have broken your fountain pen.'
10 'Sure, I don't mind at all if you use my typewriter. Go ahead.'

2.5 Verbs followed by *-ing, to . . .* and *that . . .* *Use of English*

A Can you match up the words and phrases below to make well-known collocations? The first is done for you as an example.

to answer	to a letter
to call	a letter/the phone
to contact	someone a letter
to drop	someone a line
to get	someone on the phone
to give	someone by phone/by post
to keep	someone a ring
to reply	someone a story
to tell	through to someone on the phone
to write	in touch with someone

B Use suitable collocations from the list overleaf to complete each of the following sentences. You may have to add a suitable preposition, and in some cases several possible versions are correct. Look at the example first.

1 I'm sorry ....*not to have kept*.... in touch with you.
   or ....*for not having kept*.... *or* ....*that I didn't keep*....
2 Is there any point .... by post?
3 I'm not looking forward .... all these letters.
4 Make sure that you remember .... a thank-you letter for your birthday present.
5 Have you heard him .... about the penguin and the polar bear?
6 I strongly advise you .... his letter by return of post.
7 He never writes letters because he's so used .... on the phone.
8 Her number was engaged all day but I finally succeeded .... in the evening.
9 Don't forget .... a line to let me know how you are.
10 It may be worth .... a ring if you ever need any advice.

2.6 Hello, darling *Questions and summary*

Read the text below and answer the following questions about it. Before you write down your answers (in complete sentences, please!), it may help to decide with a partner what you're going to write.

'Hello, darling', says a man to his wife. He says 'Hello, darling' to his neighbour's wife. He says 'Hello, dear' to his wife. An old lady says 'Hello, dear' to her pussy-cat. I write to the Commissioner of Taxes, beginning 'Dear Sir'. A young man says 'Hello, darling' to another young man. I call you 'Dear Reader'. I address the Commissioner of Taxes as 'Darling Sir'. A young man says 'Hello, dear' to another young man. A man says 'Hello, dear' to his neighbour's wife. I call you 'Darling Reader'. An old lady says 'Hello, darling' to her pussy-cat.

All very friendly. But we know that not all these events are equally likely to happen. This is because we have sifted from our experience of people saying things a pattern of language and another pattern of circumstances in which language is used, and we expect the language to fit the circumstances. We can see that in many cases words are interchangeable, that cats, unlike commissioners of taxes, may equally well be called 'dear' or 'darling', but we also know that these are different words, and that in other circumstances one word might be more appropriate than the other. Our knowledge of our language is immensely complex; we carry with us not only a knowledge of a vast, intricately patterned code, but also an experience of its varying surrounding circumstances. This guides us in making choices from approximately similar items in the code to fit particular occasions.

We know what language is in the sense that we can identify it or simply construct a sample of it. We would agree that I am using language now, though there is, when we think about it, something unusual about this language. As I sit at a desk in an outer suburb of Adelaide, looking from time to time out of my window on a day more overcast than we usually have, rather cold, in fact, for September, to see wind stirring our loquat tree and the gums beyond it, you are in London, or Canberra, or Leeds or Kuala Lumpur at another time and in circumstances quite unknown to me, so that the way you and I are using language in the present discussion is not the most normal one. As a matter of fact, it is more abnormal than I have suggested, since I have later revised and amended the words I wrote in Adelaide, looking out from time to time on a colder, more overcast day in Hampstead in March, taking account of comments made by two editors on a first draft of my text. Writing is a special, careful, elaborated, shuffled, pruned and tidied form of language, very different from the everyday, spontaneous, precarious adventures of speech which make up, and have made up, most of the world's linguistic activity and are in that sense 'normal language'.

(from *Stylistics* by G. W. Turner)

1 Can you explain why a man wouldn't normally say 'Hello, darling' to his neighbour's wife?
2 Which of the examples given in the first paragraph would be considered *appropriate* language?
3 What knowledge is essential to be able to use language accurately?
4 What experience is essential to be able to use language appropriately?
5 Why does the writer describe the style he is using as 'unusual' or 'abnormal'?
6 What are the differences between speech and writing, according to the text?
7 What personal information have you discovered about the writer and the process of his writing the book?

2.7 Speaking with an accent *Listening*

Ann and Ken are having a conversation with Kerry, an American friend. Listen carefully and decide which of the alternatives in the multiple-choice questions below best represents the meaning of the speakers. You'll probably need to hear the conversation twice to get all the answers.

1 Ken says that regional accents in Britain . . .
have low status.
are less common than they used to be.
are no longer looked down on.

2 Kerry says that Britain has . . .
a surprisingly large number of different accents.
more different accents than the USA.
more delightful accents than the USA.

3 The object of the New York City experiment was to discover . . .
the status of the customers of different stores.
the class of the staff of different stores.
whether different social classes used different pronunciations.

4 The New York experimenters couldn't ask people to say 'Fourth floor' . . .
because they would have tried to use the 'best' pronunciation.
because they might have refused to cooperate.
because they would have wanted to know the reasons for the experiment.

5 Ann implies that her feelings about rural and urban accents are . . .
common idiosyncratic uncommon

6 Presidents Johnson and Carter . . .
did get laughed at because of their Southern accents.
did not get laughed at because of their Southern accents.
did not have Southern accents.

7 Ann says that in some circumstances an RP accent may sound . . .
impressive out of place prestigious

8 Which of these reasons are given to explain why RP has become a model for foreigners learning English? (Tick several answers.)
It is the accent of educated Southern middle-class Britain.
Teachers used RP.
All teachers still speak with an RP accent.
All learners of English use RP as their model.
RP was used by the BBC.
All BBC announcers still use RP.
A standard is needed to avoid confusion.
RP still has prestige in Britain.

2.8 Who's talking? *Listening*

You're going to hear five different people talking. In each case it's not immediately obvious what they're talking about or even who they're talking to, so you'll have to pick up 'clues' to get the answers. You'll need to hear the recording more than once to get all of the clues and answers.

FIRST SPEAKER
1 How does the speaker feel and where is she?
2 Who is she talking to?
3 She says: '. . . they're all over the place . . .' – who or what are 'they'?
4 She says: '. . . it's almost time to pick them up . . .' – who or what are 'they'?
5 She says: '. . . don't look like that . . .' – how is the listener looking?
6 Why is the listener silent?

SECOND SPEAKER
7 Who is the speaker talking to?
8 Why has he started talking to her?
9 Who are all the people he refers to?
10 Why is the listener silent?

THIRD SPEAKER
11 What is the speaker's profession?
12 She says: '. . . there's a tendency for some of them to think it's syllable-timed just like theirs . . .' – who are 'they' and what is 'it'?
13 Is she talking to one person or to several, do you think?

FOURTH SPEAKER
14 What kind of person is the speaker?
15 Who is she talking to?
16 She says: '. . . I know there are lots of them . . .' – what are 'they'?
17 She says: '. . . don't get so upset, there's no need to . . .' – can you complete her sentence?
18 Why is the listener silent?

FIFTH SPEAKER
19 Who is the speaker?
20 Who is he speaking to?
21 He says: '. . . it couldn't have happened . . .' – what is 'it'?
22 Is the speaker telling the truth, do you think?

2.9 Blurbs *Pronunciation*

Work in pairs. One of you should look at communication activity 2 while the other looks at 40. You will have part of the 'blurb' from the back cover of a book to read to your partner and then discuss. Pay particular attention to your pronunciation.

2.10 Meanings of words *Communication activity*

Can you explain the difference between these pairs of words?
dialect – accent slang – jargon idiom – collocation irony – sarcasm
antonym – synonym phrasal verb – prepositional verb grin – chuckle
scowl – frown

Work in pairs. One of you should look at activity 5 (where some of the words are explained), the other at activity 38 (where the other words are explained). Together you should pool your information.

2.11 Writing a short report *Composition*

'Write a short report about the different languages, dialects and accents used in your country.'

1 Look at the questions below and note down your answers to them. If some of them seem to be irrelevant or if you can't answer some of them, leave a blank.

a) How many people speak your language? Which countries do they live in?
b) How many different languages are spoken in your country? Is there one 'official language'?
c) What language (and which dialect of it) is used in schools? Do the children in your area speak the same language or dialect when they are at home?
d) Do you use a different variety of your language (or different dialect) when talking with friends or family to the one which you use with strangers or people from other parts of the country? Is there a 'high' and 'low' variety of your language? What situations are the different varieties used in? What are some of the differences in vocabulary and grammar? Can you give any interesting examples?
e) What are the main regional accents and dialects that most people can recognise? Do people in the capital regard the speakers of any of these as 'funny' or 'stupid'?
f) Do the people in the regions where different languages or dialects are used feel they have less power than the people in the capital? Do they have TV and radio programmes in their own language or dialect?
g) Do middle-class people talk differently to working-class people? Are there any regional accents which are considered to be less 'educated' or less socially acceptable than others? What is considered to be the 'best accent' in your language?
h) Are there any other relevant or interesting points not covered by the questions above that you think would help to give a clearer picture about your country?

2 Rearrange the notes you have made (perhaps using arrows or different colours) to make the sequence of ideas and information as coherent as possible. Then

explain to another student what you're going to write and add any further points that now seem necessary.
3 Write your report. Draw a sketch map if you think this is useful.
4 Before handing your written report to your teacher, show it to the same student you talked to earlier and ask for comments.

"Funny how you soon forget his regional accent."

3 People

3.1 Vocabulary

A Complete each of these sentences with a suitable word.

1 When my mother remarried, I found it hard to get on with my new s................................
2 My mother had a son by this second marriage and this child is my h................................
3 When she died I was sent to my m................................ grandmother's house.
4 On the death of my grandmother, my uncle became my g................................
5 I was lucky to have had relations to look after me, otherwise I might have had to be cared for by f................................ parents or even put in a home.

B Fill each gap below with suitable words.

6 He's a hard man to get to know and people find it hard to .... friends .... him.
7 We haven't been on speaking terms since the day I had that .... her.
8 They say they don't believe in getting married and that's the reason why they are ....
9 She hardly knows her husband-to-be because the marriage has been .... by her parents.
10 After seven years of marriage she has decided to get .... her husband.

C The adjectives below can be used to describe negative aspects of people's disposition or behaviour. Find a suitable antonym for each which can be used to convey the opposite, more positive, characteristics.

Example: diffident *confident*

conceited
deceitful
lazy
malicious
mean
narrow-minded
secretive
sullen
solitary
touchy

D These idiomatic expressions are often used when describing people, sometimes unkindly and usually behind their backs. Can you match the words in the two columns? The first is done for you as an example.

muscular – He's as strong as . . .	a bat
short-sighted – She's as blind as . . .	a cucumber
hard of hearing – He's as deaf as . . .	a fiddle
well-behaved – They were as good as . . .	gold
stupid – She's as thick as . . .	a hatter
unemotional – He's as cool as . . .	a horse
tough – She's as hard as . . .	a mouse
self-effacing – He's as quiet as . . .	nails
healthy – She's as fit as . . .	a picture
crazy – He's as mad as . . .	a post
attractive – She looks as pretty as . . .	two short planks

E Look at the photos of the people below and decide how you would describe each of them. Follow the guidelines suggested below to make sure you describe each person adequately.

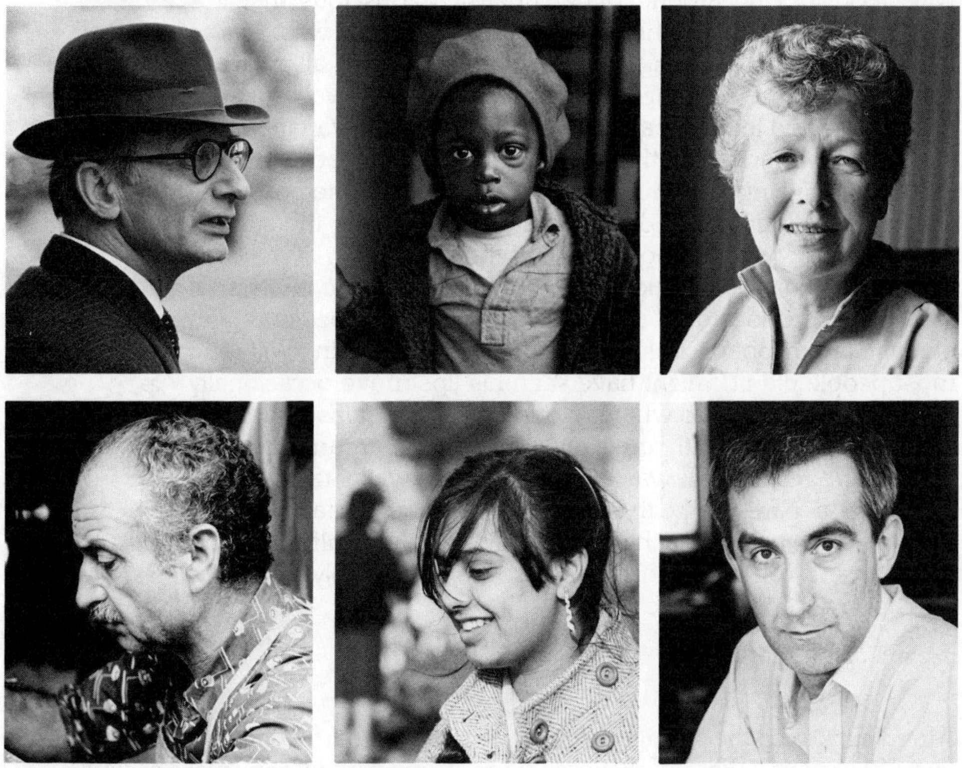

When describing a person you might refer to:

your own first impression of the person
the person's appearance and clothes
the person's age
the person's face and hair
the person's character and the way he or she behaves
what you know about his or her background and occupation

3.2 Wilt *Reading*

Whenever Henry Wilt took the dog for a walk, or, to be more accurate, when the dog took him, or to be exact, when Mrs Wilt told them both to go and take themselves out of the house so that she could do her yoga exercises, he always took the same route. In fact the dog followed the route and Wilt followed the dog. They went down past the Post Office, across the playground, under the railway bridge and out on to the footpath by the river. A mile along the river and then under the railway line again and back through streets where the houses were bigger than Wilt's semi and where there were large trees and gardens and the cars were all Rovers and Mercedes. It was here that Clem, a pedigree Labrador, evidently feeling more at home, did his business while Wilt stood looking around rather uneasily, conscious that this was not his sort of neighbourhood and wishing it was. It was about the only time during their walk that he was at all aware of his surroundings. For the rest of the way Wilt's walk was an interior one and followed an itinerary completely at variance with his own appearance and that of his route. It was in fact a journey of wishful thinking, a pilgrimage along trails of remote possibility involving the irrevocable disappearance of Mrs Wilt, the sudden acquisition of wealth, power, what he would do if he was appointed Minister of Education or, better still, Prime Minister. It was partly concocted of a series of desperate expedients and partly in an unspoken dialogue so that anyone noticing Wilt (and most people didn't) might have seen his lips move occasionally and his mouth curl into what he fondly imagined was a sardonic smile as he dealt with questions or parried arguments with devastating repartee. It was on one of these walks taken in the rain after a particularly trying day at the Tech that Wilt first conceived the notion that he would only be able to fulfil his latent promise and call his life his own if some not entirely fortuitous disaster overtook his wife.

(from *Wilt* by Tom Sharpe)

After you've read the passage through, work with a partner and answer these questions about it. Each of them can be answered with just one word or with a short phrase.

1 Who decided what time Clem should go for a walk?
2 Who decided on the route for the walk?
3 What do you think a 'semi' (line 10) is?
4 Why did Clem feel more at home where the houses were larger?
5 Why did Wilt feel uneasy there?
6 What did Wilt do during the rest of the walk?

7 What were the three directions in which his thoughts took him?
8 How do you think Wilt fared in arguments in real life?
9 What do you think Wilt does at 'the Tech'?
10 What might 'some not entirely fortuitous disaster' be?

Which bits of the passage amused you most? Can you explain why? (If it didn't amuse you at all, what did you find annoying about it?)

3.3 Two short poems *Reading*

Not Waving but Drowning

NOBODY heard him, the dead man,
But still he lay moaning:
I was much further out than you thought
And not waving but drowning.

Poor chap, he always loved larking
And now he's dead
It must have been too cold for him his heart gave way,
They said.

Oh, no no no, it was too cold always
(Still the dead one lay moaning)
I was much too far out all my life
And not waving but drowning.

(by Stevie Smith)

Epitaph

I AM old.
Nothing interests me now.
Moreover,
I am not very intelligent,
And my ideas
Have travelled no further
Than my feet.
You ask me:
What is the greatest happiness on earth?
Two things:
Changing my mind
As I change a penny for a shilling,
And,
Listening to the sound
Of a young girl
Singing down the road
After she has asked me the way.

(by Christopher Logue)

Before you answer the questions, ask your teacher to read the two poems aloud – or read them aloud yourself. If you find it hard to follow their meaning, read them as if they were prose.

1 In the first poem, how did the man die?
2 Which are the words uttered by the 'dead man'?
3 Which are the words uttered by his friends?
4 What does 'larking' mean in line 5?
5 What was 'too cold' in line 7? What was 'too cold' in line 9?
6 In what way was he 'too far out' in line 11 and 'drowning' in line 12?
7 In what way was he 'not waving' in line 12?

8 In the second poem, what was different for the poet when he was young?
9 How influential have his ideas been?
10 Why does he say that 'changing my mind' makes him happy?
11 Why does he feel happy at the 'sound of a young girl'?
12 Why is the poem entitled 'Epitaph'?

3.4 Articles *Use of English*

Fill each of the gaps in this paragraph with a suitable article or determiner. Be careful though because many of the gaps require the 'zero article' (Ø). Other gaps may require: *a an the her*

Clara never failed to be astonished by ...the... extraordinary felicity of ...1... own name. She found it hard to trust herself to ...2... mercy of fate, which had managed over ...3... years to convert ...4... greatest shame into one of ...5... greatest assets, and even after ...6... years of ...7... comparative security she was still prepared for, still half expecting ...8... old gibes to be revived. But whenever she was introduced, nothing greeted ...9... amazing, all revealing Clara but ...10... cries of, 'How delightful, how charming, how unusual, how fortunate,' and she could foresee ...11... time when ...12... friends would name their babies after her and refer back to her with ...13... pride as ...14... original from which ...15... inspiration had first been drawn. Finally ...16... confidence grew to such ...17... extent that she was able to explain that she had been christened not in ...18... vanguard but in ...19... extreme rearguard of ...20... fashion, after ...21... Wesleyan great aunt, and that ...22... mother had formed ...23... notion not as ...24... unusual and charming conceit, but as ...25... preconceived penance for ...26... daughter, whose only offences at that tender age were ...27... existence and ...28... sex. For Mrs Maugham did not like ...29... name any more than Clara and ...30... school friends did, and she chose it through ...31... characteristic mixture of ...32... duty and malice. When Clara explained this to ...33... people, she found that they merely laughed, and ...34... thought of ...35... people laughing, however indirectly, at ...36... mother's intentions, gave her ...37... deep and secret pleasure.

(from *Jerusalem the Golden* by Margaret Drabble)

3.5 Idioms with GET

Use of English

Rewrite each of the sentences so that it still means the same, using the words on the left together with the correct form of the verb GET. Look at the example first.

1 NERVES His refusal to commit himself does annoy me.
His refusal to commit himself gets on my nerves.
2 DOWN This cloudy weather is making me feel depressed.
3 OUT OF BED You seem to be very grumpy this morning.
4 OVER WITH I would like to finish this meeting as quickly as possible.
5 THROUGH You won't be able to make her understand what she has to do.
6 WRONG FOOT We made a bad start by having a row on our first meeting.
7 WORD IN EDGEWAYS Once he starts talking you won't be able to interrupt.
8 OWN BACK They retaliated by pouring cold water over my head.
9 BACKS UP He tends to antagonise people by telling them exactly what's on his mind.
10 ALONG Thomas and David are very good friends.
11 WRONG END OF THE STICK Don't get me wrong – you seem to have misunderstood what I was getting at.
12 ROUND One of these days I must find time to reply to all this correspondence.

" 'AUTUMN', by Alicia Teabury Shrum."

3.6 Women's rights *Questions and summary*

Read the passage through and then answer these questions in writing.

1 Explain the meaning of these words and phrases used in the passage:
oppression (line 2) chattels (line 8) legal reprisals (line 13)
gains (line 40) maternal deprivation (line 43)
(Underline the words in the passage, so that you can see them in context.)

2 The passage describes several changes in the law affecting women. Complete each of the sentences below to explain *in your own words* what the legal position of women was before each of the changes.
Before 1803 . . .
Before 1832 . . .
Before the 1831–72 Factory Acts . . .
Before 1882 . . .
Before 1918 . . .

3 How did the attitude of the British government towards women change during and then after the two world wars? Write a short paragraph, using your own words where possible.

The authority which men exercise over women is a major source of oppression in our society – as fundamental as class oppression. The fact that most of the nation's wealth is concentrated in the hands of a few means that the vast majority of women *and* men are deprived of their rights. But women are doubly deprived. At no level of society do they have equal rights with men.

At the beginning of the nineteenth century, women had virtually no rights at all. They were the chattels of their fathers and husbands. They were bought and sold in marriage. They could not vote. They could not sign contracts. When married, they could not own property. They had no rights over their children and no control over their own bodies. Their husbands could rape and beat them without fear of legal reprisals. When they were not confined to the home, they were forced by growing industrialization to join the lowest levels of the labour force.

Since then, progress towards equal rights for women has been very slow indeed. There have even been times when the tide seemed to turn against them. The first law against abortion was passed in 1803. It imposed a sentence of life imprisonment for termination within the first fourteen weeks of pregnancy. In 1832 the first law was passed which forbade women to vote in elections. In 1877 the first Trades Union Congress upheld the tradition that woman's place was in the home whilst man's duty was to protect and provide for her.

Nevertheless, the latter half of the nineteenth century saw the gradual acceptance of women into the unions and the informal adoption of resolutions on the need for equal pay. Between 1831 and 1872 the major Factory Acts were passed, which checked the exploitation of women workers by placing restrictions on hours and conditions of labour and by limiting their employment at night. In 1882 married women won the right to own property.

Wartime inevitably advanced the cause of women's rights – women became indispensable as workers outside the home, as they had to keep the factories and government machinery running while the men went out to fight. They were allowed into new areas of employment and were conceded new degrees of responsibility. In 1918 they got the vote. Again, during the Second World War, state nurseries were built on a considerable scale to enable women to go out to work. When peace came, however, women were unable to hold on to their gains. Men reclaimed their jobs, and women were forced back into the home and confined to their traditionally low-paid, menial and supportive forms of work. The government closed down most of the nurseries. Theories about maternal deprivation emerged – women who had been told it was patriotic to go out to work during the war were now told that their children would suffer if they did not stay at home. Little progress was made for the next two decades.

(from *Women's Rights: A Practical Guide* by Anna Coote and Tess Gill)

3.7 Sex discrimination *Listening*

Read the questions through and then listen to the recording to find out which of the following cases are illegal according to English law. Put a cross (✗) beside the cases that represent actions which are illegal, and a tick (✓) beside the actions which are not illegal.

1 A barman in a pub refuses to serve a woman. ☐

2 A barman in a private drinking club refuses to serve a woman. ☐

3 Jack and Jill are pupils in a mixed school: Jack is not allowed to join the cookery class that Jill goes to but has to do carpentry instead. ☐

4 John is a pupil in a boys' school where no cookery lessons are given. His sister Mary's school does have cookery classes. ☐

5 Girl pupils in a mixed school are discouraged from specialising in maths and science subjects. ☐

6 A school textbook on 'Famous Writers' describes 34 male writers but no women writers at all. ☐

7 Job advertisement: ENTHUSIASTIC GIRL REQUIRED AS PERSONAL ASSISTANT. ☐

8 Job advertisement: CHAMBERMAIDS REQUIRED FOR SUMMER SEASON. ☐

9 A woman is refused a job as warden of a men's hostel. ☐

10 Job advertisement: MEN REQUIRED FOR WORK IN MIDDLE EAST. ☐

11 Three men and one woman apply for the same job, all equally qualified. The three men are interviewed but the woman is not and no reason is given. ☐

12 A woman is refused a manual job on a building site because she is not strong enough. A man gets the job later. ☐

13 A café owner with a staff of four advertises for 'a waitress'. ☐

14 A female factory worker, working a 40-hour week, is required to work 10 hours overtime during one week. ☐

15 A factory manageress is required to start work at 6.30 a.m. ☐

"Just what is it that you people WANT?"

3.8 Who tells the truth? *Listening*

Listen to the radio report of a public opinion survey which asked people in the street what kinds of people they thought could be trusted to tell the truth. Fill in the missing information in the spaces (a) to (o) in the chart below.

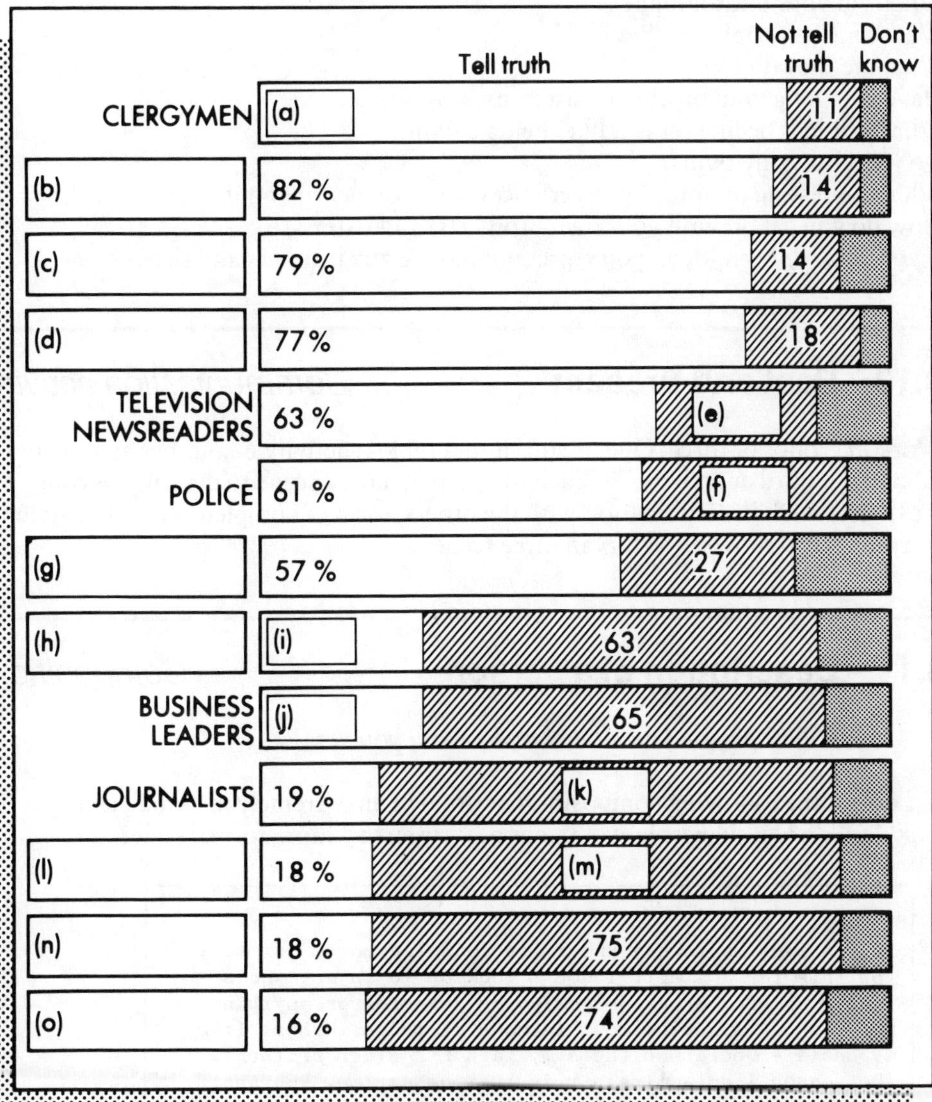

Do your own views accord with those of the members of the public interviewed? Carry out a similar poll among the members of your class.

3.9 Twins *Picture conversation*

Work in pairs. One of you should look at communication activity 3, while the other looks at 42. Each of you will have a different photograph to talk about and your partner will ask you these questions:

What's in your photograph?
What kind of people are they?
What are they doing?
Have you got a twin brother or sister, by any chance?
What would it be like (or is it like) being a twin?
Do you know any twins?
What interesting or amusing experiences have you heard about twins?
How do you get on with your own brother(s) and sister(s)?
If you're an only child, do you regret not having any brothers and sisters?

3.10 Past and Present *Communication activity*

Work in groups of three. One of you should look at activity 6, another at activity 73 and the third at activity 79. Each of you will have a scene to describe to your partners, which in combination with the others, forms a complete Victorian-style 'cartoon strip' showing a story in three scenes.

3.11 Description of a person *Composition*

'Describe a person you admire or *a person you detest.'*

1 Look at the following composition, written in an extremely informal, chatty style. Can you suggest how it might be written in a more formal style?

```
If you want me to say who it is I admire most, let me tell
you this for a start: I don't look up to anyone who's
famous or rich or good-looking or powerful or anything.
No, the guy I admire most is none of those things. It's
my uncle - Uncle Bob (he's my father's elder brother).
The reason I do admire him is that he's nice, you see.
Not just nice to me (though he is) but nice to everyone,
even to blokes that I'd probably just tell to clear off.
(It's amazing the way he can stay patient all the time!)
If you go to ask him for his advice about something or
other, he doesn't just come out with some old cliché
like some people do. What he'll do is this: he'll sit
down with you and let you talk and talk while he
```

listens and asks questions and so on, and then when you've had your say he'll tell you what he thinks and somehow or other he'll make you find your <u>own</u> solution to whatever problem it is. I mean, that's <u>great</u>, being able to do that.

Oh, and another reason why I admire him is that he takes the trouble to do everything he does as well as he can. I mean, even boring things like doing the washing-up or cleaning shoes he seems to enjoy and he seems to take pleasure in doing them well. He seems to relish every moment of the day and it doesn't seem to make any difference whether he's doing something he appreciates like listening to music or something he <u>has</u> to do like shopping, he still finds what's good about the activity and makes an effort to enjoy every moment of it. I suppose the best way to describe it is: he loves <u>living</u>.

But best of all is when you talk to him (not about problems but just chatting). It's not just interesting to listen to him and hear about his experiences and all that, but he makes you feel that what <u>you</u>'ve got to say is interesting too. I mean, that's great, isn't it?

2 Write your own composition on the same topic.

3 Before you hand your completed composition in to your teacher, show it to another student and ask for his or her comments on it.

4 Other places

4.1 Vocabulary

A Fill in the gaps in the description of the area shown in this map, using the words given on the right.

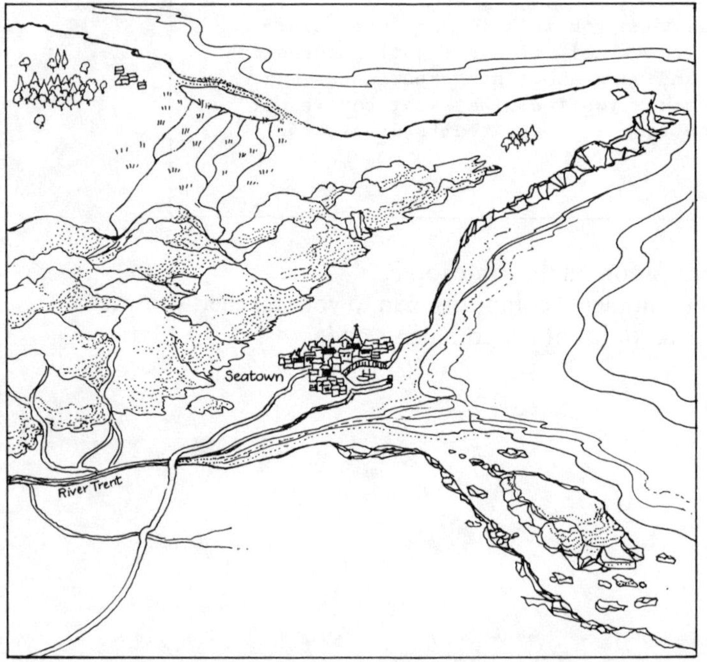

bay
cliffs
coastline
currents
estuary
harbour
headland
high tide
lagoon
low tide
marshes
mouth
plain
port
range of hills
sandbank
scenery
source
streams
tributaries
view

Seatown itself is a small fishing ...1... lying at the centre of a sheltered ...2... which forms a natural ...3... . It occupies the south-east corner of a fertile ...4... separated from the north coast by a ...5... . An interesting feature of the north coast is a freshwater ...6... enclosed by a ...7... and surrounded by ...8... . To the east is an impressive ...9... with high ...10... where seabirds nest. The River Trent, at whose ...11... Seatown lies, widens into a tidal ...12... several miles upstream. The river is fed by many small ...13... , which rise in the hills to the north, but its ...14... is over 100 miles to the west. To the south of the town across the river the ...15... is rocky and it is possible to walk across to an offshore island at ...16... , though at ...17... the crossing should not be attempted as there are dangerous ...18... . For those who enjoy coastal ...19... there is a splendid ...20... from the island.

B In each of the sentences below, choose *three* of the six words given that make sense in the gaps.

21 The Vatican in Rome is visited every year by millions of ....
commuters holidaymakers passengers pilgrims
vagrants travellers

22 I enjoy visiting places abroad where the people are ....
churlish courteous easygoing hospitable sulky sullen

23 Not liking crowds, I prefer a holiday spot that's ....
abandoned deserted godforsaken off the beaten track
out of the way secluded

24 Seeing different places and meeting new people ....
broadens the mind dulls the senses expands your consciousness
gives you new experiences widens your horizons

25 Next week I'm leaving for the continent and I'll be .... till June.
absent away from home in foreign parts on the run
out in the country out of the country

C Draw a sketch map of your own country and of the countries that surround it, giving the English names of the countries you have shown. What is the English word for an inhabitant of each country? What languages do they all speak? What are the principal cities called and how are they pronounced in English?

D Which ten countries in the world would you like to visit one day? And which ten countries have you no desire to visit ever? Give your reasons for your choices.

4.2 Learning the language *Reading*

Find the answers to these questions in the passage that follows.

1 How did many Turks demonstrate that they didn't understand that some people do not understand Turkish?
2 Who was more confused when she said her 'useful phrase': the Turks or the author herself?
3 Why was the hotel porter the first to understand her?
4 What exactly was the mistake that she had made?
5 Did she discover her mistake before or after meeting Mr Yorum?
6 Why did Mr Yorum point to himself when she said she didn't understand Turkish?
7 Why did she *think* he was pointing to himself?
8 Did Mr Yorum speak any English at all?
9 Why did the writer not try to resolve the confusion with him?
10 What does the word 'yorum' mean in Turkish?

What do you think happened afterwards in the story? ⟶

I studied my Turkish phrase book, and learned a few of the most useful ones by heart. One was about how I did not understand Turkish well, which I copied into my notebook and carried about with me. Many Turks can't understand that any one really does not understand Turkish; they think that if they say it often enough and loud enough it will register. They did this whenever I said this phrase; it seemed to start them off asking what seemed to be questions, but I only said my piece again, and after a time they gave up. Sometimes they said "Yorum, yorum, yorum?" as if they were asking something, but I did not know what this word meant, and I thought they were mimicking what they thought I had said.

This was all that happened about it for a few days, then one day when I said my piece to the porter he nodded, and went to the telephone and rang someone up, and presently a man came downstairs and bowed to me as I stood in the hall and said something to me in Turkish. I had better explain here that there was a misunderstanding which was my fault, for I discovered some time afterwards that I had copied the phrase in the book which was just below the one which meant "I do not understand Turkish," and the one I had copied and learnt and had been saying to everyone for days meant "Please to phone at once to Mr Yorum," though this seems a silly phrase to print in a book for the use of people who do not know Mr Yorum at all and never would want to telephone to him. But one day this Mr Yorum turned up at the Yessilyurt to stay, and the porter saw then what I wanted him to do, and he rang Mr Yorum in his room and asked him to come down. But I did not know then about the mistake, and when Mr Yorum spoke to me I said again that I did not understand Turkish, and he bowed and pointed to himself. I thought he must be offering to interpret for me, but when I tried English on him he shook his head and said, "Yok, Yok," and I could see he knew none. So I looked up the Turkish for "What can I have the pleasure of doing for you?" and said it, but of course I did not understand his answer, and that is the worst of foreign languages, you understand what you say in them yourself, because you have looked it up before saying it, but very seldom what the foreigners say to you, because you have not looked up that at all. So I looked through the book till I found, "Who are you, sir?" and he said in reply, "Yorum, Yorum, Yorum." I saw there was some confusion somewhere, but there is always so much confusion in Turkey that I let it go, and ordered drinks for both of us, and we drank them, then he went away, quite pleased that I had telephoned to him to come and have a drink.

(from *The Towers of Trebizond* by Rose Macaulay)

MAURITANIA

The sand baggers

Nigel Cross sees signs of success in the battle to hold back the dunes

IT WAS a pleasant day by Mauritanian standards. In the football match between the home side and Libya the players could hardly spot the ball. A fog of pink sand hung over the stadium. Outside parked cars were covered in a film of dust. Men shovelled away sand blocking the road to the coast. Three o'clock in the afternoon, and the light faded as in a partial eclipse.

Nouakchott, the capital of the Islamic republic of Mauritania, is a city under siege. To the west it faces the Atlantic, on the land side it is surrounded by desert. Twenty years ago the climate of the Sahara used to be 250km further north. But years of overgrazing, poor land management, and changing weather patterns have taken their toll. Today the dunes edge towards the city.

There has been a massive social upheaval as people have been pushed south by the desert. In the 1960s three-quarters of the population of 1.5 millions were nomads. Now more than three quarters are settled, either in the spreading towns, or along the Senegal river to the south, or in the "temporary" camps that line the new 1100km road joining Nouakchott to the eastern town of Nema. Most people now live off food aid.

But even this precarious way of life is being threatened by sand. Every day bulldozers struggle to clear mountains of it from that road, the main route for food aid traffic. Trucks carrying urgent supplies often fail to get through.

In 1982 the Mauritanians launched a three year $4.5 millions dune offensive on 15 fronts funded jointly by Denmark and a group of United Nations agencies. The result is the most intensive battle of the dunes south of the Sahara.

How do you "fix" a dune? The surest way, says Dr Axel Martin Jensen, the Food and Agriculture Organisation's consultant forester, is to build a large town. But as this is rarely practicable, the next best thing is to plant trees, shrubs, and grasses. Planting in sand is not easy.

At a project site along the Nema road Jensen and his colleagues hope that they have virtually halted dune movement. Brushwood fences have been erected along the crests of the dunes to the north. The effect is like an undulating chequer board. Drought resistant species — prosopis juliflora, acacia tortilis, parkinsonia aculeata — are planted within the fenced dunes. The fencing protects seedlings from wind-blown sand and browsing animals.

Water is a constant problem. It is carried to the site in tankers but with a minimum of annual rainfall a useful supply of water stays trapped in the sand. The top of the dune dries out immediately, but below 50cm it can retain moisture for at least a year.

The trick is to breed long-stemmed seedlings which can be planted below the surface with their roots resting on the moisture level. Eventually the roots, which can grow to a depth of 50 metres or more, will bind the sand and stop dune movement.

To the north of the site the project team is building a super dune by repeatedly raising the perimeter fence to allow the sand to build up behind it. The dune is now so massive it has been stopped in its tracks by its own bulk, and it also helps to protect the rest of the site from the Saharan winds.

Another novel idea exploits Mauritania's two limitless

→

commodities — sand and food aid bags. But sand-bagging the dunes has not worked very well.

Brilliant improvisation and patient scientific research is useless if there is no defence against animals and people. Barbed wire and keep-out notices are impractical. Instead Jensen argues for a sustained education programme which will teach people how to exploit vegetation without destroying it.

A more immediate problem is the search for suitable fencing material. Dry vegetation is in short supply. Other kinds of fencing material will have to be found. Jensen believes the best material may be fibre glass.

The arcane world of dune fixation could capture the public imagination by combining life-saving technology with grand modern art. Commissioning an artist to design coloured fibre glass panels to encase the Mauritanian dunes, could make the Nouackchott-Nema road one of the most exciting shows on earth.

The United Nations Sudano-Sahelian office is currently casting around for some $10 millions to take the dune project into a second, five-year phase. It is not a lot of cash to the art world of Gettys and Mellons and Sainsburys.

A What do you think is the meaning of each of these words used in the passage? You should be able to work this out from the context.

shovelled (line 16) overgrazing (line 30) nomads (line 40)
precarious (line 51) funded (line 63) super dune (line 115)
barbed wire (line 135)

B Each of these questions has **several** correct answers. Tick the answers that are correct and put a cross beside the ones that are not correct.

1 What have been the causes of the Sahara moving south?
Animals eating too much vegetation
Not enough care being taken by farmers
Strong winds from the north
Alteration in climate

2 What have been the results of the Sahara moving south?
Main road to east keeps getting blocked
Most people now have semi-permanent homes
There is virtually no agricultural produce available
The weather is much hotter

3 What methods have been successful in preventing the further encroachment of the Saharan dunes?
Building cities
Erecting wooden fences
Erecting fibre glass fences
Planting seedlings with long roots
Planting seedlings with long stems
Planting seedlings that will eventually grow very long roots
Creating an abnormally large dune
Filling bags with sand for use as barriers

4 Why is education considered to be important?
The people are unable to read the notices
The people allow their animals to eat any plants available
The people must learn that plants can be utilised but not destroyed

5 What is the meaning of 'arcane' in line 150?
secret fascinating scientific mysterious

C What is the writer's attitude to the idea of artist-designed fibre glass panels? What is his attitude to the difficulties of the Mauritanian people? And to the efforts of the dune project scientists?

4.4 Positive and negative sentences *Use of English*

Rewrite each sentence so that its meaning remains unchanged, beginning with the words given. The first is done for you as an example.

1 I've never been anywhere nicer than here.
Everywhere . . . I've been is less pleasant than here.

2 The weather never seems as bad abroad as it does at home, does it?
The weather always . . .

3 It isn't pleasant to be alone in a strange country, is it?
It's . . .

4 Not many of the people in Britain speak a single word of my language.
Hardly . . .

5 You can't expect everyone in the world to understand your own language, can you?
Not everyone . . .

6 You can't say anything that would persuade me to live overseas.
Nothing . . .

7 I'd do anything to be able to travel to China.
There's . . .

8 All the people in Japan speak Japanese.
There's nobody . . .

9 I can't often afford to spend my holidays abroad.
I'm seldom . . .

10 There isn't anywhere as nice as your own country, is there?
Nowhere . . .

4.5 Comparative and superlative sentences *Use of English*

Using your own (or your partner's) knowledge of geography, fill the gaps in the sentences in a suitable way. Look at the example first.

1 Belgium is a far *less mountainous country than* Austria.
2 Canada is a great deal .... Egypt.
3 Switzerland is much .... Holland.
4 The Pacific is nothing like as .... Mediterranean.
5 In Brazil there are many more .... in Greece.
6 Australia is a far less .... United Kingdom.
7 Portugal is the .... Europe.
8 In Saudi Arabia there isn't .... Ireland.
9 The USA and USSR are the .... world.
10 Antarctica is the .... world.

"Mind you, I expect job prospects are just as dismal elsewhere."

4.6 The vanishing island and dog soup *Questions and summary*

Read the two newspaper articles and answer the questions in writing, using your own words if possible.

'Catastrophe' of the vanishing island

From Iain Guest in Gland, Switzerland

The conservation community has reacted with alarm to the disappearance of an island off the coast of Tanzania.

Until recently, Maziwi was the kind of place featured in holiday brochures : an idyllic 1,500 acres of palm trees ringed with white sand, and a coral reef. It was also one of the finest breeding places for the green turtle, an endangered species, off the East African coast. Then it vanished without trace.

" It is a catastrophe " said Mr James Thorsell, who works on marine parks at the International Union for Conservation of Nature and Natural Resources (IUCN), here at Gland. Mr Thorsell was formerly at the College of African Wildlife Management in Tanzania, and he heard so much about Maziwi that he went to visit the island last year. When he arrived, all he saw was a tiny sand bar a few feet wide at low tide.

" I just couldn't believe it. There was nothing left," he said yesterday.

According to a local superstition, the disappearance of Maziwi would signal the end of the world. This, in Mr Thorsell's view, may have made Tanzanians reluctant to discuss the affair.

In the absence of any official investigation, Mr Thorsell speculates that fishermen dynamited the coral reefs which surrounded the island. At the same time, he feels, local people probably cut down much of its lush vegetation and trees, for use in building or charcoal. This left the island hopelessly vulnerable to the ferocious monsoon, known in Swahili as the Kazi Kazi, which washed the island away.

Another possibility, more remote, is that the island was built on coral which was smashed and damaged by tourists collecting shells. If they unwittingly opened up a hole, it is conceivable that the island poured away into the sea. It is still legal to export shells from Tanzania.

1 Can you explain the meaning of these words used in the article?
   superstition (line 36)
   reluctant (line 41)
   lush (line 48)
   conceivable (line 60)

2 Explain what is referred to by 'it' and 'this' in these quotations from the passage:
   Then **it** vanished . . . (line 17)
   It is a catastrophe . . . (line 19)
   I just couldn't believe **it** . . . (line 33)
   This, in Mr Thorsell's view . . . (line 39)
   This left the island . . . (line 50)

3 Write a short paragraph explaining the reasons suggested for the disappearance of Maziwi.

Dog soup banned from Korean table

Seoul: The Government yesterday banned restaurants from serving traditional soup made from dog and snake meat to improve the country's image for the 1986 Asian Games and 1988 Olympics being held here.

A government statement said "The ban, which had already been enforced in Seoul, would now take effect throughout the country." Both snake and dog are eaten in several Asian countries, including China.

Seoul civic authorities reported that 300 dog meat soup shops which had served the dish in the capital had been closed and others were being phased out.

Dog meat soup (Boshintang) is believed by many Koreans to help invigorate health during the hot summer months. Snake meat soup is traditionally served in the cold winter months.

The ban has caused a lively debate in Seoul newspapers with readers' letters complaining that local habits formed over hundreds of years should not be changed to suit foreigners.

The Government, however, has received strong protests from dog-lover organisations in the US and Europe over eating dogs.

Some people breed dogs and fatten them up for the summer months like cattle or sheep are reared in other countries.

Dog meat is cooked by boiling and is eaten with a sauce of hot red peppers and garlic powder.

The meat is often seen in traditional Korean open markets, which has offended foreign tourists who have been able to identify the carcasses as canine.

Dog and snake meat are by no means the most prominent of Korea's traditional health foods. They also include fried grasshoppers, deer antler horn powder, bull testes powder and the famous ginseng root which is believed to increase sexual performance.

4 Explain the meanings of the following words used in the second passage:
image (line 8) ban (line 12) phased out (line 24) suit (line 38)

5 What are the reasons for the Korean government's banning of dog soup? Write a short paragraph.

4.7 Three island nations *Listening*

You'll hear part of a broadcast about the three countries shown below. Fill in the missing details as you listen – you'll need to hear it more than once to do this.

SINGAPORE

area: 580 km^2
population: 2.4 million
languages: ...., ..., ... and English
climate: .... all year round
scenery: .... island with many parks
annual number of tourists: ....

The attractions: shopping, varieties of ethnic .... and ....
The drawbacks: there are few good ....;
the weather can be very ....

NEW ZEALAND

area: .... km^2
population: 3.2 million
languages: English and Maori
climate: .... winters, ... summers
scenery: attractive countryside; mountains over .... m; glaciers and fiords
annual number of tourists: ....

The attractions: .... scenery; beaches; seafood
The drawbacks: difficult and costly to reach; weather can be ....,
.... and ....

PAPUA NEW GUINEA

area: 460,000 km^2
population: .... million
languages: English, ... and
.... local languages
climate: .... all year round.
scenery: thick forests and mountains over ....m
annual number of tourists: ....

The attractions: the island is ...., wild and primitive
The drawbacks: the weather can be very ....

4.8 The impact of tourism *Listening*

Listen to the interview about the way that tourism has affected Fiji in the South Pacific. Decide whether the following statements are true (**T**) or false (**F**), according to what is said in the interview.

1 A few of the islands of Fiji are uninhabited.
2 In 1970 tourism was still a relatively recent phenomenon.
3 Most of the tourists who go to Fiji are from Australasia.
4 About half of the population of Fiji is of Indian origin.
5 Most of the money earned by tourism does not benefit the local people.
6 New Zealand exports orange juice to Fiji.
7 Fiji cannot provide enough food for its visitors because it is not fertile enough.
8 Schoolchildren in Fiji sometimes earn money as 'shopping guides' instead of going to school.
9 The Fijians are just as friendly as they used to be.
10 Tourists rarely find out anything about the local people's lives.
11 One effect of tourism is that visitors and locals look down on each other.
12 The relationship between visitors and Fijians is likely to deteriorate in the future.

"Before we came out here, Stanley and I took one of them sun-lamp courses so we wouldn't stand out too much from the crowd."

4.9 Beauty spots *Pronunciation*

Work in groups of three. One of you should look at activity 4, another at 45 and another at 71. You'll have to listen carefully to a description of the three places shown below and decide which one each of you is describing.

4.10 Faraway places *Communication activity*

Work in groups of three. One of you should look at activity 8, another at 47 and the other at 76. Follow the instructions there. You will be exchanging information about different faraway places.

4.11 Description of a place *Composition*

'Write a description of a country for the benefit of a foreign visitor who has not yet been there. Point out some of the drawbacks as well as the country's attractions.'

1 Look at the notes below and, working with a partner, decide how they could be turned into a piece of continuous prose. What points could be left out, do you think?

Bamburi Beach Hotel, Mombasa

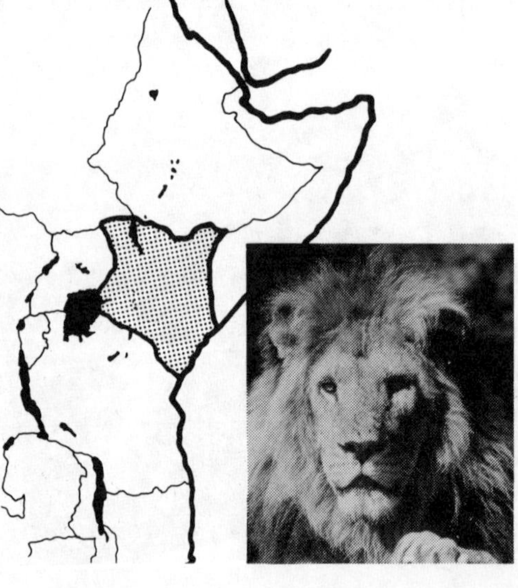

KENYA

Pros

RELAXING ON PALM-SHADED CORAL BEACHES

SWIMMING AND SNORKELING IN REEF-SHELTERED WATERS

WILDLIFE IN GAME RESERVES

SNOWY SLOPES OF MOUNT KENYA

WARM WEATHER ALL YEAR ROUND

DRY WEATHER ALL YEAR (EXCEPT THE 'LONG RAINS' IN APRIL AND MAY + 'SHORT RAINS' IN NOVEMBER)

Cons

SERVICE IN HOTELS SLOWER + MORE EASYGOING THAN EUROPE

FOOD NOT ALWAYS TOP QUALITY

SAFARIS ARE VERY DUSTY

ROAD MAPS MAY SHOW STONY TRACKS AS WIDE MAIN ROADS

DARKNESS FROM 6 P.M. TO 6 A.M.

INSECTS AND SNAKES MAY HIDE IN CORNERS OF ROOMS

2 Rewrite the notes above as a piece of continuous prose, leaving out any points you think need not be mentioned.

3 Write a similar description of your own country for the benefit of a first-time visitor from abroad. Begin by discussing this task with a partner and then make notes before you write the composition.

5 The arts

5.1 Vocabulary

A Fill the gaps in the following sentences with a suitable word or phrase.

1 Lovers of classical music don't always appreciate ....
2 My own favourite musical instrument is the ....
3 It's not my favourite opera, but I did enjoy the .... very much.
4 Before a performance actors spend many hours ....
5 A theatre programme gives the names of all the members of the ....
6 Before getting the part she had to attend a(n) ....
7 A sculpture by Henry Moore fetched £1 million at a(n) .... last year.
8 The gallery's latest acquisition is a wonderful medieval ....
9 And don't miss Rembrandt's magnificent ....
10 The most important people involved in the making of a film are the ...., ... and ....
11 Three string instruments are the ...., ... and ....
12 Three wind instruments are the ...., ... and ....
13 Three keyboard instruments are the ...., ... and ....

B Choose suitable adjectives from the list below to fill the gaps in these sentences:

14 It's a really .... film.
15 It was a very .... performance.
16 The acting was really ....
17 The plot was very ....
18 The production was really ....
19 This painting is very ....
20 The play was extremely ....

amateurish	astonishing	crude
compelling	elegant	flashy
entertaining	harrowing	brilliant
stirring	remarkable	great
second-rate	superb	tasteless
overrated	unremarkable	moving
revolting	pathetic	poor

→

C In each of the sentences below, choose *three* of the five words given that make sense in the gaps.

21 Shakespeare's *Hamlet* is one of the world's greatest ....
comedies dramas plays shows tragedies

22 Although I play the piano quite well, I still can't ....
play by ear play the notes read the notes read music read a score

23 I haven't seen the film yet, but I've seen the ....
criticisms propaganda reviews trailer write-ups

24 They sometimes play together in a ....
quintet solo trio quartet quarto

25 He's a well-known soloist but he also plays in a(n) ....
band company group orchestra team

5.2 Silent movies *Reading*

Talk to people who saw films for the first time when they were silent, and they will tell you the experience was magic. The silent film, with music, had extraordinary powers to draw an audience into the story, and an equally potent capacity to make their imagination work. They had to supply the voices and the sound effects, and because their minds were engaged, they appreciated the experience all the more. The audience was the final creative contributor to the process of making a film.

The films have gained a charm and other-worldliness with age but, inevitably, they have also lost something. The impression they made when there was no rival to the moving picture was more profound, more intense; compared to the easily accessible pictures of today, it was the blow of a two-handed axe, against the blunt scraping of a tableknife.

The films belong to an era considered simpler and more desirable than our own. But nostalgia should not be allowed to cast a Portobello Road quaintness over the past, for it obliges us to edit from our mind the worst aspects of a period and embrace only those elements we admire. The silent period may be known as 'The Age of Innocence' but it included years unrivalled for their dedicated viciousness. In Europe, between 1914 and 1918 more men were killed to less purpose than at any other time in history. In America, men who stood out from the herd—pacifists, anarchists, socialists—were rounded up and deported in 1919, and were lucky to avoid being lynched. The miseries of war culminated in the miseries of disease when the Spanish flu swept Europe and America and killed more civilians than the war had killed soldiers. With peace came the Versailles treaty—collapse and starvation in Central Europe—the idealism of Prohibition—gangsterism in America.

The benefit of the moving picture to a care-worn populace was inestimable, but the sentimentality and charm, the easily understandable, black-and-white issues were not so much a reflection of everyday life as a means of escape from it. Again and again, in the publications of the time, one reads horrified reactions against films showing 'life as it is'.

You did not leave the problems of home merely to encounter them again at the movies. You paid your money, initially, for forgetfulness. As the company slogans put it: 'Mutual Movies Make Time Fly' . . . 'Selznick Pictures Create Happy Hours'. And if the experience took you out of yourself and excited you, you talked about it to your friends and fellow-workers, creating the precious 'word of mouth' publicity that the industry depended upon. You may have exaggerated a little, but the movies soon matched your hyperbole. They evolved to meet the demands of their audience.

Gradually movie-going altered from relaxation to ritual. In the big cities, you went to massive picture palaces, floating through incense-laden air to the strains of organ music, to worship at the Cathedral of Light. You paid homage to your favourite star; you dutifully communed with the fan magazines. You wore the clothes they wore in the movies; you bought the furniture you saw on the screen. You joined a congregation composed of every strata of society. And you shared your adulation with Shanghai, Sydney and Santiago. For your favourite pastime had become the most powerful cultural influence in the world—exceeding even that of the Press. The silent film was not only a vigorous popular art; it was a universal language—Esperanto for the eyes.

(from *Hollywood, The Pioneers* by Kevin Brownlow)

These questions about the passage can all be answered very briefly.

1 Why did the audiences of silent movies appreciate them so much?
2 What do modern audiences find attractive about silent movies?
3 Why do modern audiences appreciate silent movies less than their original audiences did?
4 What is the writer's attitude to present-day nostalgia?
5 Why did people go to the cinema in the days of silent movies?
6 What did they *not* want to see in a film?
7 What was the most effective publicity for a film?
8 What was a large city cinema like?
9 What influence did movies have on their fans' lives?
10 What kinds of people went to see silent movies?
11 Why is the power of Hollywood weaker nowadays?
12 Who is being referred to as 'you' in the last two paragraphs? What is the effect of this stylistic device?

What seem to be the writer's feelings about silent movies?
Do you share these feelings at all, or have you been influenced by his views?

Profits may be falling but sponsorship lives

COMPANIES may be cutting expenses to the bone, but arts sponsorship is doing better than ever. The Philharmonia Orchestra, for instance, receives £800,000 from its five or six company backers, and British archaeological groups receive generous help from one giant insurance company.

The trend is steadily upwards. Sponsorship overall now takes up perhaps £50 million, or three times as much as it did five years ago. Most of that may go on sport—but the spending on arts has risen fastest of all and may now be worth £4 million a year.

Rising benevolence and falling profits seem a paradox at the best of times. It is all the more curious when the tax laws in Britain are relatively tight. Companies have to show that the expenses they have incurred are "wholly and exclusively incurred" as part of the business and though they can claim that what they give to some events is at least part of their public relations and advertising budget, that does not extend indefinitely.

The rules in America, where companies are expected to provide $500 million for charities this year, are considerably more generous.

The extra help is easy to explain. Banks, insurance companies, the oil industry and tobacco firms provide three quarters of the funds going into arts sponsorship. All four groups tend to be unpopular—which makes them all the keener to display their social concern and so build up at least some good will.

Insurers help archaeologists, perhaps with quick money, because companies are vast property developers. The arts are a perfect way for most aid to appear, for the tradition of private personal benevolence is dying on its feet—and the massive cuts in the Arts Council grants make orchestras, and arts festivals very anxious for the money.

That is certainly the reason that the companies themselves put forward—and it is probably part of the truth. Costs of doing so come cheap when measured against an overall advertising budget. "We'll sponsor a festival for the cost of a 30-second television commercial and though we'll only reach a microscopic fraction of the number we hit on television, the impact will be far more long lasting," said one advertising man yesterday.

What is more, there may be a direct spin-off. Lloyds Bank provides £250,000 on sponsoring the National Youth Orchestra (as part of an overall advertising budget of £1 million) and finds it always brings in a mass of student customers.

The biggest reason, though, lies in the rules on cigarette advertising. Since the rules prevented companies from producing commercials for cigarettes—leaving them only with the right to push cigars and pipe tobacco—the stress has been on poster advertising, even though the companies have agreed not to attempt to bring in new young smokers, but restrict themselves to adults.

Now further restrictions have appeared. They have had to accept a 10 per cent cut in volume this year, and the prospect of another fall of 30 per cent next year.

Sports sponsorship was the immediate reaction after the television ban. When John Player started to sponsor the county cricket series, the name John Player appeared in every sports news—as indeed it still does. The tobacco firms, though, seem to have reached saturation point, and with very few other places for money to go arts sponsorship has done very well from them.

Tax changes, too have provided at least some help. Companies do not have to commit themselves for as long as in the past.

Almost every orchestra, non-commercial theatre and touring group is a charity—and regular contributions bring in tax relief if they are made over three years. The old rule used to restrict the relief to covenants lasting seven years—or more accurately for longer than six years and a day.

The standard criticism is that the sponsors stick to established events like the Proms, rather than going for more innovative work. That may be true. But certainly the arts generally would be feeling an even colder wind without the companies' help.

Tom Tickell

Answer each of these questions with a few words or a *short* sentence.

1 Explain the meaning of these words and phrases used in the article: cutting expenses to the bone (lines 3–4) good will (line 43) dying on its feet (line 49) push (line 78) feeling an even colder wind (line 117)
2 How much money was spent on sponsorship in Britain five years ago?
3 How much is spent currently on the sponsorship of non-artistic events?
4 Why is the increased spending on the arts by companies 'paradoxical'?
5 Why, for example, do banks give so much?
6 Why do insurance companies contribute to archaeology?
7 Why do companies prefer arts sponsorship to TV advertisements?
8 Why does Lloyds Bank support the National Youth Orchestra?
9 What happened after cigarette commercials on TV were banned?
10 Why has arts sponsorship by tobacco companies been growing recently?
11 How have recent changes in tax laws in the UK affected arts sponsorship?
12 What is the writer's attitude to the unadventurousness of commercial sponsorship of the arts?

5.4 Linking words *Use of English*

Fill each of the gaps in the passage below with a suitable linking word or phrase. Choose from this list but be careful – some are to be used more than once!

and but that unless although since because
when what while even
however
in order to
after all for example incidentally

The critic should never imagine that he is powerful, ..1... it would be culpable of him not to realise ..2... he is bound to be influential. There is no reason, ..3... , to be crushed flat by the responsibility of the job. It is, ..4... , a wonderfully enjoyable one, ..5... at its most onerous. The onerousness, ..6... , springs more from the fatigue of trying to respond intelligently than from the necessary curtailment of one's night-life. Any television critic soon gets used to being asked about how he supports the loss of all those dinner parties. Doesn't he pine for intelligent conversation? The real answers to such questions are usually too rude to give, ..7... the interrogator is a friend. Formal dinner parties are an overrated pastime, barely serving their nominal function of introducing people to one another, ..8... nearly always lamentably devoid of the intelligent conversation they are supposed to promote. Most people severely overestimate their powers as conversationalists, ..9... even the few genuinely gifted chatterers tend not to flourish when hemmed about by bad listeners. The talk on the little screen is nearly always better than the talk around a dinner table. For my own part, I hear all the good conversation I need ..10... lunching with drunken literary acquaintances in scruffy restaurants. In London, the early afternoon is the time for wit's free play. At night, it chokes in its collar.

..11... I miss in the evenings is not dinner parties ..12... the opera house. ..13... I finally give up reporting the tube, it will probably be ..14... the lure of the opera house has become too strong to resist. ..15... sitting down to be bored ..16... eating is an activity I would willingly go on forgoing. The box is much more entertaining – a fact which even the most dedicated diners-out occasionally admit, ..17.. from time to time it becomes accepted in polite society that the long-drawn-out gustatory proceedings may be interrupted ..18.. watch certain programmes. It was recognised, ..19.. that *The Glittering Prizes* might legitimately entail a concerted rush from the dinner table to the television set, ..20.. I confess that in this one case my own inclination was to rush from the television set to the dinner table.

(from an article by Clive James in *The Observer*)

5.5 Idioms with PUT *Use of English*

Rewrite each of the sentences so that it still means the same, using the words on the left together with the correct form of the verb PUT. Look at the example first.

1 ON They are producing a version of 'Cinderella' on ice.
They are putting on a version of 'Cinderella' on ice.
2 OFF We discouraged him from giving up his job to become a painter.
3 OFF The opening of his one-man show has been postponed until he recovers from his illness.
4 ON THE MAP The success of our local theatre has made our city famous.
5 PRESSURE ON They tried to persuade the Arts Council to subsidise the newly-formed orchestra.
6 WORDS INTO MY MOUTH Don't misquote me: I never said I hated ballet!
7 MY FINGER ON I can't specify exactly what it was that I disliked about the performance.
8 DOWN TO The show's lack of success can be attributed to the poor reviews it received in the press.
9 BEHIND Never mind your previous failures – try to forget them and think of what your next venture might be!
10 FORWARD A plan has been suggested to prevent valuable paintings being sold to collectors and galleries abroad.
11 PAID TO Lack of government support has destroyed the plan to build the new museum in the city.
12 YOUR FOOT IN IT You really blundered when you told him that he had no talent as a painter!

5.6 Guernica *Questions and summary*

The passage that follows describes Pablo Picasso's 'Guernica', which was painted after the bombing of a Basque town during the Spanish Civil War. The painting itself is huge, but the reproduction below gives an idea of what it looks like and will help you to follow the description in the first paragraph.

Guernica is the most powerful invective against violence in modern art, but it was not wholly inspired by the war: its motifs – the weeping woman, the horse, the bull – had been running through Picasso's work for years before Guernica brought them together. In the painting they become receptacles for extreme sensation – as John Berger has remarked, Picasso could imagine more suffering in a horse's head than Rubens normally put into a whole Crucifixion. The spike tongues, the rolling eyes, the frantic splayed toes and fingers, the necks arched in spasm: these would be unendurable if their tension were not braced against the broken, but visible, order of the painting ...

... it is a general meditation on suffering, and its symbols are archaic, not historical: the gored and speared horse (the Spanish Republic), the bull (Franco) louring over the bereaved, shrieking woman, the paraphernalia of pre-modernist images like the broken sword, the surviving flower, and the dove. Apart from the late Cubist style, the only specifically modern elements in *Guernica* are the Mithraic eye of the electric light, and the suggestion that the horse's body is made of parallel lines of newsprint, like the newspaper in Picasso's collages a quarter of a century before. Otherwise its heroic abstraction and monumentalized pain hardly seem to belong to the time of photography and Heinkel 51s. Yet they do: and Picasso's most effective way of locating them in that time was to paint *Guernica* entirely in black, white, and grey, so that despite its huge size it retains something of the grainy, ephemeral look one associates with the front page of a newspaper.

A Explain the meaning of the following words that are used in the description of the painting:

invective (line 1) archaic (line 10) bereaved (line 12)
paraphernalia (line 12) ephemeral (line 20)

B Now read the continuation of the passage and answer the questions that follow.

Guernica was the last great history-painting. It was also the last modern painting of major importance that took its subject from politics with the intention of changing the way large numbers of people thought and felt about power. Since 1937, there have been a few admirable works of art that contained political references – some of Joseph Beuys's work or Robert Motherwell's *Elegies to the Spanish Republic.* But the idea that an artist, by making painting or sculpture, could insert images into the stream of public speech and thus change political discourse has gone, probably for good, along with the nineteenth-century ideal of the artist as public man. Mass media took away the political speech of art. When Picasso painted *Guernica*, regular TV broadcasting had been in existence for only a year in England and nobody in France, except a few electronics experts, had seen a television set. There were perhaps fifteen thousand such sets in New York City. Television was too crude, too novel, to be altogether credible. The day when most people in the capitalist world would base their understanding of politics on what the TV screen gave them was still almost a generation away. But by the end of World War II, the role of the 'war artist' had been rendered negligible by war photography. What did you believe, a drawing of an emaciated corpse in a pit that looked like bad, late German Expressionism, or the incontrovertible photographs from Belsen, Maidenek, and Auschwitz? It seems obvious, looking back, that the artists of Weimar Germany and Leninist Russia lived in a much more attenuated landscape of media than ours, and their reward was that they could still believe, in good faith and without bombast, that art could morally influence the world. Today, the idea has largely been dismissed, as it must be in a mass media society where art's principal social role is to be investment capital, or, in the simplest way, bullion. We still have political art, but we have no *effective* political art. An artist must be famous to be heard, but as he acquires fame, so his work accumulates 'value' and becomes, ipso facto, harmless. As far as today's politics is concerned, most art aspires to the condition of Muzak. It provides the background hum for power. If the Third Reich had lasted until now, the young bloods of the Inner Party would not be interested in old fogeys like Albert Speer or Arno Breker, Hitler's monumental sculptor; they would be queuing up to have their portraits silkscreened by Andy Warhol. It is hard to think of any work of art of which one can say, *This* saved the life of one Jew, one Vietnamese, one Cambodian. Specific books, perhaps; but as far as one can tell, no paintings or sculptures. The difference between us and the artists of the 1920s is that they thought such a work of art could be made. Perhaps it was a certain naïveté that made them think so. But it is certainly our loss that we cannot.

(from *The Shock of the New* by Robert Hughes)

1 How did artists before 1937, when 'Guernica' was painted, believe that they could make political statements?
2 How do people in the West nowadays form their political opinions?
3 Why did it become meaningless to paint scenes of war during the Second World War?
4 What is the function of art in the modern capitalist world?
5 What is the role of art in politics nowadays?

C In one paragraph, using your own words as far as possible, summarise the changing role of art in Western society between the 1920s and the present day.

5.7 Terms of Endearment *Listening*

A As you listen to the recording for the first time, match the names of the people on the left to the parts they played or their roles in the making of the film, 'Terms of Endearment'.

James L. Brooks	Aurora Greenway
Jeff Daniels	Emma, her daughter
John Lithgow	Flap Horton, Emma's husband
Shirley MacLaine	Emma's lover, a banker
Larry McMurtry	Garrett Breedlove, an ex-astronaut
Jack Nicholson	Director
Debra Winger	Writer of the screenplay
	Writer of the original novel

B Listen to the recording again and decide whether the following statements are true (T) or false (F), according to what is said in the recording.

1 Shirley MacLaine won an Oscar for her performance in the film.
2 Emma's father is still alive.
3 Aurora hates her son-in-law, Flap.
4 Aurora cries during her daughter's wedding ceremony.
5 Aurora admires her daughter very much.
6 Flap and Emma go to live in another state, remote from Aurora.
7 Flap is unfaithful to his wife.
8 Emma has an affair to punish Flap for his infidelity to her.
9 Aurora's neighbour drinks heavily.
10 Aurora and Garrett get married in the end.
11 Emma dies in childbirth.
12 The critic thinks the film was less effective in the cinema than it is on video.

5.8 Starlight Express *Listening*

Answer these multiple-choice questions about the hit musical 'Starlight Express'. Pay particular attention to the *tone of voice* used by the speakers.

1 Celia seems to think the story of 'Starlight Express' is . . .
comic silly stupid witty

2 Celia thinks the songs were . . .
banal brilliant somewhat disappointing wonderful

3 Musically, the songs are all in . . .
different styles similar styles the same style

4 Celia thinks the best singer was . . .
Jeffrey David Frances Ruffelle Stephanie Lawrence Jeff Shankly

5 The best song, according to Celia was . . .
'AC/DC' 'Only You' 'Uncoupled' 'Don't Cry for Me, Argentina'

6 Celia couldn't make out the lyrics because . . .
the singers didn't enunciate clearly.
the audience were speaking during the songs.
the sound system was very loud.

7 She says the tunes of the songs were . . .
easy to remember forgettable remarkable

8 She thought the design and the set were . . .
incredible unusual shocking unspeakable

9 During the races she felt . . .
annoyed bored scared scornful

10 Ray Shell's performance as Rusty the Steam Engine was . . .
exciting inspiring pathetic touching

11 When Paul left the theatre he felt happy and . . .
dissatisfied excited inspired fulfilled

12 Celia felt that the whole show lacked . . .
excitement humour profundity good performances

13 Celia agrees with Paul that the show will be . . .
critically acclaimed a flop popular unpopular

5.9 Two paintings *Picture conversation*

Work in pairs. One of you should look at activity 26, while the other looks at 44. You will each have a work of art to describe and discuss.

5.10 What do you enjoy? *Communication activity*

Work in pairs. One of you should look at activity 9, while the other looks at 46. You will be finding out about each other's tastes in the arts and entertainment.

"No encores – I know only two numbers."

5.11 A day in the life *Composition*

Look at the photograph and information that follow. When you have discussed the subject with a partner or with other members of the class, you will have to put yourself into the shoes of *one* of the performance artists whose work is described and continue the account of either his or her experience of the 'performance'.

Linda and Tehching have promised to stay together for one year and never be alone, but never to touch each other during the year. They will always be in the same room when they are indoors.

Write your composition as if it is the continuation of one of the accounts on the next page. Imagine how your daily life would be affected by the rope joining you to your fellow-performer.

On Wednesday – America's Independence Day – Tehching Hsieh and Linda Montano will cut an eight-foot rope which has connected them since last summer. They are performance artists, and this bizarre feat is their latest "work of art". Tehching Hsieh, 33, grew up in Taiwan. Since coming to New York, he has completed three year-long performances: the first in a cage without reading, writing or speaking; the second punching a time clock every hour; and the third living entirely out of doors. Linda Montano, 42, is from New York State. She has spent five years in karate school, two years in a Zen centre and two years in a convent. She sees this performance as an artistic continuation of her training in mental discipline. Interview by Rose Kernochan. Photograph by Louise Gubb

July, 1983

STATEMENT

We, LINDA MONTANO and TEHCHING HSIEH, plan to do a one year performance.

We will stay together for one year and never be alone.

We will be in the same room at the same time, when we are inside.

We will be tied together at the waist with an 8 foot rope.

We will never touch each other during the year.

The performance will begin on July 4, 1983 at 6 p.m., and continue until July 4, 1984 at 6 p.m.

Linda Montano
LINDA MONTANO

Tehching Hsieh
TEHCHING HSIEH

111 Hudson St. 2 Fl. New York, N.Y. 10013

Information: EXIT ART 966-7745

■LINDA MONTANO

Why am I doing this piece? I felt that to put myself in a difficult situation would challenge me emotionally, and force me into changes I needed to make. I needed to learn lessons about interdependence and compromise, because I knew I wasn't going to have children.

Also, in 1973, I was handcuffed for three days to a curator for a museum of conceptual art. That piece allowed me to see that art could be made without being in the studio. I'm interested in extending art into life, not separating it

■TEHCHING HSIEH

The rules for the piece state that we always have to be in the same room at the same time. When one person goes to the bathroom, for instance, the other often stands in the doorway. Also, we can't have physical contact. I'd say, however, that we've touched about 60 times so far; we write it down each time we do. The rope is comfortable and very strong.

Every day we take a 3in × 5in colour photograph of ourselves. We tape all of our conversations. The tapes are not replayed; we seal them permanently to show that the piece will go on for ever. So far, we've accumulated about 600 of these tapes.

I feel that the piece is a symbol of human beings and their survival. All of us are tied up together and we struggle among ourselves for we are all individuals. The

(from *The Sunday Times*)

6 The news

6.1 Vocabulary

A Find a suitable word to fill the gaps in the sentences below. Sometimes there may be several words that would make sense.

1 A newspaper expresses its opinions about the news in its ....
2 Small-format papers (eg *The Sun*) are known as ....s.
3 After the conference the leaders issued a .... to the press.
4 There's a good report in the paper from their Moscow ....
5 The news was released to the press by a government ....
6 Thousands of people have been killed in a(n) ....
7 I prefer *The Guardian* because it has excellent .... of the arts.
8 The articles in a week-old paper are no longer ....
9 It says the baby's mother is 123 – that must be a ....
10 The first part of the paper I turn to is the sports ....

B Here are some typical, mostly genuine, newspaper headlines. Each has been 'translated' into everyday language, with some words missing. Can you supply the missing words?

11 **Jobless total tops 3m**
.... 3 million people are now ....

12 Storm over pit closures
There has been an angry .... to the announcement that some .... are to be closed.

13 ***QUAKE TOLL RISES***
The number of .... of the .... has risen.

14 Tories set to win poll
The .... party is expected to win the forthcoming ....

15 **Peace moves in docks**
There has been an .... to .... both sides in the port workers dispute.

16 Jobs blow for second city
There has been much .... about the announcement that workers are to be made redundant in Birmingham.

→

17 ***ENVOY'S CONCORDE DASH TO UN TALKS***
The British .... has .... by Concorde to .... at the United Nations.

18 **Teachers to be axed**
Some teachers are going to lose ....

19 Africa arms dog premier
The .... has been facing further .... over the supply of weapons to an African country.

20 ***POLICE NAME MR BIG***
The police have revealed the .... of the .... of the robberies.

21 **Trio on kidnap charge**
.... people have been .... in connection with the kidnapping.

22 Mayor goes in bribes storm
After the discovery that he had .... bribes, the mayor has ....

23 ***KREMLIN UPS ARMS SPENDING***
The .... government have .... their defence budget.

24 **£3m drugs haul at Heathrow**
Customs officers at Heathrow Airport have .... drugs .... £3 million.

25 Fish talks in Copenhagen
.... between EEC .... ministers are to be .... in Copenhagen.

6.2 Three news reports *Reading*

To show that you can't necessarily believe everything you read in the newspapers, look at the three reports that follow. Decide which of the reports gives the 'facts' listed below. The first is done for you as an example.

The amount of damage caused by the fire was . . .
£4 million A
£1 million B
less than £1 million C

The 007 sound stage at Pinewood is . . .
1) the largest in the world
2) 400 feet long
3) 336 feet long

The fire was fought by . . .

4) over 100 firemen
5) about 70 firemen

Flames from the fire could be seen . . .

6) five miles away
7) eight miles away

The stage was first used for the filming of . . .

8) 'The Spy Who Loved Me'
9) 'Thunderball'

The people who received treatment were . . .

10) a carpenter and a wardrobe worker
11) four firemen and two stagehands
12) four firemen, an actress and one other person

The next James Bond film due to be made at Pinewood is . . .

13) 'A View To A Kill'
14) 'A View For A Kill'

The film being shot at Pinewood when the fire broke out is called . . .

15) 'Legend'
16) 'Legends'

A

Home of 007 movies destroyed in £4m fire

By BAZ BAMIGBOYE

IN a real-life drama more spectacular than any 007 movie, the world's biggest film set went up in smoke yesterday.

The sound stage at Pinewood Studios — home of the James Bond films — was destroyed in a massive blaze, causing an estimated £4 million damage.

The stage was being used for a £25 million fantasy epic, Legend, which has been shooting at the legendary Buckinghamshire studios for several months.

The main set, a vast artificial forest of wood and polystyrene, was wiped out. But the crew and cast of the picture, with stars Tom Cruise and Tim Curry, were at lunch when the blaze broke out.

Firemen say they would have been killed if filming had been going on.

The blaze was so fierce that a foam tender at a nearby oil depot was put on alert. As the fire became a raging inferno, the studio's metal walls and roof turned white hot and 100ft flames could be seen eight miles away.

More than 100 firemen from Buckinghamshire, Greater London and Berkshire fought the blaze for two hours.

Six people, four of them firemen, were treated at the scene. Two stage hands suffered minor burns and shock.

The fire broke out near some gas cylinders and is thought to have been started by an explosion.

The 400ft sound stage was built for the James Bond epic, The Spy Who Loved Me, and opened by Sir Harold Wilson in 1976.

Since then all the Bond movies starring Roger Moore have been shot there

(from *The Daily Mail*)

B

£1m thunderball destroys James Bond set

A £1m fire has destroyed the film set where the Superman and James Bond films were made.

An explosion ripped through the set at Pinewood studios near Iver Heath, Buckinghamshire, minutes after nearly 200 actors and workers had left for lunch.

Flames leapt more than 100ft into the air and the clouds of smoke could be seen more than five miles away.

More than 100 firemen fought the blaze but there was nothing they could do to stop the corrugated steel building becoming a mass of twisted and buckled wreckage.

The studio said the stage, the biggest in the world and known as the 007 set because of its link with the Bond films, would cost more than £1m to rebuild.

Six people, including four firemen, were treated for burns, smoke inhalation and shock, but no one was seriously hurt.

The 007 set was being used to make a multi-million pound science fiction film called *Legends*. The film involves hundreds of spectacular special effects and gas cylinders were on the set, although the cause of the fire is not yet known.

Much of the scenery was made of polystyrene and wood and the blaze spread quickly.

Prop shifter Mr Barry Gibbs, aged 23, was one of the few people left inside the building when "suddenly there was a huge explosion. It was like a bomb going off" he said. "There was a blinding flash and everything went up."

Hundreds of pigeons, a fox and a cow being used in the film were saved from the flames. Mrs Gladys Haywood, from the agents "Animal Action" said: "We bashed down the shed where they were kept and dragged their cages to safety through the smoke. None of them was hurt."

The actress who rescued the animals was overcome by fumes and was given oxygen, but she did not have to go to hospital.

It is understood that the filming of *Legends* was almost complete and the film is not likely to be delayed. But a new Bond film, *A View For a Kill*, was due to start shooting there in August and it will now have to be postponed or switched to another studio.

The 007 stage was built in the 1960s to cope with the Bond films' demand for an indoor set capable of holding the series' panoramic visual stunts. The 336ft x 139ft stage contained a 249ft long tank which was flooded to double as an underground submarine compound in one of the films.

It was first used on *Thunderball*, and then for the *Superman* series, it was turned into an exotic outer space location.

(from *The Times*)

C

007 stage destroyed in fire at studio

THE 007 sound stage at Pinewood film studios in Buckinghamshire — the largest in the world, and where many of the James Bond films were made — was destroyed by fire yesterday.

"It's like something from Hiroshima Now," said a studio executive after the fire, which started in the lunch-hour when the set was almost unattended.

The set of Arnold Ridley's film, Legend, worth £500,000 was incinerated as gas cylinders exploded, driving back firemen. A wardrobe worker and a carpenter escaped with only slight burns and shock, and they were the only injured.

Legend, with a fairyland set of forests, waterfalls, and hills, had been shooting since March, and was only 11 days from completion. The company had hired at least three other stages at the studio, and work will be switched to these.

The latest Bond film, A View to a Kill, was due to go to the studio in August, and will now be restricted to the smaller sound stages at Pinewood.

"The whole thing is agonising," said a Pinewood executive. "Half a million pounds worth of set was destroyed, with hundreds of thousands of pounds worth of film equipment."

There were 200,000 gallons of water on the set that could have helped put out the fire, but 70 firemen could not reach it because of the heat.

(from *The Guardian*)

"You'd think he'd have learnt by now that every page smells exactly like every other page."

6.3 Three sports reports *Reading*

Each of the reports that follow is about the same day's play at Wimbledon. Don't worry if tennis is a closed book to you – you don't have to be an expert either to appreciate the reports or to answer the questions.

1 How many paragraphs do *The Daily Mail* and *The Guardian* devote to Connors' behaviour?
2 What does *The Times* have to say about Connors' bad language?
3 Which of the reports show(s) that Connors did actually use bad language?
4 How many paragraphs does each report devote to the match itself?
5 Was Connors' behaviour the day's worst at Wimbledon?
6 Results of other matches that day: True or False?
   Arias beat Ocleppo
   Colombo beat Krishnan
   Annacone beat Van Rensberg
   Dickson beat Doyle
   Lendl beat Tarr
7 Unlike the other two, somewhat conventional, sports reports, *The Times* report is full of extravagant imagery ('. . . buzzing with life like a hive at springtime') and idiomatic phrases ('within a whisker of . . .'). Can you find five more examples of these – or perhaps even more?

Connors finds stomach for fight

By Geoffrey Green

When Jimmy Connors beat the young Swede Stefan Simonssen 6-2, 6-1, 6-3 on the Centre Court, one could scarcely call it a pageant of rich language nor even a vignette. Yet there were moments in the third set which got the gallery buzzing with life like a hive at springtime.

At that point Connors stood at love-40 on service and within a whisker of being 1-4 down. Suddenly the Swede unfurled his colours with some penetrating two-fisted backhands down the line and dipping top spin forehand passes à la Borg.

Connors, serving and diving for volleys, grunted even louder, which made one think of Lord Emsworth's favourite sow the Empress of Blandings, grunting in her sty. The American for that spell clearly was off his feed, but put his digestion right in time to save that game and roll on to victory by taking the last four games with two breaks of service. That was the heart of the matter.

The odd fact was that not a single ace was unleashed by either man until the third set – a big relief from the usual heavy barrage of serve and swift volley. Simonssen set the example then, as he went to 2-0, followed soon by four from Connors, the last to seal the match. This happily led to some dignified exchanges which suggested that the Swede may some day have something to say for himself.

His second service for one thing was largely meat and drink to Connors as he broke twice to take the last five games for the first set in spite of two doubles in the eighth game. The second set was an echo of the first as Connors put three more breaks into the margin of his effort.

But it was the concluding set that embellished the affair. Base-line barter saw each man use every inch of the canvas artistically. By then Connors was back on his feed, but as he said at his press interview later: "I shall hope to do better next time." He was certainly not on his usual high plateau.

(from *The Times*)

brilliant plot to which the 18-year-old had no answer, and as the pressure grew his shots became increasingly wild and uncontrolled. His day will come, but experience has to be learned the hard way and Kriek gave him a lesson.

Two of the tournament's aristocrats were in action. Lendl seemed totally unconcerned at being sent to Court Two, known as The Graveyard, and overwhelmed Derek Tarr 6-3, 6-1, 6-3, in 90 minutes. Jimmy Connors had his first match on the Centre Court and was almost equally abrupt in dismissing Stefan Simonssen 6-2, 6-1, 6-3 to equal Arthur Gore's record, set between 1888 and 1927, of winning 64 singles matches in the championships.

It should have been a happy occasion and it would have been but for an incident in the third set, when Simonssen had two points for a 4-1 lead after a disputed call. Connors was heard to say to the umpire Malcolm Huntington: "You piss me off. If you both think that ball was out, you should both be dismissed." Just the sort of insubordination officials had warned against.

Alan Mills, the referee, said they will be studying the TV tape this morning. Action could follow. It was clearly a breach of the code of conduct. Such matters, happily, were far from the thoughts of two 21-year-olds who last night found themselves scheduled to play one another for a place in the fourth round.

Almost a fortnight ago, Paul Annacone, an American, and Christo Van Rensberg of South Africa entered the qualifying tournament at Roehampton; yesterday, they joined the 14 other second-round winners. Annacone beat the vastly more experienced Mark Dickson 7-6, 7-6, 6-1 and Van Rensberg defeated the lone Irishman, Matt Doyle, 4-6, 6-2, 7-5, 7-6.

● Simone Colombo, a 20-year-old Italian, was fined £250 yesterday for spitting at a linesman during his first-round defeat by India's Ramesh Krishnan.

(from *The Guardian*)

Connors faces trial by video

WIMBLEDON referee Alan Mills will today head a trial-by-video investigation into the behaviour of Jimmy Connors on Centre Court yesterday.

He will try to discover if the No. 3 seed was abusive to umpire Malcolm Huntingdon during his straight sets win over Stefan Simonsson.

The matter reached his office after BBC commentator John Barrett had raised the subject during yesterday's broadcast.

Mills said last night: 'If Connors swore and it was heard on TV then something would have to happen.'

After talking to BBC production staff last night I believe the American was not heard to swear on air. He is believed to have said to the umpire: 'If you both think the ball is out you should both be dismissed.' Mills must decide if that was abusive.

Connors was never threatened by Simonsson and whipped through his second round match 6-2, 6-1, 6-3.

Jimmy Arias, the 19-year-old street-wise No. 5 seed reached the third round at his first attempt, beating Italian Gianni Ocleppo 7-5, 5-7, 3-6, 7-6, 6-4, and afterwards listed his deficiencies on a surface that is alien to him.

Useless

'I don't know how to hit a second serve,' he admitted. 'My kicker is a useless sitter and now I am trying to slice it, but that means I double-fault five or six times.

'Grass is tough on my thighs and I get cramp. I feel I am improving every day, but I need to come to the net more often. But I am such a chicken, especially in the fifth set.'

A linesman has been rebuked for failing to report Italian Simone Colombo for spitting at him. Colombo was fined $350 after the umpire's report. MALCOLM FOLLEY

(from *The Daily Mail*)

6.4 Past, present and future forms *Use of English*

Rewrite each of the headlines below to show their meanings. The first is done for you as an example.

1 Bid to save heart man fails
Surgeons . . . have not succeeded in saving the life of a patient suffering from heart disease.

2 **Charges to go in museums**
Admission charges . . .

3 Cane head is cleared in court
A headmaster who . . .

4 *GUNMAN KILLS 3 IN BANK DRAMA*
A man . . .

5 **Riddle of missing heiress solved**
The police . . .

6 Police attacked in clashes
The police . . .

7 *'POLICE ATTACKED' SAYS STUDENT LEADER*
A student leader . . .

8 **Storm grows over long hair in school**
Parents and pupils . . .

9 Councillors to act on strip shows
The city council . . .

10 *CUSTOMS SWOOP NETS £1m AT PORT*
Customs officials . . .

6.5 Reporting speech *Use of English*

Use suitable words to complete each of the sentences below. The first is done for you as an example.

1 An eyewitness described ......how ten people had been killed...... in the fire.
2 The Prime Minister announced that government spending .... cut.
3 The report disclosed .... workers .... made redundant next year.
4 A spokesman explained .... no danger to the public.
5 The star's press agent announced .... from the film as she was suffering from food poisoning.
6 The manager of the England team commented .... with the team's performance.
7 The minister warned .... no settlement unless the strikers returned to work at once.
8 One of the survivors described .... by the lifeboat.
9 In a press release British Rail have announced .... £20 million .... the modernisation of rolling stock.
10 A survey published today reveals .... electorate .... vote the present government back into power if an election were held tomorrow.

6.6 A correspondent's life *Questions and summary*

A CORRESPONDENT'S LIFE

Michael Buerk tells of the luck, pleasures and pains in having 'the world's most wonderful job'

It must have been the shuffling on the landing outside the room that did it. Strange how the mind works. All night gunfire had stuttered and crashed and rolled around the town and I had slept on through everything. It had, after all, been an exhausting couple of weeks, criss-crossing El Salvador, watching — from both sides and often at dangerously close quarters — the guerrillas as they were resolutely attempting to disrupt the national elections.

We had arrived in San Vicente late in the evening after another hair-raising day in which the rebels and government troops took turns at different points on the road to push their guns through the windows of our car. We had spent half the afternoon in a ditch that marked the precise centre of a gun battle ... I, scared beyond rational thought, attempting to use my face as a trowel to wriggle further into the ground, my two camera crew colleagues discussing gun calibres and overtime rates with an insouciance which did begin (along with a considerable amount of dirt) to get right up my nose.

There had not been much point in being choosey over where to spend the night. There was, we were told, only one place. A shabby two storey quadrangle, the room bare concrete with an iron bed, draped in grey sheets that made you scratch just to look at them. None of that had mattered. Gunfire and lice did not wake me up ... it was the shuffling of those feet.

I rolled out of bed and opened the door. Outside nearly all the other rooms was a long queue of Salvadorian soldiers waiting, with varying degrees of patience, for their turn in what, it was now clear, was San Vicente's biggest brothel. Not to put too fine a point on it, we were staying in the busiest knocking shop in the whole of Central America.

The thought was not conducive to sleep. In the itching, noisy darkness I fell to thinking about all the other strange nights I had spent in a career as a home then foreign correspondent.

The night in the back of a hired car, lit by the bloody glow of a burning chemical factory at a place nobody had ever heard of then — Flixborough. The night in a Turkish jail after I had been rash enough to sail a chartered fishing boat through the Turks' invasion fleet as it prepared to invade Cyprus. A fortnight later, several hilarious nights trapped in a UN post in what had become no-man's-land between Turkish and Greek-Cypriot forces. The post was manned by Danish policemen, liberally supplied with good meat and wine by the UN — and several thousand pornographic magazines sent by sympathetic colleagues on the Copenhagen vice squad.

I had spent nights staring at the sea as I threw up over the side of a lobster boat sailing round the Orkney Islands ... a lifetime, or so it seemed, pursuing an apparently deranged Army commander through the African bush in a single decker bus ... and, the worst of all, a night trying to catch a scorpion by match-light. I had found it when I pulled back the sheet of my bed in a mudwalled cell in northern Ethiopia (we foreign correspondents learn to check these things). But it gave me the slip and I hunted for it all night in vain.

I have spent most of my adult life doing the world's most wonderful job. I am actually *paid* to go all over the world to see the most fascinating, the most important, or the most entertaining things that might be happening. It is a life of hasty departures, airline schedules and charter planes, satellites and deadlines.

Few people wake up each morning not knowing for certain they will even be on the same continent by nightfall. Few wives would put up with it. Christine is special. She used to be a journalist herself, which helps. She's tolerant, good-humoured, and capable, but then she has had to be. Our social life is a series of gambles, our last four holidays have been disrupted. I even missed the christening of our twin sons, an occasion that's gone down in the family history as 'the day Christine was jilted at the Font'.

We *did* have a brief period of predictability in our lives. For eighteen months my itchy feet were kept under the newsreading desk on the BBC 'Nine o'Clock News' ... a job I had thought not worthy of a grown man, let alone a trained journalist. I was wrong of course. Fronting a live programme, often still being prepared as it goes on air, is like spending half an hour on a high wire that's only properly fixed at one end. Some nights it felt wonderful, relaxed confidence oozing through gallery and studio. Other nights only professionalism stood between tension and panic as the crew struggled to dovetail late breaking news into an already complex programme. 'You need a sense of humour', a veteran newsreader told me once ... a memorable understatement. He himself had once concluded a particularly shambolic programme by signing off: 'If it looked a bit odd to you people out there ... you should have been where *I* was sitting'.

It *was* fun. Wonderful for the ego to be recognised about the place (don't let anybody tell you otherwise). Pleasant to be treated as somebody important ... even though it's a spurious importance, based only on the ability to read out loud and the technology of television which projects you into ten million living rooms each night.

It was a seductive life. In many ways I regret leaving it. But the opportunity I had wanted for years finally came up — to become a proper foreign correspondent and *live* abroad. So we left the comfortable house in Surrey we had created out of the wreck we had recently bought. We settled in Johannesburg, wrestling with the problems of houses and schools familiar to all expatriates, and began to learn about Africa.

It's a continent of paradox. So much beauty and so much ugliness. Fertility and famine. A continent of unrealisable dreams and fading hope.

It's an infuriating place for a journalist to work. Where governments do not actively discourage what we in the west would regard as objective reporting, their bureaucracies raise endless obstacles that you have to be both tireless and ingenious to overcome. But it's worth it. The harsh African sun shines on stark issues ... the supremacy of one race over another, of one tribe over another. Dictatorships dally with disaster. And, of course, the ultimate human issue ... survival itself.

Ethiopia proved a personal watershed for me. To experience, at first hand, suffering on such a scale is to change your life ... or at least the way you look at it.

A year ago a trainee journalist asked me what was the most important advice I could give a would-be correspondent. 'Don't have your injections in the bum if you've got a long flight', I said. If I was asked that question now I would say: 'Stay human.' I would probably also add, '... don't tell anybody else about your job, or they'll all want to do it'. □

Answer these questions about the passage in writing.

1 Explain the meaning of these words and phrases used in the passage:
shuffling on the landing (line 4) insouciance (line 26)
itchy feet (line 104) fronting (line 108) dovetail (line 116) ⟶

2 Why was Michael Buerk unable to sleep in San Vicente?
3 Why were his nights in a UN post 'hilarious'?
4 Why couldn't he sleep in northern Ethiopia?
5 Why is a correspondent's life 'wonderful'?
6 Why did he enjoy his time as TV newsreader?
7 How many times does the writer use this punctuation device: ... ? What is the effect of this?
8 In one paragraph, summarise the dangers, discomforts and distress that Michael Buerk has encountered in his life as a foreign correspondent.

(When you have completed this exercise, your teacher will give you some further instructions.)

6.7 What do you read? *Listening*

You'll hear eight people describing a paper or magazine they buy regularly. Fill in the questionnaire form for each, showing their preferences with a tick (✓) or a cross (✗).

NAME *Bill*
- Type of publication: MORNING DAILY ☐ EVENING DAILY ☐ WEEKLY ☐ SUNDAY ☐ [tick one]
- Country of publication: UK ☐ USA ☐ ELSEWHERE ☐ [tick one]
- Tick features enjoyed (✓), or put a cross beside features disliked (X):

NEWS OF BRITAIN ☐ NEWS OF USA ☐ WORLD NEWS ☐ ENTERTAINMENT ☐ GOOD WRITING ☐
PHOTOGRAPHS ☐ ADVERTISEMENTS ☐ CARTOONS ☐ ARTS ☐ BINGO ☐ BUSINESS ☐
TV ☐ EDITORIALS ☐ POLITICAL STANDPOINT ☐ QUALITY OF PRINTING ☐ COLOUR ☐
TAKES A LONG TIME TO READ ☐ TAKES A SHORT TIME TO READ ☐ PRICE ☐

NAME *Jerry*
- Type of publication: MORNING DAILY ☐ EVENING DAILY ☐ WEEKLY ☐ SUNDAY ☐ [tick one]
- Country of publication: UK ☐ USA ☐ ELSEWHERE ☐ [tick one]
- Tick features enjoyed (✓), or put a cross beside features disliked (X):

NEWS OF BRITAIN ☐ NEWS OF USA ☐ WORLD NEWS ☐ ENTERTAINMENT ☐ GOOD WRITING ☐
PHOTOGRAPHS ☐ ADVERTISEMENTS ☐ CARTOONS ☐ ARTS ☐ BINGO ☐ BUSINESS ☐
TV ☐ EDITORIALS ☐ POLITICAL STANDPOINT ☐ QUALITY OF PRINTING ☐ COLOUR ☐
TAKES A LONG TIME TO READ ☐ TAKES A SHORT TIME TO READ ☐ PRICE ☐

NAME *Ann*
- Type of publication: MORNING DAILY ☐ EVENING DAILY ☐ WEEKLY ☐ SUNDAY ☐ [tick one]
- Country of publication: UK ☐ USA ☐ ELSEWHERE ☐ [tick one]
- Tick features enjoyed (✓), or put a cross beside features disliked (X):

NEWS OF BRITAIN ☐ NEWS OF USA ☐ WORLD NEWS ☐ ENTERTAINMENT ☐ GOOD WRITING ☐
PHOTOGRAPHS ☐ ADVERTISEMENTS ☐ CARTOONS ☐ ARTS ☐ BINGO ☐ BUSINESS ☐
TV ☐ EDITORIALS ☐ POLITICAL STANDPOINT ☐ QUALITY OF PRINTING ☐ COLOUR ☐
TAKES A LONG TIME TO READ ☐ TAKES A SHORT TIME TO READ ☐ PRICE ☐

NAME Ken

- Type of publication: MORNING DAILY ☐ EVENING DAILY ☐ WEEKLY ☐ SUNDAY ☐ [tick one]
- Country of publication: UK ☐ USA ☐ ELSEWHERE ☐ [tick one]
- Tick features enjoyed (√), or put a cross beside features disliked (X):

NEWS OF BRITAIN ☐ NEWS OF USA ☐ WORLD NEWS ☐ ENTERTAINMENT ☐ GOOD WRITING ☐
PHOTOGRAPHS ☐ ADVERTISEMENTS ☐ CARTOONS ☐ ARTS ☐ BINGO ☐ BUSINESS ☐
TV ☐ EDITORIALS ☐ POLITICAL STANDPOINT ☐ QUALITY OF PRINTING ☐ COLOUR ☐
TAKES A LONG TIME TO READ ☐ TAKES A SHORT TIME TO READ ☐ PRICE ☐

NAME Michael

- Type of publication: MORNING DAILY ☐ EVENING DAILY ☐ WEEKLY ☐ SUNDAY ☐ [tick one]
- Country of publication: UK ☐ USA ☐ ELSEWHERE ☐ [tick one]
- Tick features enjoyed (√), or put a cross beside features disliked (X):

NEWS OF BRITAIN ☐ NEWS OF USA ☐ WORLD NEWS ☐ ENTERTAINMENT ☐ GOOD WRITING ☐
PHOTOGRAPHS ☐ ADVERTISEMENTS ☐ CARTOONS ☐ ARTS ☐ BINGO ☐ BUSINESS ☐
TV ☐ EDITORIALS ☐ POLITICAL STANDPOINT ☐ QUALITY OF PRINTING ☐ COLOUR ☐
TAKES A LONG TIME TO READ ☐ TAKES A SHORT TIME TO READ ☐ PRICE ☐

NAME Yvonne

- Type of publication: MORNING DAILY ☐ EVENING DAILY ☐ WEEKLY ☐ SUNDAY ☐ [tick one]
- Country of publication: UK ☐ USA ☐ ELSEWHERE ☐ [tick one]
- Tick features enjoyed (√), or put a cross beside features disliked (X):

NEWS OF BRITAIN ☐ NEWS OF USA ☐ WORLD NEWS ☐ ENTERTAINMENT ☐ GOOD WRITING ☐
PHOTOGRAPHS ☐ ADVERTISEMENTS ☐ CARTOONS ☐ ARTS ☐ BINGO ☐ BUSINESS ☐
TV ☐ EDITORIALS ☐ POLITICAL STANDPOINT ☐ QUALITY OF PRINTING ☐ COLOUR ☐
TAKES A LONG TIME TO READ ☐ TAKES A SHORT TIME TO READ ☐ PRICE ☐

NAME Ted

- Type of publication: MORNING DAILY ☐ EVENING DAILY ☐ WEEKLY ☐ SUNDAY ☐ [tick one]
- Country of publication: UK ☐ USA ☐ ELSEWHERE ☐ [tick one]
- Tick features enjoyed (√), or put a cross beside features disliked (X):

NEWS OF BRITAIN ☐ NEWS OF USA ☐ WORLD NEWS ☐ ENTERTAINMENT ☐ GOOD WRITING ☐
PHOTOGRAPHS ☐ ADVERTISEMENTS ☐ CARTOONS ☐ ARTS ☐ BINGO ☐ BUSINESS ☐
TV ☐ EDITORIALS ☐ POLITICAL STANDPOINT ☐ QUALITY OF PRINTING ☐ COLOUR ☐
TAKES A LONG TIME TO READ ☐ TAKES A SHORT TIME TO READ ☐ PRICE ☐

NAME Harry

- Type of publication: MORNING DAILY ☐ EVENING DAILY ☐ WEEKLY ☐ SUNDAY ☐ [tick one]
- Country of publication: UK ☐ USA ☐ ELSEWHERE ☐ [tick one]
- Tick features enjoyed (√), or put a cross beside features disliked (X):

NEWS OF BRITAIN ☐ NEWS OF USA ☐ WORLD NEWS ☐ ENTERTAINMENT ☐ GOOD WRITING ☐
PHOTOGRAPHS ☐ ADVERTISEMENTS ☐ CARTOONS ☐ ARTS ☐ BINGO ☐ BUSINESS ☐
TV ☐ EDITORIALS ☐ POLITICAL STANDPOINT ☐ QUALITY OF PRINTING ☐ COLOUR ☐
TAKES A LONG TIME TO READ ☐ TAKES A SHORT TIME TO READ ☐ PRICE ☐

6.8 Here is the news *Listening*

Listen to the radio news broadcast and decide which of the following pieces of information are true (T) or false (F), according to what is reported.

1 The strike at London's airports is over working hours, not pay.
2 Flights from Heathrow will be less badly affected than flights from Gatwick.
3 Some flights into Heathrow will be landing at other airports.
4 Some flights into Gatwick will be landing at other airports.
5 Twenty per cent of flights from Gatwick will be delayed by two hours or more.
6 Flight information on Heathrow services is available on 01 795 2525.
7 The strike at Heathrow will continue tomorrow.

8 Fourteen coach passengers were seriously injured by a falling tree near Barnstaple.
9 Six people escaped from a cinema fire at Appledore.
10 The M5, A30 and A303 are still closed to traffic.
11 Drivers in the South West should put off their journeys if possible.

12 There have been many casualties in a typhoon in Japan.
13 The typhoon looks as if it may claim further victims.

14 Next month's summit meeting will be attended by six Western leaders.
15 Experts are surprised at the choice of the meeting place.

16 John Lloyd beat John MacEnroe in a three-set match.
17 The winner meets Vitas Gerulaitis in the next round.

18 It will be wetter in the West than yesterday.
19 The weather in the East will improve during the day.
20 There will be more heavy rain at the weekend.

6.9 Animal stories *Pronunciation*

Work in groups of three. One of you should look at communication activity 10, another at 48 and the third at 77. You will each have a short news item to read out to your partners.
Listen carefully to your partners' news items for the answers to these questions:

What happened to Mr Watling?
How many times was the Italian attacked?
How many rats are there in China?

Which of the items appeals to you most? Find another similar item from a recent newspaper and tell your partners about it.

6.10 Sweet revenge *Communication activity*

You will each have different parts of a newspaper article to summarise in your own words. Here, to start you off, are the first and last paragraphs of the article:

Peter Chapman on how the Mexicans make a mint out of small change

Finding a slot for sweet revenge

MANY Mexicans remember as if it were yesterday the loss of Texas and California to the US midway through last century, not to mention the vast tracts of land that went under the 1803 Louisiana Purchase, for which Mexico believes it was blatantly short-changed.

In the old days, of course, the US might have been more inclined to send in the marines to protect US interests — a point which Mexico remembers very well and which will now incline Mexico City towards telling Washington that if it does not like the new, devalued peso then it will just have to lump it.

One of you should look at activity 11 and the other at 50.

6.11 Two narratives *Composition*

The two articles on the next page appeared on successive days in the same newspaper. After you have read them through, make notes on the events described in chronological sequence – starting with the events that occurred before the court hearing and ending with the outcome of the hearing. ⇢

Write *two* narratives describing the events. The first should give the story from the point of view of Mr Monty Cohen; the second from the point of view of Mrs Anna Sewell. Make sure both narratives include the relevant facts as well as the narrators' reactions and feelings.

The cat sat on the witness box

By Penny Chorlton

A LARGE neutered ginger tom cat behaved himself impeccably in the witness box at Snaresbrook Crown Court, Essex, yesterday. The cat stared impassively at the 12 jurors summoned to assess rival claims of ownership and to decide whether he is called Marmaduke or Sunny.

In the dock was 57-year-old Mr Monty Cohen, of Woodford Bridge, Essex, who denies stealing the cat and assaulting his neighbour, PC John Sewell.

PC Sewell, who was asked by Judge Worthington to show the cat to the court, said that he and his wife had returned home from holiday last September to find their cat missing. A friend who had been looking after him said that he disappeared soon after they went away.

The cat's real name, he said, was Marmaduke Gingerbits, but this had been shortened because it was no longer strictly true.

"He was christened before his operation," said PC Sewell.

Mr Kenneth Macrae, prosecuting, said that meanwhile a large, well-fed ginger cat had started visiting another neighbour, Mrs Doreen Smythe.

She said that one evening she saw Mr Cohen trying to catch it. He said that he thought it was his missing cat, Sunny.

Despite the animal's reluctance to go to him, Mrs Smythe said that she let him take it. "The cat wouldn't go near him. He crouched and was spitting and laid on the floor, all hunched up."

Then she saw a picture of Marmaduke in a shop window with an advertisement offering a £10 reward for his return and contacted the Sewells to say that she might have made a mistake.

PC Sewell, a 6ft 4ins juvenile bureau officer said that Mr Cohen was hostile but showed him the cat.

"The cat immediately turned his head and we knew at that moment that it was our animal. He was struggling to get free and get away from Cohen towards myself and my wife." Mr Cohen would not free him and there was a struggle.

PC Sewell produced his warrant card but failed to calm the situation. As he started to leave, Mr Cohen and a friend, who said he was a karate black belt, attacked him. PC Sewell said that he was aching for days afterwards.

Mr Andrew Trevan, a vet who treated Marmaduke a year earlier for an eye injury, told the court that he was now employed by the veterinary group given custody of the cat pending the case. The disputed animal had the same, uncommon, eye scar.

Mr Cohen is expected to give evidence today.

Cat goes into care while 'owners' fight on

By Penny Chorlton and Anne McHardy

"EXHIBIT B," the ginger tom cat that might be Marmaduke Gingerbits or might be Sunny, was transferred to the custody of the RSPCA yesterday after Judge Worthington, sitting at Snaresbrook Crown Court, Essex, had decided that his court had no jurisdiction to decide who owned the animal.

Rival claimants PC John Sewell and Mr Monty Cohen, neighbours at Woodford Bridge, Essex, both declared their intention of taking the matter to the other courts after the Snaresbrook jury had found 57-year-old Mr Cohen guilty of assaulting PC Sewell, aged 37, but not guilty of stealing the cat.

Mrs Anna Sewell said later at her home that she and her husband would be seeking an order at Redbridge magistrates' court today which they hoped would give the cat to them within 10 days.

PC Sewell had told the court that his wife's cat, Marmaduke Gingerbits, disappeared last September while they were on holiday. When they returned a neighbour told them a stray cat had been taken from her garden by Mr Cohen. Mr Cohen said that his cat, Sunny, disappeared at the same time as Marmaduke and he had twice recovered it from local gardens.

The cat produced in court has been in a cattery since the argument flared between PC Sewell and Mr Cohen when the Sewells tried to claim the cat from him. Yesterday Judge Worthington expressed concern at the escalating cost of keeping the cat in custody—already more than £300—and said he would accept the offer of the local RSPCA secretary to look after it. Immediately, Mr Cohen's counsel, Mr Dermott Hynes, asked for the cat to be given to Mr Cohen.

Judge Worthington replied: "I am not going to deal with the question of access to a cat."

PC Sewell, a juvenile bureau officer, said he was badly bruised when Mr Cohen and a friend attacked him when he tried to take the cat away. Mr Hynes said that when police officers arrived at Mr Cohen's house Mr Cohen had already been told that his rival was a policeman. "From start to finish Mr Sewell, working with other police officers, was on the inside rail, so to speak.... There was no proper consideration of Mr Cohen's account."

7 Consumers

7.1 Vocabulary

Find a suitable word to fill the gaps in the sentences below. In some cases there may be several possible words that make sense.

1 People who buy goods or services are known these days as ....
2 Large groups of stores obtain goods from manufacturers at a good ....
3 During the past year the store's .... has increased by 55%.
4 I haven't heard of Snibbo Coffee before; is it a new ....?
5 Secondhand furniture can be bought cheaply at an .... sale.
6 Market traders in many countries expect their customers to ....
7 The store's policy is to prosecute anyone who is caught ....
8 An ironmonger's is also known as a .... store.
9 Fish shops are usually called ....
10 A shop where you buy office supplies, pens and paper is a ....
11 Fine foods from all over the world can be bought in a ....
12 Ready-cooked hot food to eat at home can be bought in a ....
13 Food shops are controlled by strict laws affecting ....
14 The owner of a shop can be fined if he .... the law.
15 If you want a shopkeeper to reserve an article for you until a later date, he'll probably ask you to pay a ....

In the next ten sentences, *three* of the alternatives are correct in each sentence and *two* are wrong. Decide which are correct and why the wrong alternatives seem to be incorrect.

16 The .... was thronged with crowds of shoppers on Saturday.
arcade kiosk shopping precinct shopping centre department shop

17 The goods they have on offer at the moment are certainly ....
value for money good value priceless invaluable a bargain

18 There are consumer protection laws that affect every ....
retailer trader vendor patron purchase

19 Complaints about goods should be made to the seller, not the ....
creator manufacturer supplier wholesaler author

20 Sales staff are often told that 'the .... is always right'.
customer client stockist dealer purchaser

21 A modern cash register keeps a record of every ....
contract transaction sale deal purchase made

22 The food in that restaurant is really ....
delicious tasteful tasty wholesome savoury

23 'What would you like to drink: a .... or something stronger?'
cider soft drink liqueur lager short

24 New products are announced to the public ....
on posters in commercials in press releases by mail order
by propaganda

25 I enjoy eating there because the staff are so ....
subservient courteous helpful obsequious good-natured

7.2 Tide turns against the Devil *Reading*

After you have read the article, answer the questions that follow it briefly:

Tide turns against the Devil

From Christopher Reed in San Francisco

Procter & Gamble, manufacturer of Tide detergent, Crest toothpaste, Ivory soap and other household products and food, is trying to cleanse the Devil from its corporate image.

Satanic soap suds and the presence of Lucifer in the loo would seem to be unlikely competition for the multinational giant. But the company has felt compelled to go to court to exorcise the charge that it promotes devil worship.

The satanic smear originates from the company's curious logo—a hirsute male face as a quarter moon against a black background with 13 stars. It goes back 131 years to the time when the moon face was a popular image. The 13 stars represent the original American colonies.

Rumours began two years ago that the trade mark was linked to Old Nick. They were taken up by religious fundamentalists and turned into a virulent whispering campaign until P. & G.'s Cincinnati head office was receiving 3,000 enquiries a week.

P & G's "Old Nick" logo

Company executives decided they could no longer ignore the Antichrist allegations when pastors in the South began preaching against P & G products and fundamentalist pamphlets urging Christians to boycott the company were distributed outside supermarkets. The firm sent disclaimers to 48,000 southern churches but still the rumours persisted.

P & G finally lost patience when cultists, projecting one of their own customs, began suggesting that a tithe of the firm's considerable profits went to satanism—a 10 per cent dividend for The Devil.

Now the firm has defamation suits against a couple in Florida and a man in Georgia as perpetrators of the rumour campaign and threaten more suits if the gossip continues.

P & G's UK subsidiary in Newcastle has also been under the gun from British religious critics.

Invoking Mephistopheles in the market place is only one example of malignant legends that bedevil companies. In 1978 McDonald's, the world-wide fast food chain, had to fight allegations of using worms in its Big Mac hamburger. The fact that worms would cost the company more than its beef did nothing to stop the tongues wagging.

The firm placed large ads denying the story but it spread to rival companies — and then just as mysteriously died out.

A persistent tale is the "Kentucky fried rat" in which a woman — it is always a woman — finds a rat tail protruding from a piece of batter-coated meat in her bucket of fried chicken.

Coca-Cola has long suffered from wild allegations. As a child you may remember being told that a tooth left in a glass of coke would dissolve by the next day. Another favourite is of a rodent or parts of it being found in a bottle.

Rodents, spiders and snakes often feature. The reason, author Jan Harold Brunvand believes, is because they also crop up in folklore, for these company tales are what he calls urban folklore. He has made a collection in a new book called The Vanishing Hitch-Hiker (Norton) in which he says they will always be around.

He offers one consolation: no big company has ever been put out of business because of unfounded rumours.

---

1 What do these words used in the article mean? You should be able to work out their meanings from the context:
   hirsute (line 23)   tithe (line 58)   bedevil (line 76)
2 The writer uses five different synonyms for 'the Devil' – what are they?
3 The writer uses alliteration for humorous effect – can you find some examples of this? (Your answers to the previous question will help you to do this!)
4 What are the true reasons for the moon face and the 13 stars in Procter and Gamble's logo?
5 Why are P & G taking the rumours so seriously?
6 What unsuccessful attempt did they make to allay fundamentalists' fears?
7 What have they done more recently about the rumours?
8 Did McDonalds take seriously the rumour that their hamburgers contained worms?
9 Is it true that Coca Cola can dissolve a tooth?
10 Are such rumours about big companies likely to recur?

Describe the tone of the article. What is the writer trying to do and how does he achieve this? Give examples to support your answer.

7.3 How we test fridges

Reading

The captions below come from a report in the consumer magazine *Which?* Can you decide which of the photographs on the next page the captions belong to? The first is done for you as an example on the next page.

1 This print-out from the computer shows how the fresh food storage compartment temperature (middle line) and frozen food storage compartment temperature (bottom line) changed with room temperature (top line)

2 Frozen food compartments are filled with test-freezing packages made of a synthetic, jelly-like material that responds to temperature changes as lean beef would, but, unlike real food, doesn't deteriorate and so is a good substitute for food in long-term tests. The fine wires are from thermocouples – type of thermometer – embedded in some of the packages.

The temperatures measured by the thermocouples are recorded throughout the tests by a computer. It can provide any detail that's required: for instance, what the highest temperature was anywhere in the cabinet, or how the temperature of the cabinet has averaged out over a long period

3 As part of the convenience tests, compartments and doors are filled with a variety of food

4 Every fridge is checked for electrical safety. In this test a high voltage is applied to the fridge via the plug. Any fault in the electrical insulation shows up straightaway

5 The laboratory has two rooms in which temperature and humidity can be closely controlled. They can take up to 16 appliances. These fridge/freezers are being tested to see how they manage against room temperatures varied between 10°C and 32°C

6 This is a simple, yet effective test: if the strip of paper shut in the door stays put against a gentle pull, the seal is working properly. The test is repeated all round the door

7 Each appliance is connected to an electricity meter, but unlike the one in your house which is read by the meter man, this one is read by the ubiquitous computer

»»→

HOW WE TEST FRIDGES

Meanwhile, back at the lab . . .
Twenty years' experience of fridge and freezing testing has led to a pretty impressive set-up at the *Which?* laboratory. And our fridge and freezer testing isn't, nowadays, just for *Which?*: the laboratory carries out work for the World Health Organisation; and is in the process of testing for a number of European consumer organisations. In these pictures you see fridge/freezers from the UK (being tested for a *Which?* report later this year), alongside ones from Belgium, France and the Netherlands

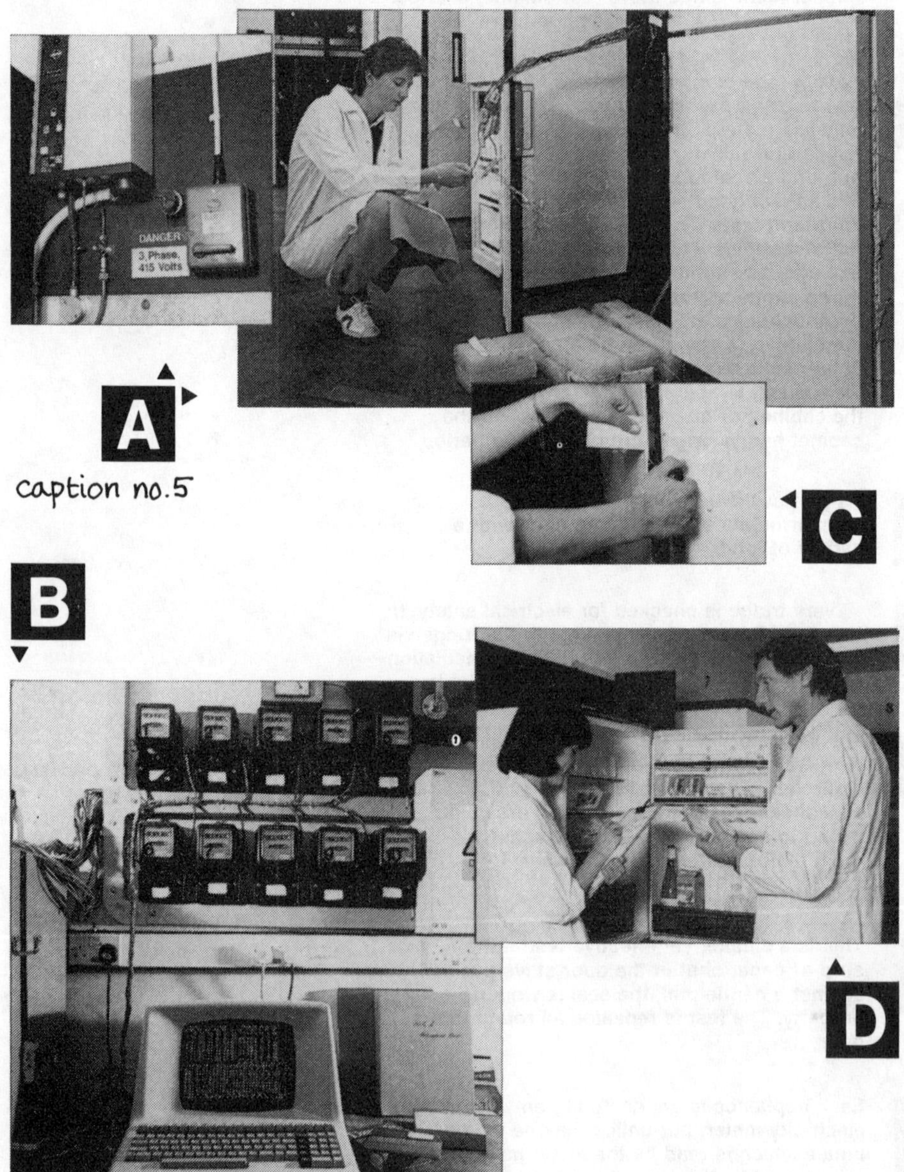

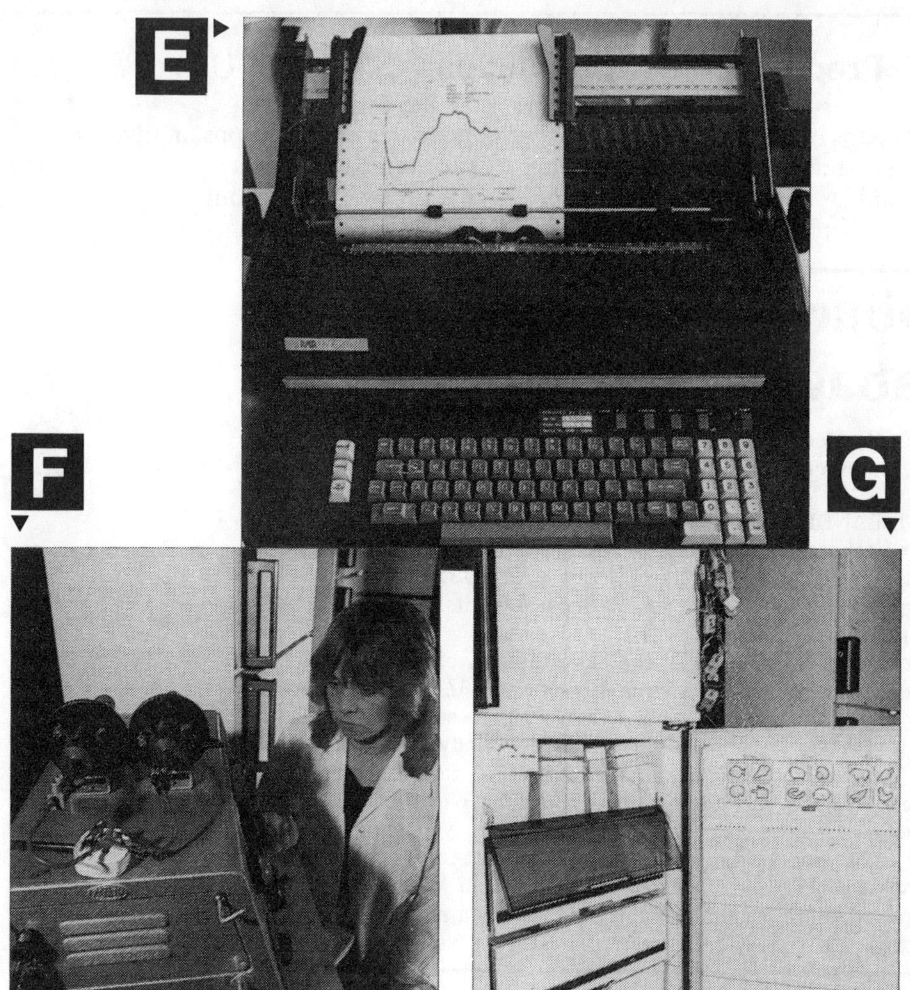
E
F
G

7.4 Prepositions and particles

Fill the gaps in the newspaper article with one of these prepositions or adverbial particles – but be careful because some are used more than once.

around between by for in of on out
since to with

Tobacco for chewing – teabag style

By Derek Harris
Commercial Editor

SKOAL BANDITS (a brand ....1.... chewing tobacco dispensed ....2.... a slim, one-inch sachet like a teabag) are ....3.... the way ....4.... Britain's shops, imported ....5.... US Tobacco, which ....6.... the United States has defied sliding tobacco market trends ....7.... its new product.

US Tobacco has been ....8.... the tobacco business, including the production ....9.... chewing tobacco, ...10.... 1822, but packing chewing tobacco ....11.... the "teabags" has proved more profitable and attractive ....12.... a wider range ....13.... people intent ....14.... taking nicotine.

Chewing tobacco, teabag style, means a third less tobacco is used, so enhancing profits, Mr Louis Bantle, chairman and president ....15.... US Tobacco, says. The Skoal Bandits, which are being backed ....16.... television as well as other advertising, let smooth flavour get ....17.... while the tobacco stays ....18...., according ....19.... the company's advertising slogan.

Nicotine fanciers are told: "You don't chew it. Just place a pouch ....20.... your upper lip and gum." Most users let the tiny pouch roam ....21.... the mouth ....22.... half an hour ....23.... average, Mr Bantle says.

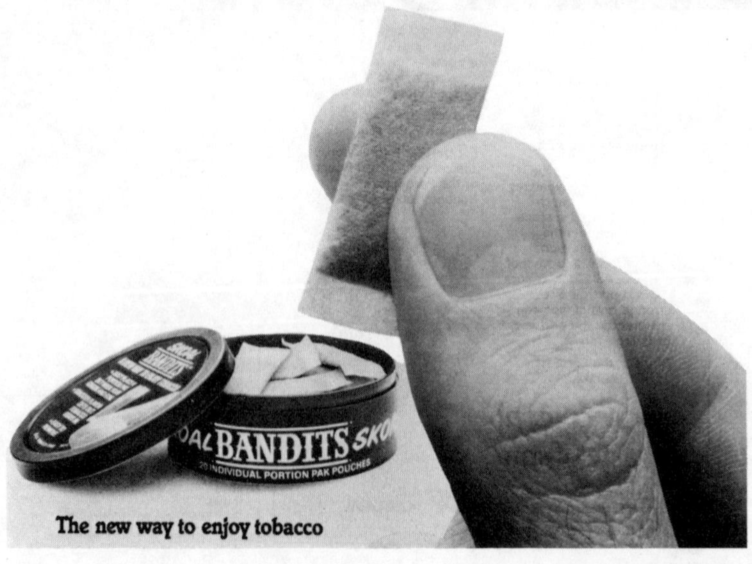

7.5 Idioms with GO *Use of English*

Rewrite each of the sentences so that it still means the same, using the words on the left together with the correct form of the verb GO. The first is done for you as an example.

1 DOWN Prices have fallen as a result of the fall in VAT.
Prices have gone down as a result of the fall in VAT.
2 TO HIS HEAD His success in business has made him very conceited.
3 OUT OF BUSINESS His shop has now stopped trading after making heavy losses.
4 BAD TO WORSE Trade has deteriorated and staff are being laid off.
5 FOR Supplies are so scarce that any models available are fetching high prices.
6 OFF By the time I opened the carton its contents were no longer fit to drink.
7 OVER I'll explain how it works before you try it yourself.
8 HAYWIRE My new watch seems to be working strangely and erratically, so I'd better take it back to the shop.
9 BACK ON I was told that it would be repaired free of charge but the man in the shop refuses to honour his promise.
10 OFF When I bought it I thought it was a beautiful colour, but I don't like it any more.
11 ROUND The book was so popular that there weren't enough copies to supply the demand.
12 LIKE A BOMB Sales dropped before the Budget, but since then it has been selling at a phenomenal rate.

7.6 Distorting the truth? *Questions and summary*

Look at the advertisement and answer the following questions about it in writing.

1 Explain the meaning of these words and phrases used in the passage:
a handful (line 9) weakling (line 19) pledging (line 40)
akin (line 41) ditch (line 58) yardstick (line 68)
breach (line 92) unwittingly (line 93) monitor (line 97)
sceptical (line 128) levy (line 141)

2 Look at the passage and explain who or what is referred to by the words ringed in the quotations below:
with the people (they) are addressed to (line 8)
(They) misrepresent the products (line 9)
would have (us) flexing our muscles (line 29)
(it) must not require an Olympic athlete (line 50)
to do (it) in the time (line 52)
what (they) can and cannot say (line 75)
any advertising (they) are asked to publish (line 78)
any advertisements (they) think ought not to have (line 101)

If (they) cannot (line 109)
or withdraw (them) completely (line 111)
sceptical about (its) effectiveness (line 128)
For (this) to be credible (line 133)

3 What examples of misrepresentative advertisements are given?
4 How does the ASA act on complaints made by members of the public?
5 How does the ASA maintain its independent status?
6 In one paragraph, describe the role of the ASA and how it operates.

DO ADVERTISEMENTS SOMETIMES DISTORT THE TRUTH?

The short answer is yes, some do.

Every week hundreds of thousands of advertisements appear for the very first time.

Nearly all of them play fair with the people they are addressed to.

A handful do not. They misrepresent the products they are advertising.

As the Advertising Standards Authority it is our job to make sure these ads are identified, and stopped.

WHAT MAKES AN ADVERTISEMENT MISLEADING?

If a training course had turned a 7 stone weakling into Mr Universe the fact could be advertised because it can be proved.

But a promise to build 'you' into a 15 stone he-man would have us flexing our muscles because the promise could not always be kept.

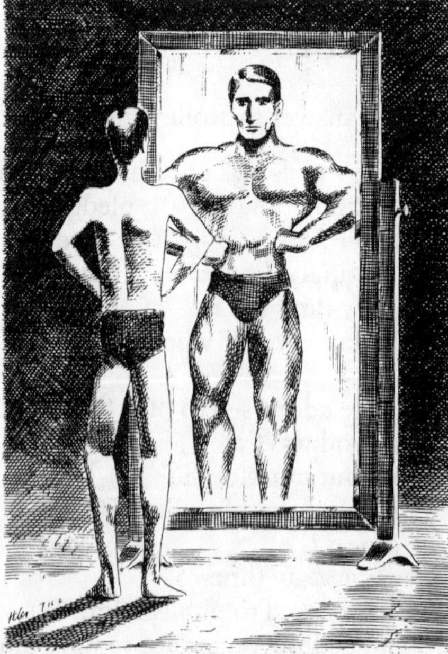

'Makes you look younger' might be a reasonable claim for a cosmetic.

But pledging to 'take years off your life' would be an overclaim akin to a promise of eternal youth.

A garden centre's claim that its seedlings would produce 'a riot of colour in just a few days' might be quite contrary to the reality.

Such flowery prose would deserve to be pulled out by the roots.

If a brochure advertised a hotel as being '5 minutes walk to the beach', it must not require an Olympic athlete to do it in the time.

As for estate agents, if the phrase 'overlooking the river' translated to 'backing onto a ditch', there would be nothing for it but to show their ad the door.

HOW DO WE JUDGE THE ADS WE LOOK INTO?

Our yard-stick is The British Code of Advertising Practice.

Its 500 rules give advertisers

precise practical guidance on what they can and cannot say. The rules are also a gauge for media owners to assess the acceptability of any advertising they are asked to publish.

The Code covers magazines, newspapers, cinema commercials, brochures, leaflets, posters, circulars posted to you, and now commercials on video tapes.

The ASA is not responsible for TV and radio advertising. Though the rules are very similar they are administered by the Independent Broadcasting Authority.

WHY IT'S A TWO-WAY PROCESS

Unfortunately some advertisers are unaware of the Code, and breach the rules unwittingly. Others forget, bend or deliberately ignore the rules.

That is why we keep a continuous check on advertising. But because of the sheer volume, we cannot monitor every advertiser all the time.

So we encourage the public to help by telling us about any advertisements they think ought not to have appeared. Last year over 7,500 people wrote to us.

WHAT DO WE DO TO ADVERTISERS WHO DECEIVE THE PUBLIC?

Our first step is to ask advertisers who we or the public challenge to back up their claims with solid evidence.

If they cannot, or refuse to, we ask them either to amend the ads or withdraw them completely.

Nearly all agree without any further argument.

In any case we inform the publishers, who will not knowingly accept any ad which we have decided contravenes the Code.

If the advertiser refuses to withdraw the advertisement he will find it hard if not impossible to have it published.

WHOSE INTERESTS DO WE REALLY REFLECT?

The Advertising Standards Authority was not created by law and has no legal powers.

Not unnaturally some people are sceptical about its effectiveness.

In fact the Advertising Standards Authority was set up by the advertising business to make sure the system of self control worked in the public interest.

For this to be credible, the ASA has to be totally independent of the business.

Neither the chairman nor the majority of ASA council members is allowed to have any involvement in advertising.

Though administrative costs are met by a levy on the business, no advertiser has any influence over ASA decisions.

Advertisers are aware it is as much in their own interests as it is in the public's that honesty should be seen to prevail.

If you would like to know more about the ASA and the rules it seeks to enforce you can write to us at the address below for an abridged copy of the Code.

The Advertising Standards Authority

If an advertisement is wrong, we're here to put it right.

ASA Ltd, Dept. T, Brook House, Torrington Place, London WC1E 7HN.

7.7 Improving the customer's way of life *Listening*

You'll need to hear the recorded conversation at least twice. The first time through, answer questions 1 to 8:

1 Apart from its main store, there are .... Mitsukoshi branches in Japan.
4 14 40 44

2 The 'Ladies Club' provides . . .
companionship discounts free lunches lectures

3 To help foreigners, brochures are available in . . .
most European languages Japanese English Japanese and English

4 English is spoken by .... of the sales staff.
all most none some

5 When you step off an escalator a girl in uniform . . .
can give information helps you off greets everyone
tells everyone what is available on that floor

6 The facilities offered at other Japanese department stores are . . .
exactly the same as Mitsukoshi more numerous than Mitsukoshi
very different from Mitsukoshi very similar to Mitsukoshi

7 Japanese department stores are open . . .
every day of the week every day except Sunday
every day except national holidays six days a week

8 Japanese department stores are in direct competition with . . .
discount stores each other mail order houses supermarkets

As you hear the recording for the second time, fill in the gaps in the sentences below:

9 Mitsukoshi was founded .... years ago.
10 Unlike the policy of a supermarket, the emphasis in Mitsukoshi is on 'ways of .... of customers' lives'.
11 The audience in the theatre is given a .... containing *sushi*, which is .... with ....
12 Shoppers' babies can be looked after in a '.................... babies'.
13 The lift girls wear a uniform consisting of skirt, waistcoat and a little .... hat with .... and beautiful little white ....
14 On the roof there is a .... for children and a .... with a view of Tokyo.
15 Some department stores in Japan even have their own ....
16 At Odakyu or Keio department stores you can take the lift down to the .... where your .... is waiting.
17 Department stores in Japan are open from .... to ....

18 The speaker thinks that the Japanese concept of department stores cannot be .... to the West.
19 Western department stores compete in terms of .... and ....
20 Japanese department stores compete in terms of .... and ....
21 At Mitsukoshi in Regent Street, London, the staff happily spend time helping people who have lost their .... or ...., or who can't find their .... or can't find ....

7.8 Knowing your rights *Listening*

Listen to the interview in which an expert outlines a customer's rights in law when buying goods. Fill in the gaps and answer the questions below.

1 Whenever a purchase is made, the buyer and seller enter into a ....

2 The trader has three main obligations:
A that the goods are 'of .... quality' (this includes .... goods) – eg pair of shoes that .... after two weeks don't meet this obligation.
B that the goods are 'fit for any particular .... made known to the ....' – eg wrong advice given by salesman fails to meet this obligation.
C that the goods are 'as ....' by the seller or on the packet – eg frozen prawns illustrated as .... and .... (but which are in fact ....) don't fulfil this obligation.

3 What should a buyer do if goods are faulty? Tick only the actions that the speaker recommends.
a) Take the item back to the shop
b) Ask the retailer to collect the item
c) Accept a cash refund
d) Accept a credit note
e) Accept a replacement
f) Agree to the item being repaired
g) Send the item back to the manufacturer

4 A trader is not legally obliged to give a refund . . .
– if you examined the goods before purchase and didn't notice any ....
– if you were told of any specific .... at the time of purchase
– if you .... the seller's advice on the .... of the product
– if you .... the seller's claim that he wasn't .... enough to offer advice
– if you .... about wanting the goods
– if you .... the item as a ....

5 When can a shopkeeper refuse to sell you something?

6 Why is it advisable to keep your receipt in a safe place?

7 Why is it unusual for a dissatisfied customer to take a seller to court?

8 If a trader refuses to give you a cash refund, you should go to your local C.................. A.................. B.................. or to the T.................. S.................. Office (sometimes called the C.................. A.................. Centre).

7.9 Advertisements *Picture conversation*

Work in pairs. One of you should look at activity 13, while the other looks at 51. You will each have part of an advertisement to describe and discuss.

7.10 Shopping in Moscow *Communication activity*

Work in pairs. One of you should look at activity 14, the other at 52. You will each have part of a news story, which you must retell in your own words.

7.11 Writing a balanced, relevant essay *Composition*

Look at the notes below and decide which you would include in an essay on this topic, bearing in mind that the points must all be relevant to the topic:

'*Outline the harmful and the beneficial effects of advertising.*'

- Need created for totally unnecessary products (eg kitchen gadgets)
- Plethora of brands of goods, different only in name (eg detergents)
- Goods more expensive due to costly advertising budgets
- Young people may be harmed by certain advertisements (eg alcoholic drink)
- Ads stimulate envy among the less well-off; may lead to rise in crime rate (eg thefts of expensive cars)
- Commercials on TV interrupt programmes - very annoying
- Ads create desire for more and more material possessions

- Ads lead to dissatisfaction with one's standard of living - may lead to people trying to live beyond their means

- Many commercials on TV have insidious tunes that linger in the brain

- Many ads are amusing and informative - often more amusing than the programmes on TV or articles in a magazine

- Ads stimulate competition between companies, thus keeping prices down

- Ads create consumer awareness, giving information about a range of products

- Ads in newspapers and magazines keep their cost down - many couldn't survive without advertisements

- The world would be dull and drab without amusing and colourful ads

Add any further points you would like to make to the notes above. Then write a composition on the topic. Try to give examples of particular advertisements that seem to support your arguments.

"We have high quality and low prices. Which do you want?"

8 Books

8.1 Vocabulary

Fill each gap in these sentences with a suitable word.

1 Although he is best known for his verse, he has also published several volumes of p..................
2 She's taking a c.................. writing course in the hope of becoming a novelist.
3 Although his later novels are heavy going, his early works are very a..................
4 When he wrote that his father was an old fox, it was just a f.................. of s..................
5 'My love is like a red, red rose' is an example of a s..................
6 'The roses in her cheeks' is an example of a m..................
7 Both of the above examples can also be described as i..................
8 'Sing a song of sixpence' is an example of a ....
9 'The greatest book ever written' is an example of hy..................
10 'The less I eat the fatter I get' is an example of a p..................
11 The whole novel is an a.................. of the battle between good and evil.
12 On the surface it seems a very lightweight book but it has a serious m..................
13 The plot is fairly predictable but the c.................. is masterly.
14 Poking fun as it does at contemporary life and manners, the book is one of the best s.................. novels I've read.
15 The book was underrated by the critics but now, 40 years on, it has become a modern c..................

In the remaining ten sentences *three* of the alternatives given are correct and *two* are wrong.

16 As I prefer fiction to non-fiction I often read ....
thrillers memoirs biographies whodunits best-sellers

17 Before buying a book it's a good idea to read the ....
sleeve dustjacket contents blurb bibliography

18 The opening page of a book often has a(n) ....
appendix foreword preface index dedication

19 I've just read the reviews of a newly-published .... of poetry.
collection gathering album book anthology

20 I prefer to read books for enjoyment rather than have to .... them.
dissect study analyse criticise review

21 The plot of a romantic novel is not usually very ....
involved multiple complex intricate mixed

22 It was a very long book and it took me ages to .... through it.
struggle wade flip thumb get

23 His books are not only exciting but also ....
well-written thought-provoking gripping readable thrilling

24 The language he uses can be interpreted literally or ....
symbolically metaphorically figuratively descriptively illustratively

25 Reading a good novel is like escaping into a world of ....
dreams daydreams illusion the imagination fancy

8.2 Three American novels *Reading*

Imagine that you are browsing in a bookshop and you are looking at the first page of three well-known novels. Read the opening paragraph to get an impression of each book *before* you look at the questions on page 101.

Chapter One

1 To the red country and part of the grey country of Oklahoma the last rains came gently, and they did not cut the scarred earth. The ploughs crossed and recrossed the rivulet marks. The last rains lifted the corn quickly and scattered weed colonies and grass along the sides of the roads so that the grey country and the dark red country began to disappear under a green cover. In the last part of May the sky grew pale and the clouds that had hung in high puffs for so long in the spring were dissipated. The sun flared down on the growing corn day after day until a line of brown spread along the edge of each green bayonet. The clouds appeared, and went away, and in a while they did not try any more. The weeds grew darker green to protect themselves, and they did not spread any more. The surface of the earth crusted, a thin hard crust, and as the sky became pale, so the earth became pale, pink in the red country and white in the grey country.

In the water-cut gullies the earth dusted down in dry little streams. Gophers and ant lions started small avalanches. And as the sharp sun struck day after day, the leaves of the young corn became less stiff and erect; they bent in a curve at first, and then, as the central ribs of strength grew weak, each leaf tilted downward. Then it was June, and the sun shone more fiercely. The brown lines on the corn leaves widened and moved in on the central ribs. The weeds frayed and edged back toward their roots. The air was thin and the sky more pale; and every day the earth paled.

In the roads where the teams moved, where the wheels milled the

2

1

We drove past Tiny Polski's mansion house to the main road, and then the five miles into Northampton, Father talking the whole way about savages and the awfulness of America – how it got turned into a dope-taking, door-locking, ulcerated danger-zone of rabid scavengers and criminal millionaires and moral sneaks. And look at the schools. And look at the politicians. And there wasn't a Harvard graduate who could change a flat tyre or do ten push-ups. And there were people in New York City who lived on pet food, who would kill you for a little loose change. Was that normal? If not, why did anyone put up with it?

'I don't know,' he said, replying to himself. 'I'm just thinking out loud.'

Before leaving Hatfield, he had parked the pick-up truck on a rise in the road, and pointed south.

'Here come the savages,' he said, and up they came, tracking across the fields from a sickle of trees through the gummy drizzling heat-outlines of Polski's barns. They were dark and their clothes were rags and some had rags on their heads and others wide-brimmed hats. They were men and boys, a few no older than me, all of them carrying long knives.

Father's finger scared me more than the men did. He was still pointing. The end of his forefinger was missing to the big knuckle, so the finger stump, blunted by stitched skin folds and horribly scarred, could only approximate the right direction.

'Why do they bother to come here?' he said. 'Money? But how

CHAPTER I

3 In the late summer of that year we lived in a house in a village that looked across the river and the plain to the mountains. In the bed of the river there were pebbles and boulders, dry and white in the sun, and the water was clear and swiftly moving and blue in the channels. Troops went by the house and down the road and the dust they raised powdered the leaves of the trees. The trunks of the trees too were dusty and the leaves fell early that year and we saw the troops marching along the road and the dust rising and leaves, stirred by the breeze, falling and the soldiers marching and afterwards the road bare and white except for the leaves.

The plain was rich with crops; there were many orchards of fruit trees and beyond the plain the mountains were brown and bare. There was fighting in the mountains and at night we could see the flashes from the artillery. In the dark it was like summer lightning, but the nights were cool and there was not the feeling of a storm coming.

Sometimes in the dark we heard the troops marching under the window and guns going past pulled by motor-tractors. There was much traffic at night and many mules on the roads with boxes of ammunition on each side of their pack-saddles and grey motor-trucks that carried men, and other trucks with loads covered with canvas that moved slower in the traffic. There were big guns too

You will need to refer back to the three extracts in answering the following questions.

1 Which extract conveys an impression of time passing?
2 Which extract conveys an impression of movement?
3 Which extract conveys an impression of a degenerating, violent world?
4 How are these impressions conveyed? What stylistic devices are used to create the impressions?
5 Which extract uses the fewest modifying adjectives?
6 Which extract uses the simplest grammatical structures?
7 Which extract uses the style of spoken conversational English?
8 Which extract uses repetition to achieve its effect?
9 What do you think might be the theme of the book each extract comes from? What might come next in the story?
10 Which of these books do you think the extracts come from?
The Mosquito Coast by Paul Theroux (1981)
A Farewell to Arms by Ernest Hemingway (1929)
The Great Gatsby by F. Scott Fitzgerald (1926)
The Grapes of Wrath by John Steinbeck (1939)

8.3 Three British novels *Reading*

These are the opening paragraphs of three British novels. Read them through before looking at the questions.

1 I was born in the city of Bombay . . . once upon a time. No, that won't do, there's no getting away from the date: I was born in Doctor Narlikar's Nursing Home on August 15th, 1947. And the time? The time matters, too. Well then: at night. No, it's important to be more . . . On the stroke of midnight, as a matter of fact. Clock-hands joined palms in respectful greetings as I came. Oh, spell it out, spell it out: at the precise instant of India's arrival at independence, I tumbled forth into the world. There were gasps. And, outside the window, fireworks and crowds. A few seconds later, my father broke his big toe; but his accident was a mere trifle when set beside what had befallen me in that benighted moment, because thanks to the occult tyrannies of those blandly saluting clocks I had been mysteriously handcuffed to history, my destinies indissolubly chained to those of my country. For the next three decades, there was to be no escape. Soothsayers had prophesied me, newspapers celebrated my arrival, politicos ratified my authenticity. I was left entirely without a say in the matter. I, Saleem Sinai, later variously called Snotnose, Stainface, Baldy, Sniffer, Buddha and even Piece-of-the-Moon, had become heavily embroiled in Fate – at the best of times a dangerous sort of involvement. And I couldn't even wipe my own nose at the time.

Now, however, time (having no further use for me) is running out. I will soon be thirty-one years old. Perhaps. If my crumbling, over-used body permits. But I have no hope of saving my life, nor can I count on having even a thousand nights and a night. I must work fast, faster than Scheherazade, if I am to end up meaning – yes, meaning – something. I admit it: above all things, I fear absurdity.

And there are so many stories to tell, too many, such an excess of intertwined lives events miracles places rumours, so dense a commingling of the improbable

2 This much I know for sure:

My name is Peter Sinclair, I am English and I am, or I was, twenty-nine years old. Already there is an uncertainty, and my sureness recedes. Age is a variable; I am no longer twenty-nine.

I once thought that the emphatic nature of words ensured truth. If I could find the right words, then with the proper will I could by assertion write all that was true. I have since learned that words are only as valid as the mind that chooses them, so that of essence all prose is a form of deception. To choose too carefully is to become pedantic, closing the imagination to wider visions, yet to err the other way is to invite anarchy into one's mind. If I am to reveal myself then I prefer to do so by my choices, rather than by my accidents. Some might say that such accidents are the product of the unconscious mind, and thus inherently interesting, but as I write this I am warned by what is to follow. Much is unclear. At this outset I need that tedious quality of pedanticism. I have to choose my words with care. I want to be sure.

Therefore, I shall begin again. In the summer of 1976, the year Edwin Miller lent me his cottage, I was twenty-nine years old.

3 My career has always been marked by a strange mixture of confidence and cowardice: almost, one might say, made by it. Take, for instance, the first time I tried spending a night with a man in a hotel. I was nineteen at the time, an age appropriate for such adventures, and needless to say I was not married. I am still not married, a fact of some significance, but more of that later. The name of the boy, if I remember rightly, was Hamish. I do remember rightly. I really must try not to be deprecating. Confidence, not cowardice, is the part of myself which I admire, after all.

Hamish and I had just come down from Cambridge at the end of the Christmas term: we had conceived our plan well in advance, and had each informed our parents that term ended a day later than it actually did, knowing quite well that they would not be interested enough to check, nor sufficiently *au fait* to ascertain the value of their information if they did. So we arrived in London together in the late afternoon, and took a taxi from the station to our destined hotel. We had worked everything out, and had even booked our room, which would probably not have been necessary, as the hotel we had selected was one of those large central cheap-smart ones, specially designed for adventures such as ours. I was wearing a gold curtain ring on the relevant finger. We had decided to stick to Hamish's own name, which, being Andrews, was unmemorable enough, and less confusing than having to think up a pseudonym. We were well educated, the two of us, in the pitfalls of such occasions, having both of us read at one time in our lives a good deal of cheap fiction, and indeed we both carried ourselves with considerable aplomb. We arrived, unloaded our suitably-labelled suitcases, and called at the desk for our key. It was here that I made my mistake. For some reason I was requested to sign the register. I now know that it is by no m[illegible] customary for wives to sign hotel registers

Refer back to the extracts to answer the following questions.

1 Which extract uses an educated, literary style?
2 Which extract uses a bewildering, kaleidoscopic style?

3 Which extract uses a matter-of-fact, everyday style?
4 What impression does the first extract convey? And how is this achieved?
5 What impression does the second extract convey and how is this achieved?
6 What impression does the third extract convey and how is this achieved?
7 What kind of person does the narrator of each story seem to be?
8 Find an example of imagery (metaphor or simile) in the first extract.
9 Find an example of the narrator expressing his theories or ideas in the second extract.
10 Find an example of the narrator poking fun at herself in the third extract.
11 What do you think the rest of each story is likely to be about, bearing in mind that the extracts are from the following novels:
   1 *Midnight's Children* by Salman Rushdie (1981)
   2 *The Affirmation* by Christopher Priest (1981)
   3 *The Millstone* by Margaret Drabble (1965)
12 Which of the books are you tempted to read more of and why?
13 What do the three extracts have in common?

8.4 Conditional sentences *Use of English*

Rewrite each of these sentences so that its meaning remains unchanged. Look at the example first:

1 I'll let you borrow the book but you must promise to return it next week.
If . . . you promise to return the book next week, I'll let you borrow it.

2 He always has his nose in a book and never pays attention to what I say.
If he didn't . . .

3 I didn't realise he was the author and that's why I was so rude about his new book.
Had I . . .

4 Please let me know if you wish to keep the book any longer.
Should you . . .

5 I found it a very readable book, which is why I was able to get through it so quickly.
If it . . .

6 I wasn't able to buy the books I wanted because I didn't have enough money with me.
If . . .

7 You'll never be able to put it down once you've read the first chapter.
If . . .

8 It may not be in stock, but we can order it for you.
If . . .

9 If I met the author one day, I'd ask him to sign my copy of this book.
Were I . . .

10 Containing as it did such explicit descriptions of sex and violence, the book became an immediate best-seller.
If . . .

11 Picaresque novels seem to be unfashionable these days, which is why he can't get his new book published.
If . . .

12 Try to think of a book you have really enjoyed reading and recommend it to your class-mates.
If there's . . .

8.5 Linking words and phrases *Use of English*

Fill the gap in each sentence with a suitable linking word or phrase.

1 Thomas Hardy's Wessex novels, ... *Tess of the d'Urbervilles*, are much admired.
2 Charles Dickens' novels were originally published in monthly serial form, ... each instalment was eagerly awaited by readers.
3 Jane Austen's last novel, ... *Persuasion*, is a tale of love and marriage told with irony and insight.
4 Oscar Wilde's plays were considered to be very amusing in his day, ... they still seem funny today.
5 Somerset Maugham's short stories are brilliant examples of the genre, ... I'd recommend the ones he wrote later in his life.
6 I've never appreciated D. H. Lawrence .... he's supposed to be one of our greatest writers.
7 H. G. Wells was a very prolific writer; .... the quality of his output was extremely high.
8 George Orwell's *1984* has always been a best-seller; .... his other novels are much less well-known.
9 Kingsley Amis's first novel, *Lucky Jim*, is by far his best work – .... that's what some people say.
10 Graham Greene's books are as popular abroad as they are in this country; .... they have an international appeal.

8.6 Writing fiction *Questions and summary*

Read the following extract from Chapter 13 of *The French Lieutenant's Woman* by John Fowles (1969) and then answer the questions on the next page.

You may think novelists always have fixed plans to which they work, so that the future predicted by Chapter One is always inexorably the actuality of Chapter Thirteen. But novelists write for countless different reasons: for money, for fame, for reviewers, for parents, for friends, for loved ones; for vanity, for pride, for curiosity, for amusement: as skilled furniture-makers enjoy making furniture, as drunkards like drinking, as judges like judging, as Sicilians like emptying a shotgun into an enemy's back. I could fill a book with reasons, and they would all be true, though not true of all. Only one same reason is shared by all of us: *we wish to create worlds as real as, but other than the world that is.* Or was. This is why we cannot plan. We know a world is an organism, not a machine. We also know that a genuinely created world must be independent of its creator; a planned world (a world that fully reveals its planning) is a dead world. It is only when our characters and events begin to disobey us that they begin to live. When Charles left Sarah on her cliff-edge, I ordered him to walk straight back to Lyme Regis. But he did not; he gratuitously turned and went down to the Dairy.

Oh, but you say, come on—what I really mean is that the idea crossed my mind as I wrote that it might be more clever to have him stop and drink milk . . . and meet Sarah again. That is certainly one explanation of what happened; but I can only report—and I am the most reliable witness—that the idea seemed to me to come clearly from Charles, not myself. It is not only that he has begun to gain an autonomy; I must respect it, and disrespect all my quasi-divine plans for him, if I wish him to be real.

In other words, to be free myself, I must give him, and Tina, and Sarah, even the abominable Mrs Poulteney, their freedoms as well. There is only one good definition of God: the freedom that allows other freedoms to exist. And I must conform to that definition.

The novelist is still a god, since he creates (and not even the most aleatory avant-garde modern novel has managed to extirpate its author completely); what has changed is that we are no longer the gods of the Victorian image, omniscient and decreeing; but in the new theological image, with freedom our first principle, not authority.

I have disgracefully broken the illusion? No. My characters still exist, and in a reality no less, or no more, real than the one I have just broken. Fiction is woven into all, as a Greek observed some two and a half thousand years ago. I find this new reality (or unreality) more valid; and I would have you share my own sense that I do not fully control these creatures of my mind, any more than you control—however hard you try, however much of a latter-day Mrs Poulteney you may be—your children, colleagues, friends or even yourself.

But this is preposterous? A character is either 'real' or 'imaginary'? If you think that, *hypocrite lecteur*, I can only smile. You do not even think of your own past as quite real; you dress it up, you gild it or blacken it, censor it, tinker with it . . . fictionalize it, in a word, and put it away on a shelf—your book, your romanced autobiography. We are all in flight from the real reality. That is a basic definition of *Homo sapiens*.

So if you think all this unlucky (but it *is* Chapter Thirteen) digression has nothing to do with your Time, Progress, Society, Evolution and all those other capitalized ghosts in the night that are rattling their chains behind the scenes of this book . . . I will not argue. But I shall suspect you.

Answer these questions in writing:

1 According to the writer, why do novelists write novels?
2 Why can't novelists map out the plot of a novel in advance?
3 Why does he describe the characters in his novel as 'real'?
4 What is the 'freedom' that the characters in the novel have?
5 How is a modern novelist different from a 19th century novelist?
6 What does the writer mean when he says 'I shall suspect you'?
7 Taking your ideas from the extract on the previous page and from the extract below from Chapter 45 of the same book, write a paragraph summarising the writer's views on how everyone creates a 'fiction' from their own past and future lives.

I said earlier that we are all poets, though not many of us write poetry; and so are we all novelists, that is, we have a habit of writing fictional futures for ourselves, although perhaps today we incline more to put ourselves into a film. We screen in our minds hypotheses about how we might behave, about what might happen to us; and these novelistic or cinematic hypotheses often have very much more effect on how we actually do behave, when the real future becomes the present, than we generally allow.

8.7 The novels of William Wharton *Listening*

In the recording, an extract from a radio programme about books, the speaker is talking about William Wharton, a contemporary American writer. Answer the questions below briefly – you'll probably need to hear the recording more than once to get all the answers.

In *Birdy* (1978):
1 Who is the narrator of the story?
2 What is the name of Birdy's favourite canary?
3 What is the effect of Wharton's use of the present tense in the narrative?

In *Dad* (1981):
4 Who are 'Billy' and 'John'?
5 How many different 'voices' tell the story?
6 What are the 'two lives' that Dad lives?
7 How does Dad's wife 'escape from her fears'?

In *A Midnight Clear* (1982):
8 In what way are the soldiers 'unusual young men'?
9 Why is the narrator given the nickname 'Wont'?
10 What is the effect of the writer's use of the present tense to tell the story?

In *Scumbler* (1984):
11 What does 'the Scumbler' do in Paris, apart from paint?
12 Why does he go to Spain?
13 What is the effect of the use of the present tense in the narrative?

14 Which of Wharton's books is the most approachable?
15 Which of the books is his best?

AAA CON is the first name in the phone book of most large American cities. This outfit arranges drive-aways; searches out people to drive cars for delivery from one place to another.

My son Billy and I are waiting in the L.A. AAA CON office. I've had my medical exam, deposited a fifty-dollar bond, filled out forms and given references. Billy's too young to take a drive-away; the minimum age is twenty-one. A car's already been assigned to us and we're waiting now for them to drive it up.

Billy's excited because it's a Lincoln Continental. I dread telling him he isn't going to drive. I'm not a super-responsible person, but I'm *that* responsible, especially with someone else's fifteen-thousand-dollar automobile.

So, I'll be driving all the way across this huge country and I'm not looking forward to it.

The office here is grim. These places are only processing centers; ... or fancy furnishings. I figure they make a ... cross-country

(from *Dad* by William Wharton)

8.8 How to write a best-seller *Listening*

Listen to the advice given by the writer in the broadcast and fill the gaps in the notes below. During the *first* listening concentrate on getting the main points. During the *second* listening try to get the details shown in brackets.

THE INGREDIENTS OF A BEST-SELLER.

1 Be famous for .... already.
[eg Clare Francis's Night Sky sold well because of her books describing her sailing and her fame as a ....]

2 Be a .... already.
There are about 20-30 writers who are '........' by readers.
[eg for .... read Danielle Steele or Barbara Cartland
for .... read Alistair Maclean
for .... read Judith Krantz or Jackie Collins]

3 The essential ingredients are:
.... and ...., ..., ..., ...
[But .... is less easy to control.
.... is a speciality interest;
.... is out of fashion.]

4 Write a .... book on a theme that's currently ....
[Recent examples: .... or ....
Last year: ....]

5 Have your own .... and write a book from your ....
[At the end of each programme you can .... the book and the series may be ...., giving you even more sales.]

6 Write a .... of a .... - or better still: have a .... made of your ....
[People often want to read the book ...... seeing the film or buy the book .... seeing the film.]

7 Be prepared to tour giving ...., appearing on ...... and .... of your book.

8 To get more sales of a previous year's best-seller, have a .... made of it.
[eg Shirley Conran's amazingly .... and quite .... Lace; Smiley's People by John Le Carré a more .... example.]

9 The book should be .... and easy to read - so that the reader can read it ...... and .... and still keep .... of the plot.
[Winning a literary award will not boost your sales to the level of .... best-selling authors.]

10 Have lots of friends in ...., otherwise your unsolicited manuscript will be .... by a .... 'reader'.

8.9 Up the Garden Path *Pronunciation*

Work in groups of three. One of you should look at activity 15, another at 53 and another at 74. You will each have an extract from a novel to read to your partners and then discuss with them.

8.10 What did you enjoy? *Communication activity*

Work in groups of three. You should all look at activity 12, where there are questions to ask each other about your tastes and experience in reading. However, if you have started reading one of the books prescribed for optional reading for the Proficiency exam, you should all look at activity 55.

(A number of books are prescribed for optional reading for candidates taking the Proficiency exam. Your teacher can advise you which, if any, of these are suitable for you to study.)

8.11 Writing about a book *Composition*

'Describe a book you have particularly enjoyed reading.' *(about 350 words)*

'Explain what you find particularly striking or moving about the prescribed book you are reading.' (See above) *(about 350 words)*

This is the first time you have been asked to write a composition within the 350-word limit expected in the Proficiency examination. You will need to develop a feeling for this 'ideal length' and how many lines of your own handwriting this is. To help you to do this, look at one of your recent compositions and count how many words there are in ten lines of your handwriting – divide this number by 10 to find the number of words per line. Now look at your two most recent compositions and see how many words you used in each, by counting the number of lines. Are there too few or too many? Try to include more (or possibly fewer) ideas in today's composition, so that its length is approximately 350 words.

In describing the book for this composition, make sure you refer to its:
THEME PLOT CHARACTERS STYLE MESSAGE
RELEVANCE TO YOUR LIFE
Make notes on what you're going to say *before* you start writing the composition itself. Decide what your opening sentence and closing sentence are going to be too.

9 Politics

9.1 Vocabulary

Find a suitable word to fill each gap in the sentences below.

1 According to the US Constitution, the President need not be a member of either the S.................................. or C..................................
2 Unlike the USA (a federal republic), the UK is a c.................................. m..................................
3 The electorate are to be asked their opinion in a national r..................................
4 The defence minister has resigned in a scandal involving allegations of bribery and c..................................
5 After his resignation there will have to be a by-election in his c..................................
6 In the USA many members of the cabinet are not elected but a..................................
7 The PM has sacked the Home Secretary in a cabinet r..................................
8 The Chancellor of the Exchequer (finance minister) will announce several changes in taxation in next week's B..................................
9 In both the UK and the USA the finance ministry is called the T..................................
10 The legislature of many countries consists of an u.................................. and a l.................................. house or ch..................................
11 It may be unwise to assume that all right-wing politicians are r..................................
12 Or yet that all left-wing politicians are r..................................
13 However one can safely assume most middle-of-the-road politicians to be m..................................
14 You can obtain a visa to allow you to visit a foreign country from its e.................................. in your own country.
15 Should you require assistance while abroad, contact your own country's c.................................. for advice.

In the next ten sentences, *three* of the alternatives given are correct and *two* are wrong. Decide which three seem best in each case.

16 Thousands of people turned out into the streets to .... the government's repressive policy.
reform protest against demonstrate against oppose contradict

17 The government has been overthrown in a popular ....
demonstration coup revolution riot uprising

18 After the .... of the government a military junta is now in power.
collapse defeat destruction loss overthrow

19 Armed rebels are often described less derogatorily as ....
freedom fighters gorillas guerrillas revolutionaries terrorists

20 For betraying military secrets to a foreign power a high-ranking civil servant has been arrested as a(n) ....
foreign agent informer intelligence officer spy traitor

21 Excessive loyalty to one's country is sometimes described as ....
allegiance chauvinism jingoism nationalism patriotism

22 Electoral reform is not part of the new government's ....
platform policy programme schedule stage

23 The local people are calling for the .... to resign.
leader councillor counsellor mayor major

24 Dealing with civil servants can often be delayed by too much ....
bureaucracy efficiency officialdom protocol red tape

25 The President explained that the purpose of taxation was to ....
finance government spending line ministers' pockets
provide essential public services redistribute wealth rob the rich

---

9.2 Andorra *Reading*

Read the newspaper article below before answering the questions.

Opening Pandora's box in the Pyrenees

From Eve-Ann Prentice in Andorra

ANDORRA is odd ; full of geographic and cultural quirks which time may be beginning to erode.

At this time of year, the valleys, thousands of feet up in the Pyrenees, are miserably damp and bereft of orthodox mountain beauty.

A few hundred feet higher, the rain which muddies the villages still falls as snow for the benefit of a growing avalanche of ski-ing tourists. The contrast reflects the social irregularity of the principality.

It is a reformer's nightmare, where the male head of all households has been able to vote since the fifteenth century, yet where women were not enfranchised until 1970.

Independence has been assured since 1278, but only because of two overlords who still have feudal powers. However, some Andorrans are now trying to throw off the system which has protected them for 700 years.

The Government comprises 28 elected members of the Very Illustrious Council-General

—or Parliament. They have been ultimately responsible to the joint heads of state, the French Comte de Foix and the Spanish Bishop of Urgel, who can dictate the law at will, since a treaty of 1278.

Andorrans have failed so far to balk at the power of the co-lords because they were seen as protection against the gradual expansion and unification of France and Spain.

But the twentieth century arrived in the 1960s when television and tourism reached Andorra. Many young people resent the ban on trade unions and what they see as interference in their affairs by the co-lords.

The voice of the principality's two radio stations was silenced last month in what was an ominous sign of rebellion. The contract to run the stations, one held by a French company, the other Spanish, expired.

Instead of automatic renewal, the French and Spanish workers were dismissed and the Customs chief took control. Andorra plans to reopen the stations in three months and to run them independently.

Meanwhile, the Council-General wants to introduce a second legislative chamber, but the request to the co-lords has so far been met with silence.

In 1973 the heads of state decreed that all foreigners must register with their two representatives in Andorra, the *vegues*. Andorrans see this, too, as interference in their affairs.

Despite such discontent most Andorrans do not want to remove the co-lords from power—they merely want more independence. They may be loath to cut the tie completely because, when Spain joins the EEC, Andorra will become a free trade island in Europe, and a link with past stability will be reassuring.

An import tax of between 3 and 10 per cent provides the 35,000 Andorrans with revenue for roads, infant schools, and the police force. At 11, children leave home to live in Barcelona or Perpignan to complete their education.

There is no army and there are no political parties. "The people feel Catalan, but the young lean more towards France as the hope for the future," said Mr Alan Haytree, the English son-in-law of a veteran Andorran politician. "Conservative Andorrans lean to Spain and cling to the co-lords.

"The next 10 to 15 years will be crucial to us and sweeping change seems inevitable. A new working class is beginning to evolve with the growth of tourism, and this worries older people.

"De Gaulle visited Andorra in 1967 and warned that the country should be kept open to traffic between France and Spain. Then in 1978, the co-lords met for the first time in centuries for the anniversary of the 1278 treaty. Those visits changed attitudes; women got the vote in 1970, and tourism flourished, bringing outside ideas.

"Until 20 years ago, Andorrans lived mostly by cattle and tobacco farming."

If the Andorran metamorphosis continues the principality's quirks will probably vanish. The postal service, for example, is free, but so was electricity until four years ago. It may only be a matter of time before the other irregularities are smoothed away.

1 What is one of Andorra's 'geographic quirks'?

2 What is one of Andorra's 'cultural quirks'?

3 The 'social irregularity' refers to the contrast in Andorra between . . .
   Andorran men and women.
   the tourists and the Andorrans.
   the Andorrans and their rulers.

4 Decisions about changing the law in Andorra are made by . . .
   the Very Illustrious Council-General.
   the co-lords.
   the *vegues*, the co-lords' representatives.

5 In Andorra there are . . .
   a few secondary schools.
   few secondary schools.
   no secondary schools.

6 Andorrans shy away from full independence because . . .
   the co-lords rule well, in general.
   their political situation is stable.
   they fear the power of France and Spain.

7 The co-lords have . . .
   agreed to the request for a second parliamentary chamber.
   rejected the request for a second parliamentary chamber.
   not responded to the request for a second parliamentary chamber.

8 Which of the following exist or are permitted in Andorra? Tick the ones you think are correct.

an army	a police force	a working class
trade unions	free postage	free electricity
free elections	a French-run radio station	a Spanish-run TV station

9 Why is Andorra's future referred to as 'Pandora's box' in the headline?

What seems to be the writer's attitude to Andorra?
After reading the article are you tempted to find out more about the place? Why (not)?

". . . better education, lower taxes, full employment, lower crime rate, peace, better medical care, finer police and fire protection, prosperity, better public transportation and a lower cost of living OR double your taxes back if not fully satisfied."

9.3 Tired and emotional MPs

The two articles below appeared on successive days in *The Guardian*. Read them through before answering the questions on the next page.

A drop of good advice for MPs

By John Ezard

Mr Hugh Gaitskell and Sir Winston Churchill were cited yesterday as among "plenty of examples" of political leaders whose drinking habits must have impaired their intellectual capacity and judgment.

In an attack on alcohol consumption by MPs the Liberal peer Lord Avebury said that records showed that at the height of the Second World War Sir Winston was "paralytically drunk" while occupying the highest office in the land.

And "after a visit to a collective farm in Russia in 1959, Hugh Gaitskell was said to have drunk 19 tumblers of vodka and then capped it with a tumbler of brandy. It is hardly surprising that he then became unconscious and had to be carried to his car by Denis Healey and David Ennals. He then slept it off on the journey back to Moscow."

Lord Avebury, who entered Parliament as Liberal MP for Orpington in 1962, made these charges in a speech to an international conference in Liverpool on alcohol-related problems. He said that MPs and peers were "forced" to drink much more than was good for them because of the extraordinary and shocking bar opening hours at Westminster.

The bars stayed open the whole time that Parliament was sitting, including late-night sittings. "It is unthinkable that Fords of Dagenham should have a night bar, so if workers felt thirsty they could slip away for a few pints."

After his speech Lord Avebury—a teetotaller for eight years—added: "I knew contemporaries when I was an MP who died through drink. There was one MP who drank himself to death. He was always in the bar at the Commons."

Addressing the same conference, the junior Health Minister, Sir George Young, called for public debate leading to a consensus of opinion on how much freedom individuals should have to choose to damage their own health, as well as risking the health and safety of others.

As a Royal Palace, Westminster is exempt from licensing hours. Its 12 bars range from Annie's for MPs and lobby correspondents in the Commons, to the Bishops' Bar in the Lords.

Mr Gaitskell's biographer, Mr Philip Williams, said that the story of the Russian drinking session was basically true but its details were not right.

"It was one of those enormous Russian occasions when everyone is given too much to drink. He didn't have to be carried to his car but he was hopelessly asleep when he reached Moscow.

"It is the only occasion in his life when a story of that sort is told of him. To report it as in any way characteristic is quite unjustified."

Last orders called in drinking row

Peer's charge that MPs are often drunk is aired in the Commons. Colin Brown reports

LAST ORDERS were called in the Commons yesterday on the row over allegations that MPs are too susceptible to the temptation of 12 bars and long opening hours at Westminster.

The Speaker, Mr George Thomas, said: "All my predecessors have ruled that no honourable or right honourable member of this House is ever too much under the influence of drink."

Mr Thomas, a Methodist and a teetotaller, was answering a complaint by Mr Arthur Lewis, Labour MP for Newham NW about Lord Avebury. The Liberal peer made the claims about MPs' drinking at a conference in Liverpool on drink-related problems.

Mr Lewis said it was a wounding attack on MPs. Lord Avebury had tried to assert that there was "almost perpetual drunkenness" in the Commons.

Mr Lewis said a few members did have a drink occasionally, like himself. But no one was drunk in the Commons because it was against the rules. He knew that the Speaker, as a lifelong abstainer, would never allow MPs to break the rules.

The widow of Hugh Gaitskell yesterday described as "an absolute awful lie" Lord Avebury's claims at the conference that the former Leader of the Opposition drank 19 tumblers of vodka and had to be carried to his car on a trip to Russia in 1959.

Lady Gaitskell said: "I can't imagine where Lord Avebury got his information. I was with Hugh on that trip, sitting right beside him, and although the host at the function challenged him to drink brandy, there is no question of him being carried out unconscious."

● *Tom Sharratt adds:* At the conference yesterday, Mr Kenneth Oxford, the Chief Constable of Merseyside, said that young people were becoming more at risk through alcohol abuse. He said that between 1959 and 1979 the biggest rise in the proportion of people convicted of drunkenness was among those under 21.

Mr Oxford said a report by Merseyside police four months ago indicated that alcohol was a connection between young people involved in offences of violence.

Decide whether the following statements are true or false.

According to Lord Avebury:

1 Mr Gaitskell, when Leader of the Opposition, was often as drunk as a lord.
2 He knocked back 20 glasses of spirits on one trip to Russia.
3 He was so far gone that he had to be carried to his car.
4 Winston Churchill often hit the bottle when in office.
5 A lot of MPs drink very heavily.
6 Much of the time MPs are drunk in the House.
7 Opening hours of bars at Westminster should not be restricted.

According to Gaitskell's biographer:

8 Gaitskell was often intoxicated.
9 He downed 20 glasses of spirits on one trip to Russia.
10 He was so plastered that he had to be carried to his car.

According to Gaitskell's widow:

11 He was often inebriated.
12 He had 20 glasses of spirits on one trip to Russia.
13 He was so sloshed that he had to be carried to his car.

According to Mr Lewis:

14 A lot of MPs drink very heavily.
15 Much of the time MPs are drunk in the House.
16 Opening hours of bars at Westminster should not be restricted.

17 There are a dozen different bars at Westminster.
18 The bars are open round the clock there.
19 Lord Avebury and Mr Lewis never drink.
20 One of the rules of the House is that MPs are not allowed to be drunk there.

What seem to be the attitudes of the two writers to the speeches they report? Are you, as a reader, supposed to be shocked, amused or what?

9.4 Collocations *Use of English*

Fill the gaps in the newspaper article below with any words that make sense in the context. In some cases several possibilities may spring to mind – choose the one you think sounds best.

Wine at 2½p a pint for Soviets

By Ian Aitken, Political Editor

The Government admitted yesterday that the European Community was still selling food and wine to the Soviet Union and its satellite ....1.... at ....2.... low prices, although the Prime Minister clearly ....3.... her disapproval of this practice in the Commons.

Perhaps the most ....4.... revelation was that Europe's wine ....5.... was being sold off to Comecon countries at prices which ....6.... to little more than 2.5 pence a pint. Beef and veal were being sold at ....7.... 40p a pound, and butter at 54p a pound.

This information was ....8.... from Mr John McGregor, Minister of State for Agriculture, by one of the Conservative Party's most ....9.... anti-Europeans, Mr Teddy Taylor. Last night, Mr Taylor issued a ....10.... in which he raised the ....11.... of whether the EEC was actually seeking to ....12.... the Soviets by encouraging alcoholism by selling cheap ....13.... to the Communist countries.

9.5 Idioms with COME *Use of English*

Rewrite each of the sentences so that it still means the same, using the words on the left together with the correct form of COME.

1 INTO POWER The Tories won the election in 1979.
2 OUT AGAINST The opposition declared its opposition to the proposal.
3 OUT ON TOP In the election for a new party leader the favourite won.
4 IN FOR The government has had to face a lot of criticism.
5 TO TERMS WITH It's hard to accept the government's defence policy.
6 TRUE My worst fears about this government have actually happened.
7 -BACK After retiring in 1980 he has decided to make a return to the political scene.
8 UP-AND- She's a promising young backbencher, likely to succeed.
9 TO THE BOIL The situation has reached crisis point now that the government has to face a vote of confidence.
10 INTO EFFECT The tax cuts announced in the Budget do not begin to operate until next year.
11 OUT The miners went on strike in protest against the government's privatisation plans.
12 OUT BADLY The government has not done very well in the recent public opinion polls.

9.6 A party conference *Questions and summary*

Like any piece of political reporting, this article had lost its topicality within a week and seems very parochial. Nevertheless it is a typical example of its genre. To understand it better, read the background information first:

THE STORY SO FAR

Elder statesman, Roy Jenkins, with his friends David Owen, Shirley Williams and William Rodgers have left the Labour Party to form a new left-of-centre party, called the Social Democratic Party. This party has allied itself with the Liberal Party in 'The Alliance'. David Owen has become the dynamic young leader of the SDP. Now read on . . .

After reading the report of the SDP conference, answer these questions in writing:

1 Explain the meanings of the following words and phrases:
   Come off it (line 11) a one-man band (line 12) unilaterally (line 54)
   off the cuff (line 68) standing ovation (line 112)
2 Why have the media described the SDP as a 'one-man band'?
3 What does Dr Owen consider to be his role as party leader?
4 What were the main points of Miss Brennan's speech?
5 In one paragraph, summarise the main points made by Dr Owen in his speech.

Prudent Owen disbands invincible one-man party

BUXTON SKETCH

By Dennis Johnson

"ONE-man band?" asked Dr David Owen with a twisted smile during his big speech at the end of the Social Democratic Party conference yesterday. "Come off it. This is not a one-man band. This is a substantial party and it is here to stay."

It has always been, of course, something of a calumny, a media phrase picked up eagerly by his enemies and arising chiefly from his apparently invincible self-confidence in running the party his way and insisting on its independence.

Still, he evidently thought it prudent to bend a little yesterday, sensing that even some of his own members might have sneakily begun to believe it.

The policies he had put forward, he said, had not been intended as a way of imposing his views. "How could I dare?", he said wryly, earning a modest burst of dismissive laughter from the delegates. "The leader has to provoke ideas and challenge all of you, and you have the right and duty to tell him when he is talking nonsense."

What was this? An admission that he might have to concede one day that he was talking nonsense? A window in the crowded pavilion rattled ominously as the electricity discharged itself on the damp morning air.

Again, it had been said that the Council for Social Democracy had lost a little influence because of the agreement with the Liberals to work towards a joint policy statement in 1986. He did not think it had.

To win power and influence you had to act like a government and respond to the disciplines of power. Liberals and the SDP had agreed not to act unilaterally. "We've compromised," he said. "I did. I voted on the national executive for joint selection in special circumstances. It was like drawing teeth out of me."

Dr Owen succeeded, at least for the time being, in drawing the teeth of internal resentments, but such is one of the chief purposes of leaders' conference speeches. There were regular, satisfying rounds of applause, especially in those sections at the beginning and the end which he delivered off the cuff.

These, of course, were the appeals to emotion, for which Dr Owen is earning better marks for effort. Did we know the best thing that had happened to him during the past year? Holidays? No. The victory at Portsmouth South? No. "The decision which gave me the greatest pleasure was Shirley's decision to stand again as president. All I can say is that I need her probably more than you do."

Tributes fell from the born-again doctor's lips—to McNally, Thomas, Hancock of Portsmouth, Bradley, Mabon and the 43 SDP peers. Heavens above, was he ever going to praise Roy, sitting along the platform with his chin cupped in his hand? Was the very rock from which the first stones of the new Jerusalem were hewn to be condemned as a mere Liberal-lover?

He rattled through the central, prepared and analytical sections of his speech like a company boss, a trap waiting for all party leaders who feel that they have to produce what is known as content to appease pundits for whom rallying calls are synonymous with the wind.

"Be proud of the Alliance," he said, "and you will be surprised how attractive and powerful the message will be to the British people."

Maybe so. But the delegates still had ringing in their ears a salutary warning from a young woman, delivered only an hour before during a debate on inequality. Miss Ann Brennan, of Barnsbury, Islington, won a standing ovation rivalling even that of Dr Owen after criticising a prolix " background paper " on the subject prepared for the conference.

" I can hardly understand a word of it," she said. " Fancy standing on King's Cross station preaching this —they'd think you were Jehovah's Witnesses. Ninety-five per cent of you have had a university education. I haven't even got an O level.

" You are using the privilege of your education to conduct the kind of debate in which no working class people would dare to open their mouths.

" We must never forget that Bermondsey is more important to the SDP than Burgundy. I don't even read The Guardian. Since coming to Buxton I have never seen so many people reading The Guardian in all my life. Never forget, no middle-class party ever won an election on the votes of the middle-class alone."

Like masochists at an orgy, the conference loved the lash. The girl was cheered to the doors and instantly swept away by television crews, her face registering flushed and innocent astonishment.

Miss Ann Brennan, of Islington, who won an ovation after denouncing middle-class politics. She does not read The Guardian.

Picture by Denis Thorpe

"Actually, it surprises me that a man like you doesn't hold political office."

9.7 Taxes, taxes and more taxes *Listening*

Listen to the explanation of how the British and American governments collect and spend their citizens' hard-earned money. Fill in the gaps in the diagram below.

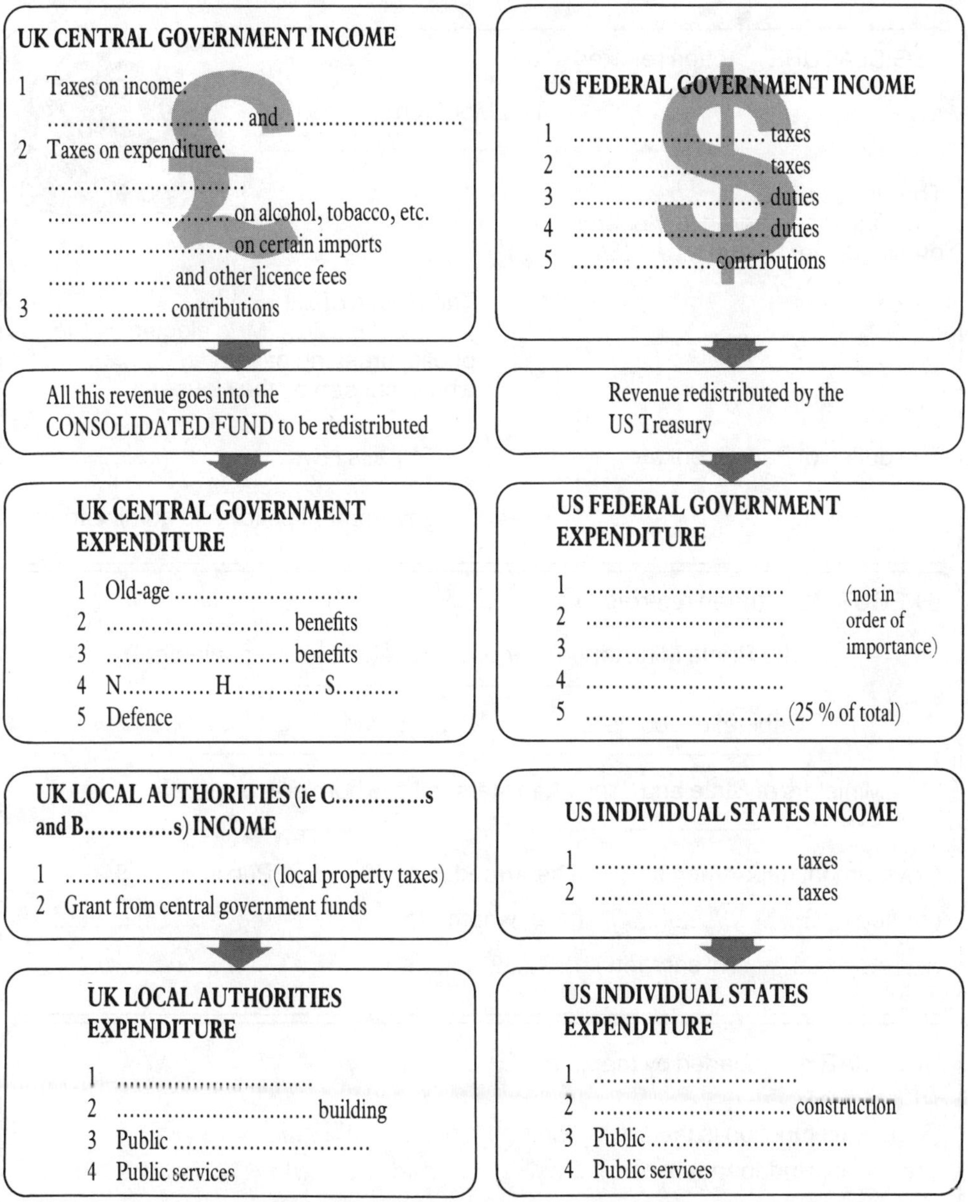

UK CENTRAL GOVERNMENT INCOME

1 Taxes on income:
.... and ....
2 Taxes on expenditure:
....
.... on alcohol, tobacco, etc.
.... on certain imports
.... and other licence fees
3 .... contributions

All this revenue goes into the CONSOLIDATED FUND to be redistributed

UK CENTRAL GOVERNMENT EXPENDITURE

1 Old-age ....
2 .... benefits
3 .... benefits
4 N............. H............. S..........
5 Defence

UK LOCAL AUTHORITIES (ie C.............s and B.............s) INCOME

1 .... (local property taxes)
2 Grant from central government funds

UK LOCAL AUTHORITIES EXPENDITURE

1 ....
2 .... building
3 Public ....
4 Public services

US FEDERAL GOVERNMENT INCOME

1 .... taxes
2 .... taxes
3 .... duties
4 .... duties
5 .... contributions

Revenue redistributed by the US Treasury

US FEDERAL GOVERNMENT EXPENDITURE

1 ....
2 ....
3 ....
4 ....
5 .... (25 % of total)

(not in order of importance)

US INDIVIDUAL STATES INCOME

1 .... taxes
2 .... taxes

US INDIVIDUAL STATES EXPENDITURE

1 ....
2 .... construction
3 Public ....
4 Public services

. . . . % of GNP goes in taxes

. . . . % of GNP goes in taxes

(cf 59% in Norway, 48% in . . . ., 28% in . . . ., 20% in . . . .)

9.8 Her Majesty's Government *Listening*

Listen to the recording of a guide talking to a group of visitors in the Palace of Westminster describing the British government to them. Add the missing information in the charts below.

LEGISLATURE (often referred to as '.......... (a) ....')

The Monarch

The House of .... (b) ....
(appointed and hereditary peers presided over by the .... (c) ....)

The House of .... (d) ....
(.......... (e) .... MPs elected by the public, presided over by .... (f) .... who is chosen by the House)

The duties of Parliament are:

1 To pass laws .... (g) ....
2 To .... (h) .... government policy and administration

EXECUTIVE (often referred to as '.......... (i) ....')

The Prime Minister (leader of .... (j) .... in parliament)

Cabinet of about 20 .... (k) .... and .... (l) ....

Ministers of State and Junior Ministers (all of whom are .... (m) ....)

Government departments (staffed by .... (n) .... civil servants)

The Armed .... (o) .... (all of whom are .... (p) ....)

Public .... (q) .... (eg .... (r) .... (s) ....)

JUDICIARY (headed by the .... (t) ....)

Its function is the .... (u) .... of .... (v) ....
It is independent of .... (w) .... and .... (x) ....

(Separate legal systems in .... (y) .... and in .... (z) ....)

9.9 Protest *Picture conversation*

Work in pairs. One of you should look at activity 16, the other at 59. You will each have some questions to ask the other about a photograph.

9.10 Freedom and the State *Communication activity*

Work in pairs. One of you should look at activity 17, the other at 56. You will be discussing individual freedoms and State control.

9.11 Guided writing *Composition*

Imagine that a newly-formed political party in your country has set out the following policy statement:

REFORMS PROPOSED BY NEW PARTY

Defence cuts – size of defence force to be cut
School-leaving age to be raised
Tighter control of pollution by motor vehicles and industry
Foreign-owned companies to be nationalised
Tighter control of trade unions – strikes may become illegal
Export of currency to be banned

Higher taxes on imported goods
Higher car tax, sales tax (VAT) and duty on cigarettes and spirits
Lower income tax and duty on wines and beer

Describe your feelings about the proposals and the probable consequences of them on life in your country if the new party comes to power. Make sure your composition is to-the-point and not too long – it should be about 200 words long in this case. Before you start writing, make notes on the points you're going to make and, if possible, discuss them with another student before you write the composition.

10 Work and business

10.1 Vocabulary

Fill the gaps below with a suitable word or phrase.

1 The board of directors are answerable to the company's s..................................s.
2 Shares are bought and sold by commercial companies and by private i..................................s.
3 A private company goes public when it raises capital by i..................................ing shares.
4 The prices of shares are q.................................. on the S.................................. E..................................
5 Profits may be passed on to the shareholders each year in the form of d..................................s,
6 or they may be ploughed back into expansion, modernisation or r.................................. and d..................................
7 A company that produces many different kinds of goods is called a c..................................
8 The word generally used in the USA to describe a firm is c..................................
9 Paramount Pictures and Columbia Pictures are s.................................. of Gulf + Western and Coca Cola, respectively.
10 Coca Cola, Shell and General Motors are all m.................................. companies.
11 Sony and Toyota both have their h.................................. in Japan.
12 In many countries the state airline has a m.................................. of internal services.
13 Someone who founds and runs their own company is called an e..................................
14 The three brothers run their company together as a p..................................
15 Engineering is not a service industry but a m.................................. industry.
16 24-hour production has been introduced by operating a three s.................................. system.
17 Management and unions have now come to an agreement on the new p.................................. scheme where increased efficiency will be rewarded.
18 The finished product is made by putting together the various components on an a.................................. l..................................
19 After the breakdown of talks a strike was called and the union organised a p.................................. l.................................. outside the factory.
20 A work-to-rule has been called by the union s.................................. s..................................
21 The selection and welfare of staff is the responsibility of the p.................................. department.
22 The co-ordination of production, advertising and sales is carried out by the m.................................. department.
23 Sales reps are paid a salary but they also receive e..................................s and may get c.................................. on sales.

24 The managing director has advertised for a p.................................. a..................................
25 The working population can be divided into two groups: b..................................
c.................................. workers and w.................................. c.................................. workers.

10.2 The telephone man *Reading*

The telephone man

By Stuart Wavell

TO THE business world, Harold Geneen is the British-born genius who built International Telephone and Telegraph into the most extensive conglomerate in the world. In his 18 years as chief executive ITT acquired 350 companies. Profits lurched to $22 billion a year.

His philosophy was simple. "You start with the end and then you do everything you must to reach it," he writes in his guide for aspiring executives, Managing (published by Granada, £7.95).

He concludes: "When all is said and done a company, its chief executive, and his whole management team are judged by one criterion alone—performance."

The general public, however, is still apt to judge ITT by one criterion alone—Chile. It was one of several scandals during Geneen's rule from 1959-77. The Watergate break-in, it was claimed, was a search for damaging material to counter revelations about ITT's alleged payments to the Republican Party during a protracted anti-trust case.

Geneen was summoned before a Senate sub-committee after one of his officials, a former director of the CIA, admitted that ITT offered the US Government a seven-figure sum to finance a political coalition to block the election of Dr Salvador Allende, Chile's Marxist President. The company maintained it was to finance public housing in Chile and won Allende's goodwill.

At 75, Geneen is an affable and persuasive talker, employing a folksy, tickertape delivery reminiscent of Victor Kayam selling a Remington razor. He does not resemble the dealer in fear depicted by Anthony Sampson in his study of ITT, The Sovereign State. Six years out of high office and a reported golden handshake of $5 million have possibly mellowed him.

I asked him about Chile, which is not mentioned once in his book.

"Our problem was very simple, Stuart. We had a $150 million company there. They just wanted to take it away and not pay us. We had a history of this kinda problem. I wasn't six months with the company before Batista and his group took our Cuban telephone company. Then we went through the same thing with the Brazilians, the Mexicans and the Peruvians.

"We would fight and argue. Generally speaking you'd get some satisfaction, but when the Communists took them over we never got a nickel back. I worked for the stockholders. I wasn't interested in politics at all. We went through half a dozen hearings in Washington. Nothing was illegal that we did."

He paused. And? "And that was the way it went. That's absolutely true. We got a lot of smear out of it. I think a lot of it was from . . . I don't know if you'd call them liberal people. We were cleared and that was the end of it. We got a lot of publicity but it could have been written up the other way. They could say 'Hell, there's a perfectly sound company.' I figure we put $7 million in that company for every dollar we took out."

He began to chuckle. "Finally we got paid, I'll say that. We had insurance with the American Government. We got paid our book value. But that's a perfectly legitimate thing."

But with its history of this kind of problem, hadn't ITT a contingency plan? "Well, our contingency plan was to keep wrestling and fighting and trying to get our Government to help us. And finally it worked, that's all. Finally he was thrown out, really. We didn't throw him out." ➳

Had the White House become an annexe of ITT, as its critics claim? His chuckles were now coming thick and fast. "No, no, no. If it were we wouldn't have had the problems we did." (A reference to the anti-trust suits against ITT.)

"It's kinda funny, in the middle of all this, Allende asked our people to check out his lines to make sure they weren't bugged. We went along and checked them out for him." This brought forth a fresh gale of mirth.

Indelible smudges remain on the slate. Cases were prepared against lesser ITT officials for lying to a senate investigating committee. These were withdrawn in 1979 when the Justice Department expressed the fear that national secrets might be revealed at the trial.

In retrospect, Geneen sees the expropriation of the Cuban Telephone Company as a blessing in disguise. "It kinda woke us up. That was one of our biggest companies. And overnight it just went Bing!"

It alerted him to the fact that ITT was dependent on 85 per cent of its revenue from overseas. In a bid to increase domestic earnings to 50 per cent he embarked on a crash programme of acquisitions in the United States. ITT swallowed Sheraton hotels, Avis, Hartford Fire Insurance and Continental Baking. To keep Hartford, ITT was forced to shed Avis.

"There were times when we were buying a company a day. None of them were hostile acquisitions. They were all available for some reason—they had reached saturation point in their mind or the management got older. So we took 'em over and made 'em grow."

He developed a new management system of open communications. Officials from all ITT's subsidiaries came face to face once a month at week-long meetings in New York and Brussels. These consumed nine years of his life.

The thorn in his side was the Justice Department's anti-trust division, which opposed two notable bids, the ABC chain and Hartford Fire. "They wouldn't let us buy two of anything. If you wanted to buy a number one company their line of argument was that you were destroying competition; you should go buy the number two company to compete with number one."

Geneen denies that conglomerates are abhorrent. To him bigness is good business, good for American clout and shelter for subsidiaries in adverse climates — "We carried our losers."

Wasn't there a limit to growth? Only his own ability to master the essential data, says Geneen — "the Geneen Machine" who at one point held titles as ITT's president, chief executive and chairman. "If I had to do it over again I think I would have tried to buy less companies and bigger ones."

He was born in Bournemouth. His mother was a light opera singer and his father a touring impresario. A series of events in his youth appear to have forged his mental toughness. His parents separated when he was three, and he was sent to a strict convent boarding school. His father went bankrupt over a land deal shortly before Geneen junior, a page at the New York Stock Exchange, witnessed the Wall Street crash (he lost $200 savings in a bank account).

He denies that he was a tough boss. "Anthony Sampson writes that everybody at ITT had bloodshot eyes, broken homes and were drinking because we beat 'em up excessively. Well, that's not exactly true. The only people I had no use for were people who didn't wanna work and people who tried to be politicians. Other than that, you lean over backwards, even to carry them on your shoulders."

He has his fans. Peru has awarded him the Order of Merit for Distinguished Service. The call from Chile may take a little longer.

A What (if any) are Harold Geneen's responses to the following allegations about ITT during his reign as chief executive?

1 'ITT was involved in the Watergate break-in.'
2 'ITT offered the US government over $1 million in an attempt to prevent Salvador Allende being elected as President of Chile.'
3 'ITT acted illegally in Chile.'
4 'ITT had the White House in its pocket.'
5 'ITT had political motives as well as business ones.'
6 'ITT officials lied to a Senate committee.'
7 'ITT managers lived in constant fear.'

B Answer each of these questions briefly:

8 How does the business world regard Geneen?
9 Why did ITT acquire Avis?
10 Why did ITT sell Avis?
11 How did Geneen help ITT's diverse subsidiaries work together?
12 What regrets does Geneen have about his time at ITT?

C What is the writer's attitude to Harold Geneen?

10.3 Payment by results *Reading*

The great American scheme: being paid on results

By Peter David

ALARMED by a 20-year decline in student achievement, American schools are considering major upheavals in the career structure of teachers. Urged on by the Reagan administration, school boards around the country are planning to abandon traditional salary schedules and single out outstanding teachers for massive pay rises. The lucky few will be called "master teachers" and earn as much as $40,000 a year instead of the present average of $19,000.

The idea is regarded with deep suspicion by the United States' biggest teachers' unions, the National Education Association and the American Federation of Teachers. They say the creation of a cadre of elite teachers will sour professional relationships and encourage teachers to compete instead of cooperate. They also question whether a fair way can be devised to tell which teachers really do perform better than their colleagues.

But heightened public anxiety about secondary education appears to have given the master teacher concept unstoppable political momentum. Florida and Tennessee are racing to introduce ambitious statewide master teacher schemes before the end of the year. Less grandiose proposals to pay teachers on the basis of merit instead of seniority have already been implemented in countless school districts. And the Secretary of Education, Mr Terrel Bell, recently promised substantial incentive grants to states which intend to follow their example.

Low pay is believed to be the single most important reason for the flight from teaching. The average salary of a teacher in the United States is just under $19,000, much less than that of an engineer ($34,700) and not much more than that of a secretary ($16,500). To make ends meet it is common for teachers to take second jobs in the evening and in their summer holidays. Women, who used to make up the bulk of teacher candidates are turning to better paid professions.

The unions insist that the answer to this problem is to increase the basic pay of all teachers, but most states would find that too expensive. They would be better able to afford schemes that confine pay increases to a small number of exceptional teachers. Champions of the idea say it would at least hold out the promise of high pay and status to bright graduates who are confident of their ability to do well in the classroom, but are deterred by the present meagre opportunities for promotion.

One of the first large-scale tests of this approach will come in Tennessee, where a year of painstaking negotiations has just overcome bitter union opposition to a wide-ranging master teacher scheme. The state has promised to pump an additional $300 million into the educational budget. In return for a chance to earn bigger salaries and faster promotion, teachers will subject themselves to closer scrutiny.

The Tennessee plan will make it harder for poor teachers to join the profession. Beginners will have to serve a probationary year before qualifying, and another three apprentice years before receiving tenure. Apprentice teachers who fail to reach a required standard will not be allowed to stay on. Survivors will be designated " career teachers " and given a chance to climb through three career rungs and earn bonuses of up to $7,000. Advancement will not be automatic. The performance of each teacher will be closely assessed by committees of teachers drawn from other districts.

Smaller but more radical schemes are being tried in other states. A North Carolina school district may extend probation a full six years, while top salaries are raised by about $17,000 to $40,000. And in some districts, merit bonuses are to be awarded on the basis of student performance, not the assessment of individual teachers. In Dallas, for example, teachers will be paid an extra $1,500 a year if their school boosts student test results above a computerised projection based on their previous showing.

The Dallas approach is vigorously opposed by teachers' unions. The American Federation of Teachers says it is " simplistic " to base teacher pay on student performance because many subtle factors—not just the ability of teachers—determine the success of particular schools. But the association also warns that it is difficult to find a completely objective way to evaluate the performance of individual teachers.

Even the unions, however, have begun to concede that pay increases restricted to talented teachers are preferable to no pay increases at all. Their strategy now is to bargain hard to win the best possible deal for serving teachers and make sure that merit pay schemes are not sullied by favouritism and patronage.

Tennessee, for example, had to make two key concessions to win over its unions. A " toe-in-the-water " clause will allow existing teachers to stay on their old salary ladder or try out the new one with the option of going back. And the unions will have ample representation on the professional committees set up to decide which teachers will be allowed to progress up the ladder.

Answer each of the questions with a short phrase or brief sentence.

1 What are the basic objections of the NEA and AFT to the master teacher scheme?
2 Why does the master teacher scheme appear to be 'unstoppable'?
3 What support is the federal government offering to states who set up a master teacher scheme?
4 Why is the master teacher scheme considered necessary?
5 How can teachers be prevented from taking jobs in industry and business, according to the union?
6 In Tennessee, what are the different grades of teachers proposed?
7 In Tennessee, how will teachers be assessed?
8 In Tennessee, how will existing teachers be persuaded to join the scheme?
9 In Dallas, how will teachers be chosen as master teachers?
10 How have the unions modified their policy towards the scheme?

What seems to be the attitude of the writer to the master teacher scheme?
Is education a 'business' or something different, in your opinion?

10.4 Obligation, necessity and probability *Use of English*

Rewrite each of the sentences so that its meaning remains unchanged.

1 You needn't make an appointment to see the personnel manager.
There's . . .

2 If I'm lucky I might get the job I've applied for.
There's . . .

3 The economic climate could deteriorate in the next few years.
It's . . .

4 Next year's turnover and profits can't be forecast.
It's . . .

5 We have to repay the loan, now that we have promised to.
We are . . .

6 The strikers will probably go back to work next week.
In all . . .

7 You don't have to have any previous experience to apply for the job.
It isn't . . .

8 There must be a good explanation for all the recent absenteeism.
I'm . . .

9 To be successful in business one must work very hard.
It is . . .

10 The company may well make a profit next year.
I wouldn't . . .

"Don't be a fool, Hempstead! It's Friday afternoon!"

10.5 Word order and inversion *Use of English*

Fill each gap with suitable words or phrases. Look at the example first.

1 Never *had I seen* so many people working so hard.
2 Seldom .... any assistance or advice.
3 Rarely .... about their appalling working conditions.
4 Scarcely .... opened the letter .... the phone started ringing.
5 No sooner .... the phone .... a knock at the office door.
6 In no way .... such a discreet man .... secrets.
7 At no time .... about it outside this office.
8 On no account .... revealed to our competitors.
9 Only in Britain .... the notion of a gentleman's agreement ....
10 Not only .... lose his job, ... his wife ....

10.6 No job to go to *Questions and summary*

Read the newspaper article on the next page and answer these questions about it in writing.

1 Explain the meaning of the following words and phrases used in the article:
 din (line 8)
 suburb of a London suburb (lines 25–26)
 discards (line 35)
 elaborate myth (line 49)
 a Standard (line 59)
 season ticket (line 90)
 fast-dwindling (line 91)
 dole (line 95)
 a precarious triumph (line 116)
 simplistic attitudes (line 184)
 camaraderie (line 207)

2 Look at the article and explain who or what is referred to by the words in bold type in the following quotations from the passage:
 He told Jean **they**'d both been fired (line 69)
 They mentioned afterwards to his friends (line 72)
 they said they'd given up the television (line 76)
 When **they** go to cut him off, Jean gives **them** a cheque (lines 104 and 105)
 they include you in their rounds (line 133)
 They think I'll ask for a handout (line 151)
 They've got to go (line 159)
 They make friends for you (line 165)
 Perhaps **they** think (line 199)

it frightens **them** away (line 235)
Didn't want **them** to know (line 258)
they hadn't got jobs any more (line 259)

3 In one paragraph, describe a typical weekday in the life of Dick Derwent.

WORKFACE

Jane McLoughlin

EVERY weekday, Dick Derwent (which is not his real name) is driven out of bed by the alarm clock he leaves outside the bedroom door. Stopping its din means he must get up first, not simply turn it off and settle back to sleep. He brings his wife Jean a cup of tea, dresses in his office suit while she makes toast and a sandwich which he packs in his brown briefcase. He leaves the house at precisely 7 55 am to walk the half mile to the station to catch the 8 15 suburban stopping train to town.

The routine hasn't changed in the 25 years since he and Jean first moved to their neat little house in a Lego-built street in a suburb of a London suburb. Dick sees the same people on the platform every morning — by now he even nods to one or two. The only difference is that until two years ago he used to buy a paper from the kiosk outside the station and now he picks one up if a fellow passenger discards it on the journey.

Two years ago, Dick was fired. He no longer has a job to go to with the others in the pin-stripe tide rushing out of Waterloo to get to the office. He starts an eight hour day doing nothing.

His wife doesn't know. He couldn't tell her he'd lost his job, so he simply carried on as though he goes to work. He believes she believes the elaborate myth he has created round his working day. His boss objects to private telephone calls, so please don't ring him at work: the other blokes at work come and go these days, he doesn't really know them well enough to talk about them at home; if he's lucky, and picks up a Standard in the afternoons, he can pretend that he had the kind of day that Bristow had at work, and she's so bored she doesn't want to hear.

Two of his ex-colleagues did drop by his home one weekend, and he rushed them down to the pub. He told Jean they'd both been fired so it was nice to see them after so long, to explain the way they greeted him. They mentioned afterwards to his friends that Dick and Jean seemed to have very little furniture around, and they said they'd given up the television because there was so much rubbish on these days. The furniture? Oh, they were going to redecorate, so they'd sold the old stuff and Jean would go to the sales when they'd got the new decor.

She *must* know. There's no way of finding out without asking her, and that's the one question no one can ever ask.

Dick pays for his season ticket out of the fast-dwindling redundancy money he put in the bank. He takes

£1 a day spending money and collects his dole weekly from the DHSS office near his old workplace. He gives Jean the same money he always did, but the bills for rates and gas and electricity he grabs up on his way out in the morning and stuffs in a wastebin near the station. When they go to cut him off, Jean gives them a cheque, thinking he has forgotten, so he doesn't really know the state of his bank account. He told her he took a pay cut last year because the firm was in trouble. " She doesn't actually think I've forgotten; she thinks I've been on a drinking spree again," he says.

His days are a precarious triumph over mind by matter, or lack of it. A typical day starts at Waterloo, when you've no idea how hard it is to hold back to his slow pace as the commuters stampede from the platform to an imperative march. " No, no tea. It's too expensive, and it's a waste of your resources because there's no chance of a return on investment. At lunchtime, if you get in the bar early and buy someone a drink, that's the first round, and when his friends come in they include you in their rounds. You've got to pick your moment to get out, of course."

He grins sideways at you and puts a lot of energy into the height of his steps rather than their length. We walk slowly along the river by the National Theatre and the Festival Hall. The wind is in the wrong direction and it's very cold. From behind, Dick's valiant old suit shows its age in the daylight and you notice how scuffed his shoes are. You can see people hurrying by, trying to avoid catching his eye. " They think I'll ask for a handout. They can smell something off me."

He sits in the park after a while, and two women on the seat break off their conversation, fidget, and loudly ask each other the time. They've got to go; never knew it was so late.

" I don't like dogs, you know, but after what I've seen I'd never speak against them. They make friends for you, for people on their own. Everyone will talk to someone with a dog in a park."

There's something which happens gradually as the hours drag by; wherever he loiters, it seems to be with intent. He can't window shop or watch the people go by without feeling that people are wondering what he's doing. During the day, we go into a public library to read the papers. He used to take the Times at home, now he reads the Sun first. It makes no demand, and provides some form of comfort in its simplistic attitudes.

" It's really irritating, reading those papers where people seem to take themselves so seriously. Same goes for the magazines."

It's the contrasts that make Dick's misery worse. It had been his slowness in the morning; and all through the morning it was having nothing to do when everyone else seemed to be busy and intent. Except the down and outs, who wouldn't speak to him. " Perhaps they think I'm a copper's nark," he joked.

At lunchtime, his drinks trick didn't work. He sat through opening hours with a half pint, a black hole among the noise and camaraderie. " I remember what it was like. You don't want some guy in trouble to bring you down when you're having a good time."

But after lunch — at closing time — his spirits pick up. The worst is over. He finds a park bench, or tramps back to Waterloo on a rainy day, and takes out his sandwiches. He has pet pigeons. " It's nice in the summer. You can sit out in the Embankment Gardens near Charing Cross and watch everyone. All sorts of stories going on, day after day. It's like Coronation

Street, down there.”

We walk past his old workplace. He does it every day. “The odd time, someone I knew comes out and thinks I'm just passing, so we have a chat. I always say I'm doing fine — it doesn't do to let people know the truth; it frightens them away from you, as though your wife had died or something.”

He says you get used to spending 9 to 5 deliberately doing nothing. “What you miss is feeling you belong somewhere. That's why I go to the same places. If I didn't go one day, someone might notice.”

One day, he'd spent 50p on a horse, sitting in the betting shop getting quite excited about the race. He'd won £5. The next day, he'd spent a wet afternoon watching a dirty movie near Trafalgar Square.

“At 6 pm sharp, everyone there got up and hurried up to Charing Cross. Home to their wives, that was it. Didn't want them to know they hadn't got jobs any more. I'm not alone, you know.”

10.7 Commuting to work *Listening*

You'll hear how changing commuting habits are affecting living patterns in south-east England. Answer the questions and fill the gaps below.

1 Which of these features did the dinner party host mention as attractions of moving to a small town outside London? Tick the ones he mentioned.
fresher air higher house prices better health services less crime
better schools better weather proximity of countryside
better shops nicer neighbours separation from family during week

2 Which of these factors did the speaker mention as stress-provoking aspects of long-distance commuting? Tick the ones she mentions.
slow trains separation from family worry about catching trains
10 hours per week travelling crowded trains high cost of travel
having to stand on trains rail timetables control your life
some trains cancelled rail strikes

3 TYPICAL HOUSE PRICES:

Bromley	3 bedroom semi-detached house	£50,000
St Leonards	3 bedroom semi-detached house	....
Bromley	4 bedroom detached house	£100,000
St Leonards	4 bedroom detached house	£....................

4 House prices also affected by closeness to the .... (houses 20 minutes or more away are ....% cheaper).

5 For a town to be a suitable commuter base the journey time must be no more than .... minutes each way and there must be at least .... trains during the period .... to .... (Bromley has .... during this period.)

6 The cost in fares for a long commute is over £.................... a year, but this is offset by lower .... and lower .... →

7 There are three trends that suggest that long-distance commuting may be unpopular:
   A Rail use is falling (increase in the use of ....)
   B Relocation of offices to .... (eg Watford)
   C Relocation of offices and factories to .... and .... (eg Swindon)

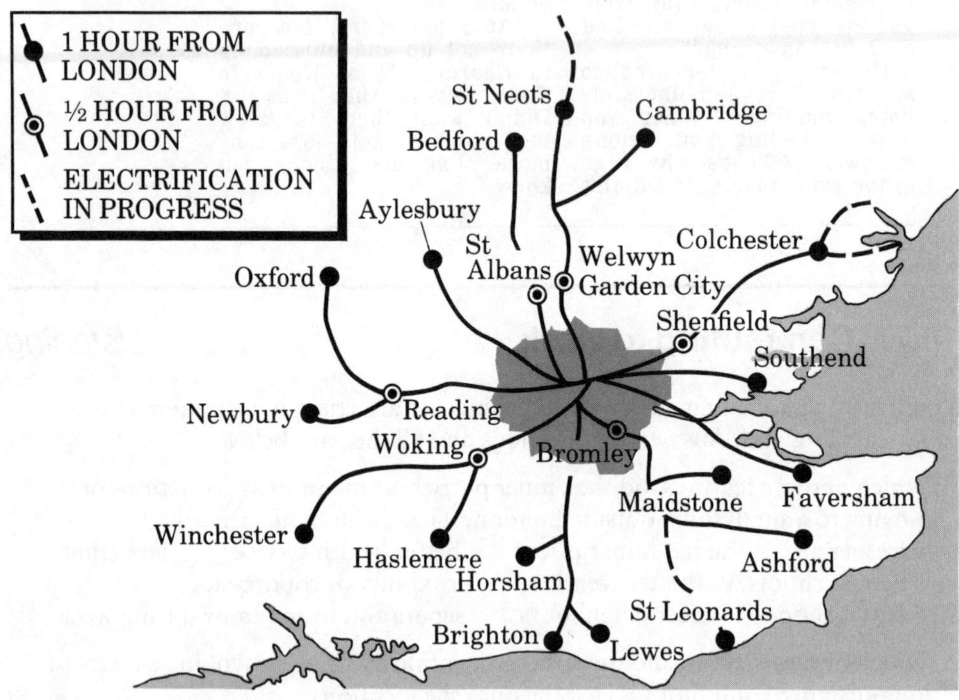

10.8 Women in business *Listening*

Listen to the conversation and answer the questions about it, by filling in the gaps or matching the items.

1 In the USA .... of managers are women – in Britain and Europe only .... of managers are women, even though they are .... of the workforce.

2 Which company does each of these successful women run? What line of business is she in? What is her position in the company? Match the items in the columns:

Marisa Bellisario	Banque Indosuez	mail order	head
Debbie Moore	Italtel	fitness	owner
Geneviève Gomez	Quelle	telecommunications	founder
Grete Schickedanz	Pineapple Dance Studios	banking	secretary general

3 Successful women like these are the .... that prove the ....

4 Many top female managers work in companies founded by their .... or .... As such, they are not suitable .... for young women who have to start at the ....

5 Young men and women have equal .... and equal .... for the first time in .... history.

6 The best way for a woman to become a boss may be to become ....: in West Germany .... of new businesses are started by women.

7 Women in Britain first started to get managerial posts about .... years ago. Now they are in their .... and in 10 years they'll be on the ....

8 The National Westminster Bank allows women who have taken up to .... years off to return to a job at the same .... – this kind of scheme is now ....

9 Many women are conditioned to believe that men are better at '....................' or at 'being the ....', according to the speaker.

10 The speaker stresses that, if women want to be equal, they must .... as equal.

10.9 On a wing and a paper clip *Pronunciation*

Work in pairs. One of you should look at activity 18, the other at 57. You will each have different parts of this news item to read and discuss.

On a wing and a paper clip

10.10 Paper engineering *Communication activity*

Work in pairs or groups of three. Following on from the previous exercise, work together to solve this problem:

> Construct a paper glider that will fly all the way across the classroom without being thrown to launch it. It may be held up high, but *not* given any other help on launching. You have just one sheet of A4 (30 × 21 cm) paper and a paper clip.
>
> You must decide on your design *before* you construct the glider, because you may only use one sheet of paper and no experimental flights are allowed. It's not as easy as it sounds!

10.11 Writing a formal letter *Composition*

> '*Write a letter to the editor of the newspaper which published the article you read in exercise 10.3 on page 127. Your letter should* **either** *support* **or** *oppose the implementation of a similar scheme in your country's schools.*'

In a newspaper, particularly in the Letters column, space is at a premium and over-long letters may be ruthlessly edited or not considered worth publishing. To make sure *your* letter is published in its entirety, limit your response to just 200 words.

Begin by discussing with a partner the points you want to make. Then make notes before writing the letter.

11 The future

"Well, let's get started—you haven't got all day."

11.1 Vocabulary

Fill the gap in these sentences with a suitable word or phrase.

1 What do you think is the o.................................. for our company's future?
2 I'm very worried about the o.................................. of the current talks.
3 I don't like the look of what might happen – it all looks o.................................. to me.
4 I have a p.................................. that something's going to go wrong.
5 I'm reasonably confident that our company has a g.................................. f.................................. ahead of it.
6 The role of computers in our lives now and in the near future would have been described until recently as s.................................. f..................................
7 Each office in the building will have its own computer t..................................
8 Each of these will be linked to a central m.................................. computer.
9 Instead of a typewriter, everyone will use a w.................................. p..................................
10 The complete system will have a very large d.................................. b.................................. and authorised staff will be able to a.................................. any information they require.
11 It is essential that young people be educated to be c.................................. l..................................
12 At the heart of every micro-computer is a m..................................
13 The computer revolution would have been inconceivable without the development of tiny m..................................s.
14 However sophisticated the hardware, the system is totally dependent on its s..................................
15 The future will bring the development of the 'fifth generation' computer, which will possess a quasi-human i..................................

In the next ten sentences, *three* of the alternatives are correct and *two* are wrong. Choose the three that make best sense in each sentence.

16 Some predictions about how life will be different in the future seem ....
alarming disturbing impending prospective worrying

17 However, the more optimistic views of some experts (see exercise 11.3) are more ....
assuring encouraging helpful hopeful reassuring

18 It's impossible to be certain about any .... events.
forthcoming future imminent unlikely unsure

19 The human race may not survive the next century, according to some ....
authorities alarms forecasters romantics prophets of doom

20 This view is, I maintain, unduly ....
dim doom-laden gloomy melancholy pessimistic

21 But the idea that we'll all be happier and better-off is ....
a castle in the air a castle in Spain a pipe dream pie in the sky wishful thinking

22 Some radical changes in our way of life are ....
in store in the offing on the air on the cards up the pole

23 For example, a reduction in the number of hours we work can be ....
anticipated envisaged expected hoped speculated

24 And many other changes in working conditions are ....
apt liable likely foreseeable predictable

25 Even changes in the way we carry on our personal relationships may ....
be about to happen be about us be imminent be up to us soon be upon us

11.2 Down with offices! *Reading*

Read the newspaper article below and answer the following questions about it. Answer each question very briefly in just one word or phrase if possible.

1 What is the likely effect of telecommuting on the distribution of population?
2 How will telecommuters be able to maintain personal contact with fellow-workers in the same company?
3 How will telecommuting save the nation money?
4 How may telecommuting clerical staff suffer from this revolution?
5 Give one example of a business transacted by telecommuting at present.
6 What is the disadvantage of telecommuting?
7 Why might hierarchical corporations find telecommuting too revolutionary?
8 Why is telecommuting attractive to many present-day commuters?
9 How many US corporations are keen to expand their telecommuting staff?
10 Why might companies find telecommuting very costly to establish?
11 How great an increase in productivity does telecommuting produce?
12 How can managers find out how hard telecommuting staff are working?

What seems to be the writer's attitude to telecommuting?
Would you like to be a telecommuter? Give your reasons.

Down with offices!

By Chris Rowley, New York

Telecommuting, otherwise known as working from home, is one of the most magical buzzwords yet to surface on the US microcomputing scene. Indeed there's a seductiveness about it that seems irresistible and the signs are that it is heading for Britain.

Americans have already demonstrated a powerful urge to deurbanize and telecommuting could spread them far beyond the most distant suburbs.

The office tower with its support net of subways, highways and power cables, could become an anachronism to place beside the mediaeval fortress.

Telecommuting office workers have the opportunity to fan out to the beauty spots of the continent from where they teleconference to swap news and views and conduct their business through computer terminals.

To retain the human element in corporate life everyone comes together several times a year for conventions in Las Vegas and Manhattan.

By one estimate 10 million Americans will be telecommuting by 1990 and in the process saving three quarters of a billion gallons of petrol. In another view a new caste of workers, the "elite creatives" will lead the charge to work in the woods where they will flourish as never before, outside the strictures of offices and their policies.

But a dark side of the telecommuting force is foreseen for basic clerical staff who may wind up as poorly paid workers in their cottage office.

Already "computer ready" housing developments are rising as in Bencia, to the north of San Francisco, where the new upmarket houses come prewired with dual phone lines and built-in computer furniture. The houses begin at about $131,500 (about £92,000) and if a prospective buyer doesn't already have a computer they'll

put in an IBM PC XT and add £2,500 to the mortgage.

The logic seems flawless, as does the contracting out of labour such as insurance claims handling to freelance workers with terminals in their own home.

For example, inmates of the Arizona women's prison have been working on terminals as reservation agents for Best Western motels since 1981. It's hard to find workers on the outside for such work, especially during the peak holiday periods.

However the memories of earlier cottage industries live on, and already clerical organizations like "9 To 5" are voicing concern for exploitable telecommuters. Will struggling single parents, isolated in rural homes, raise hungry children while processing insurance forms for pennies each?

Perhaps those likely to be the elite creatives should ponder the strengths and weaknesses of the new telecommuting life. Physical isolation goes against the corporate grain, the hierarchy being organized around the office.

Yet the impulse to give up physical commuting remains. Every morning on the Santa Monica freeway there are thousands of commuters so hungry for telecommuting they can almost taste it. What with Houston's traffic jam horror, Route 101 in Marin County, the dying commuter railway lines of the North East, there are serious physical advantages to telecommuting.

Thus approximately 250 US companies now allow employees to work from home and 30, including American Express and McDonald's, are eager to expand their telecommuter forces.

Elsewhere, however, a considerable reluctance to let the employees go has been occurring. Billions of square feet of office space are there to back up the reluctant hierarchies.

Yet Gil Gordon, a telecommuting expert, says that a study has shown that employees who work at home increased their productivity by 15 to 20 per cent. Managers have discovered that telecommuting revitalizes their skills. "Telecommuting forces managers to use discipline," says Gordon.

Indeed, there are aspects of telecommuting that we should all examine before we burn those season tickets. An increasingly popular practice at companies where everyone works on a computer terminal is to count the worker's key strokes and process the numbers with rather sophisticated software in the search for improved worker performance.

11.3 Gloom mongers at bay *Reading*

Read the article about the book *Full Circle into the Future* and complete the chart below with the information given in the article. The first gap is filled for you as an example.

	GLOOM MONGERS SAY:	THE HENLEY CENTRE FOR FORECASTING REPLIES:
1	World population will continue growing at an alarming rate in the 21st century	It will have stopped growing by 2000.
2	World population 7.5 billion in 2000	

3 Birth rates will remain high in developing countries

4 Rising living standards lead to a lower death rate and thus a higher population

5 There won't be enough food to feed the world's people

6 There is less agricultural land due to the spread of deserts

7 Food will be scarcer and more expensive

8 Population is rising faster than food production

9 We are running out of fuel reserves

10 Remaining reserves cannot be exploited because it would be too costly

11 Commodities such as copper will be exhausted

12 How does the writer use *repetition* as a stylistic device in the opening paragraph of the article? What is the effect of this?
13 How does the writer use *rhetorical questions* as a stylistic device in the article? What is the effect of this? Find some examples.
14 Whose opinion is given in the closing paragraph?
15 What are the 'real problems' referred to in the last sentence?

David Blake on a book that overturns some common misconceptions

Gloom mongers at bay

Ask most people what is happening to the world's population and they are likely to say it is exploding. Ask them whether there will be enough food next century and they will say no. Ask them about the world's energy supplies and they will say that they are running out and we will all be sitting in the dark and cold next century. Ask them about raw materials and they will say that we are using them up at a rate which will mean that there are none left for our grandchildren.

These statements have two things in common. They are all gloomy, if not about this century then the next. And they are all wrong. Or so it is persuasively argued in a book, *Full Circle into the Future*, produced last week by the Henley Centre for

Forecasting, which tries to chart our future over the next quarter century. Most of the attention the book, produced with support from Telford New Town Corporation, has received so far has concentrated on its forecasts for Britain, the way we will live and the prospect of five million unemployed. But its most important message is a very different one; the merchants of global doom have been allowed to get away with depressing people for too long. Start to examine each of the statements at the start of this article and the predictions fall apart.

Take population. There is no doubt that world population has increased, is increasing and will go on growing for many years to come. In 1950 there were about 2,500 million people in the world, now there are 4,500 million, virtually double.

The gloomy scenarios for the future see this figure growing ever more rapidly, reaching 10 billion by the year 2030 and rising to 30 billion by 2100, which really would be a pretty crowded world. The explanation for this is usually said to be that in developing countries death rates have dropped, babies which used to die now live and will grow up to have other babies. In the developing world, so the argument goes, the birth rate per couple has not dropped in response to these changes and it probably will not do so. All sorts of reasons are given for this. Some are about the difficulties of explaining contraception to an under-educated population. Some are sociological – in rural areas children are needed to take care of aged parents. Some are religious – the Catholic Church is opposed to contraception and prevents its spread in Latin America.

The only problem with these explanations is that they posit something which has not happened. Fertility rates have not stayed obstinately high since the early 1950s. They are down by more than 40 per cent in East Asia, nearly a quarter in Latin America and by about 20 per cent in South Asia. Even more encouraging, all the countries of the world show clear signs of following the path which industrial nations went down many years ago. As living standards rise, the number of children falls because potential parents become more used to the idea that they have a choice between having children and higher living standards.

Some of the impact of this is already apparent. In 1969 the United Nations forecast a population of 7,500 million by the year 2000; revision after revision has brought that figure down to just over 6,000 million.

Even the pessimists admit that population catastrophe has been delayed, pushed on to the end of the twenty-first century rather than the beginning. But if the Henley estimates are right it is not going to happen. For by the beginning of the next century the population will stop growing at all. We will have a total population figure of between 6 to 6.5 billion which will remain steady at that figure.

Will we be able to feed that many people? The short answer is yes. The projection of famine, either in polemics like *Limits to Growth* or in fictionalized versions like the film *Soylent Green,* where even western countries are half starved, show no signs of coming true. We have been through the period of greatest population growth, yet even in that time the world was able to increase

Population is stabilizing, food production is going up, vast energy sources remain untapped. The future is brighter than we have been led to believe

the amount of food per person which it produces. This has not been all good news, as British taxpayers who have to pay to buy up huge surpluses of some foods can testify. Much of the food is of the wrong kind in the wrong place. But with the significant exception of Africa, the people of the world are better fed now than 20 years ago, probably better fed than at any time in history.

Many people do not know that, which is why they feel that starvation is coming. They think that things have got worse when in fact they have got better. This ignorance is not an excuse which can be used by forecasters, however. Most of those who warn of disaster realize that things have improved but say that a reversal is in sight. One reason often put forward is that the deserts are spreading.

The truth is very different. The amount of agricultural land in the Third World is increasing, not diminishing. And the yields which farmers can get on that land are rising too. There may be severe problems in some areas of the world, especially Africa. But the balance of probability is that by the year 2000 food production will have grown faster than population. For the world as a whole, there will be more food and it will be cheaper.

We will have food to eat, but will we have anything to cook it on? The energy crisis of the early 1970s was traumatic for the western world and has led us to think that we were being given advance warning that we are running out of fuel. Now in some sense that is bound to happen. One day the sun will cease to shine and that will be the end of everything. But we have several million years before we need worry about that. In Canada there are huge deposits of oil-bearing shale. Getting the oil out is such a difficult business that it is currently not worth it. But it is still there, waiting to be removed when needed. The only drawback is that it will be more expensive.

Markets have a way of dealing with that problem. The price charged goes up and people cut back on their use. At the height of the 1974 oil crisis there were many voices heard saying energy was not like that, that Americans were so committed to gas guzzler cars that they would use them whatever the price. The years have passed and so have most of the gas guzzlers.

What does the evidence of the past tell us? It says that energy prices have fallen over the past century during a time of great growth. In the 1950s and 1960s they dropped spectacularly and there was a correcting rise in the 1970s.

What about other commodities? The first point to note is that virtually no commodities are indispensable. If there is not enough copper for the cables, we can use aluminium instead. The second is that the way this happens is that copper gets expensive, telling consumers that they ought to switch to something else. The third is that if we take this test of whether commodities as a whole are getting scarcer, they seem in fact to be becoming more plentiful. During the past century the price of commodities has tended to fall steadily.

To say that the four great harbingers of apocalypse which gained fashion in the 1970s – population, food shortages, energy shortages and commodity shortages – are all fake problems does not mean that real ones do not exist. They do. But we ought to concentrate on the real problems in our societies, not imaginary ones.

Full Circle into the Future *by the Henley Centre for Forecasting (price £85).*

11.4 Prepositions and particles

Fill each gap in this passage with a suitable preposition or adverbial particle.

Nemesis just 15 million years off

Andrew Veitch reports ...on... a theory that life will be destroyed, again

LIFE ...1... earth is wiped ...2... every 26 million years ...3... a wandering star that no one has seen but has been named appropriately Nemesis.

It is claimed to have extinguished the dinosaurs, and our turn is said to be 15 million years away.

According ...4... research ...5... US physicists to be published ...6... Nature, Nemesis is a companion star ...7... the sun orbiting the solar system ...8... distances ranging ...9... five ...10... 20 trillion kilometres.

...11... its nearest point it smashes ...12... a cloud of comets called the Oort cloud which also orbits the sun. Some of the comets are dislodged, and the planets are showered ...13... debris. The rings ...14... Saturn may be the remnants ...15... one such displaced comet.

When the debris hits the earth it is plunged ...16... darkness ...17... a million years. Most animal and plant life is extinguished. When light and heat return ...18... the planet's surface, new species emerge.

"These catastrophes give new species an opportunity. It's conceivable that if it had not been ...19... such periodic catastrophes the world might still be dominated ...20... trilobites," one of the physicists, Dr Richard Muller ...21... the University of California at Berkeley, is reported as saying ...22... New Scientist today.

Evidence ...23... periodic mass extinctions has been accumulating ...24... 1977, the magazine explains. The fossil record and impact craters suggest they happen every 26 ...25... 28 million years.

...26... three occasions — 247, 220 and 65 million years ago — 95 per cent ...27... life was wiped ...28... ...29... seven other occasions — 11, 38, 91, 125, 144, 163, and 194 million years ago — ...30... 20 and 50 per cent of species were killed ...31...

Extra terrestial objects colliding ...32... the earth are the most likely causes but the question is why do they arrive ...33... such apparent regularity? Sceptics maintain that the evidence amounts ...34... a 1,000-to-one statistical fluke.

Now Dr Muller and a team led ...35... Dr Daniel Whitmore ...36... the University of South-west Louisiana, have concluded, independently, that Nemesis is to blame. Berkeley astronomers have programmed two telescopes to search the sky automatically ...37... the star.

11.5 Idioms with KEEP and GIVE *Use of English*

Rewrite each of the sentences so that it still means the same, using the words on the left together with the correct form of the verb KEEP.

1 COMPANY Will you please stay with me for a while?
2 HIMSELF TO HIMSELF He's not going to meet anyone socially for a time.
3 A STRAIGHT FACE I couldn't help smiling when he told me of his plan.
4 IN THE DARK The staff aren't going to be told about the firm's plans for the future.
5 AN OPEN MIND I won't prejudge the issue until we've discussed it.
6 AWAY FROM I won't go near her until she's feeling more optimistic.
7 YOUR HEAD Try not to panic even if you don't know what's going to happen.
8 UP WITH THE JONESES In future we're not going to worry about maintaining the same material standards as our neighbours.

Use the correct form of the verb GIVE in the next four sentences.

9 OUT Reserves of copper and other minerals will eventually become exhausted.
10 AWAY I'll never tell you the secret information.
11 ME TO UNDERSTAND She made me think that she'd be leaving any day.
12 ME THE CREEPS All this talk about gloom and doom makes me feel very uncomfortable.

"And when you're finished cleaning upstairs, you can give me a hand in the kitchen."

11.6 Coming soon *Questions and summary*

Read the article below and answer the questions on the next page in writing.

Coming soon—a robot slave for everyone

THE HUMAN brain contains, I am told, 10 thousand million cells and each of these may have a thousand connections. Such enormous numbers used to daunt us and cause us to dismiss the possibility of making a machine with human-like ability, but now that we have grown used to moving forward at such a pace we can be less sure.

Quite soon, in only 10 or 20 years perhaps, we will be able to assemble a machine as complex as the human brain, and if we can we will. It may then take us a long time to render it intelligent by loading in the right software or by altering the architecture but that too will happen.

I think it certain that in decades, not centuries, machines of silicon will arise first to rival and then surpass their human progenitors. Once they surpass us they will be capable of their own design. In a real sense they will be reproductive. Silicon will have ended carbon's long monopoly. And ours too, I suppose, for we will no longer be able to deem ourselves the finest intelligence in the known universe.

In principle, it could be stopped. There will be those that try, but it will happen none the less. The lid of Pandora's box is starting to open.

But let us look a little closer to the present: By the end of this decade manufacturing decline will be nearly complete—with employment in manufacturing industries less than 10 per cent in Britain. The goods are still needed but, as with agriculture already, imports and technical change will virtually remove all employment.

The Japanese are aiming to make computers dealing with concepts rather than numbers with thousands of times more power than current large machines. This has triggered a swift and powerful response in the American nation. There is a large joint programme of development among leading US computer companies, and IBM, though it says nothing, may well have the biggest programme of all.

These projects are aimed at what are loosely termed fifth-generation computers. These are really a new breed of machine entirely and will be as different from today's computers as today's computer is from an adding machine.

The simple microprocessor provides sufficient intelligence for current assembly line robots. As robots learn to see and feel, their brains will grow. Eventually, and not too far in the future, they will make decisions on the production line currently delegated to a supervisor.

Outside the factory we employ men's minds in two principal ways; as founts of knowledge and as makers of decisions. The former of these attributes is now falling prey to the machine with the development of "expert systems" whereby the acquired knowledge of a man, an expert in mining for example, is made to repose in the memory of a computer. The transfer of data from human to machine mind is neither easy nor swift, but once attained it may be copied at will and broadcast. A formerly scarce resource can thus become plentiful.

The ability to reach wise conclusions, as we expect of a doctor or lawyer, from much or scant data will longer remain man's monopoly — but not always.

Fifth generation computers will share this prerogative. Tomorrow we may take our ailments to a machine as readily as to a man. In time that machine will be in the house, removing the need to journey to the doctor and providing a far more regular monitoring of the state of health than it is now economic to provide.

The computer as surrogate teacher may bring even more benefits. Today, and as long as we depend on humans, we must have one teacher to many pupils. The advantage of a tutor for each child is clear and if that tutor is also endlessly patient and superhumanly well-informed we may expect a wonderful improvement in the standard of education. What, though, is the purpose if, in this imagined future, there are no jobs ?

Curiously we can find analogies in the past. Freemen of Periclean Athens led not such different lives as we might live, for where we will have the machines, they had slaves who served both to teach and as menials. Thanks, perhaps, to their fine education, the freemen of Athens seem not to have found difficulty in filling their time.

Just as they did, we will need to educate our children to an appreciation of the finer things of life, to inculcate a love of art, music and science. So we may experience an age as golden as that of Greece.

As the intelligence of robots increases to emulate that of humans and as their cost declines through economies of scale we may use them to expand our frontiers, first on earth through their ability to withstand environments, inimical to ourselves. Thus, deserts may bloom and the ocean beds be mined.

Further ahead, by a combination of the great wealth this new age will bring and the technology it will provide, we can really begin to use space to our advantage. The construction of a vast, man-created world in space, home to thousands or millions of people, will be within our power and, should we so choose, we may begin in earnest the search for worlds beyond our solar system and the colonisation of the galaxy.

(by Sir Clive Sinclair in *The Guardian*)

1 Explain the meaning of these words and phrases used in the passage:
daunt (line 7) progenitors (line 24) deem ourselves (line 30)
triggered (line 50) founts of knowledge (line 73) falling prey (line 76)
surrogate (line 101)
2 How will it be possible for machines to become more intelligent than humans?
3 How will Britain's need for manufactured products be satisfied by 1990?
4 What is meant by an 'expert system'?
5 How will teachers be threatened by computers?
6 Using information from the article, and from this letter prompted by it, write a paragraph of about 50 words explaining how our home lives are likely to change in the future.

Chip thrills

Sir,—Struggling through Sir Clive Sinclair's ruptured syntax (April 24) it appears that what he and IBM have in store for us is a life of sitting around in long flowing robes drinking wine and eating kebabs, discussing Art, Science and Philosophy and all that stuff while just out of eye and earshot there are these silicon machines gliding effortlessly around waiting to fulfil our slightest needs in our huge tastefully furnished machine designed drawing-rooms. . . . A treacherous thought intrudes, however : if these machines are going to be so damned smart, why won't they be the ones sitting around discussing all the really interesting stuff while the little carbon-based squirts like Sir Clive and me scuttle around doing the housework ?—Yours,

Peter Smee.
13 Meadview Road
Ware, Herts.

11.7 Journey into space *Listening*

Listen to the recording in which the speaker describes what it is like to travel on the US Space Shuttle. Decide which of the statements below are true (**T**) or false (**F**), according to the speaker.

1 The speaker describes what it is like to pilot the Space Shuttle.
2 A passenger on the Shuttle doesn't need to wear a spacesuit.
3 As the Shuttle lifts off you get a tremendous feeling of speed.
4 During the first few minutes of the flight both the sea and the sky look blue.
5 Before the Shuttle breaks the sound barrier, the flight seems noisy and bumpy.
6 When you are weightless your legs get thinner.
7 When you are weightless your face gets thinner.
8 When you are weightless you get an awful headache and feel very sick.
9 About 8½ minutes after lift-off you are allowed to unstrap.
10 When you unstrap yourself your arms rise and your legs aren't straight.
11 Looking at the Earth through the window you can even make out some man-made features.
12 The sky above is a beautiful deep blue colour.
13 The sun rises every 1½ hours.
14 All the food is dehydrated to save space and weight.
15 The washbasin operates in a similar way to a washbasin on Earth.
16 There are no beds on the Shuttle.
17 Sleeping on the Shuttle is awkward and difficult.
18 A complete flight lasts less than a week.
19 Experiencing gravity again after being in space is reassuring and soothing.
20 The Shuttle lands like a conventional plane on a runway, only faster.

"I don't care what planet you're from, you can't run around earth stark naked!"

11.8 Ocean city *Listening*

Listen to the recording in which there is a report of a futuristic Japanese plan to build a floating city in the Pacific Ocean. Fill in the gaps in the notes below and complete the missing parts of the diagram with the appropriate details.

1 Population of Japan now: ..... million
Only ....% of Japan's land area of .... sq km is inhabitable

2 Kiyohide Terai's study group includes the heads of many famous Japanese companies: S......., Mitsui, Nippon S........, Nippon T....... & T......., Asahi p........ group

HOW OCEAN CITY WOULD WORK:

3 Distance from coast of Japan: .... km No. of inhabitants ...... million. To build it would need .... tonnes of steel

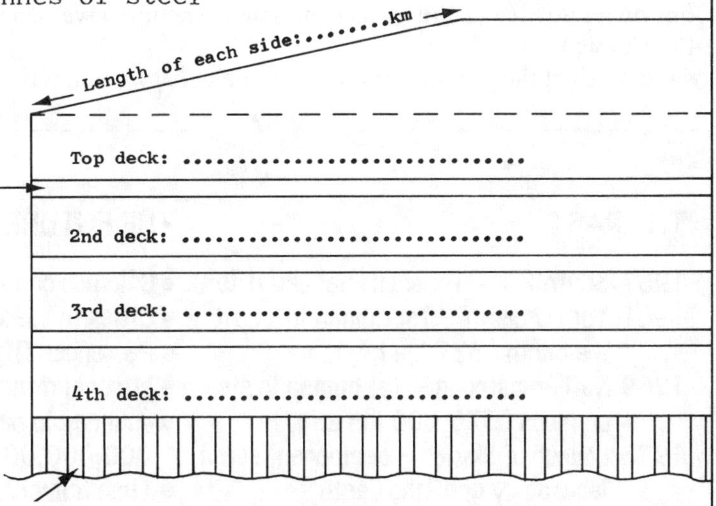

Length of each side:.......km

Top deck: ....

4 Distance between decks: ....

2nd deck: ....

3rd deck: ....

4th deck: ....

5 Total number of poles: ...., each containing a .... controlled by .....
- Not resting on sea bed but ....
- No sensation of being ....
- Not affected by rough seas because of its .... and height above ....

6 Advantages of living there: tax benefits, leisure facilities: four ....s, ... pools, ..., ... riding etc. PLUS: no ....s

11.9 Future fantasy or future fact? *Picture conversation*

Work in pairs. One of you should look at activity 19, the other at 54. You will each have a photograph to talk about.

11.10 Predictions *Communication activity*

Work in pairs. One of you should look at activity 20, the other at 60. You will each have some predictions to discuss.

11.11 Giving your opinions *Composition*

'How much truth is there in the pictures we are given of space travel by science fiction writers and film-makers?' (About 350 words)

Basing your composition on some of the facts and conjectures below, together with your own knowledge and ideas from science fiction, give your opinions on the above topic.
Make notes of the points you intend to make *before* you write the composition.

THE PAST	THE FUTURE
1957 Sputnik 1 - 1st artificial satellite	• Colonies on Moon?
1961 Yuri Gagarin - 1st human to orbit the Earth (327 km high)	• Cities in space?
	• Passenger flights into space?
1969 Neil Armstrong - 1st human to step on Moon (376,000 km away)	• Mineral mines on other planets?
	• Journey to nearest star (40, 000,000,000,000 km away)?
1973 Launch of Skylab - permanent space laboratory orbiting Earth	• Time travel?
1976 Viking I landed on Mars (55,000, 000 km away) - no life there, apparently	• Faster-than-light space ships?
	• Visitors from other planets land on Earth?
1981 1st return journey of space shuttle, Columbia	• Space exploration stops due to enormous cost?

12 One world

12.1 Vocabulary

Fill the gaps in these sentences with a suitable word.

1 The countries of the world can be divided into three groups: the West, the Eastern bloc and the T.................................. W..................................
2 The latter can also be called non-.................................. or d.................................. countries.
3 Others divide the world into the prosperous N.................................. and the poorer S..................................
4 Among these countries are some which are new i.................................. states (such as South Korea, Taiwan and Singapore), but most depend much more on a..................................
5 In many parts of Asia and Africa, p..................................s produce s.................................. crops to feed themselves and their families.
6 However, it is often more profitable for farmers to produce c.................................. crops (such as cocoa or cotton) for export.
7 Land is often used to provide luxury foods for the rich, instead of being used more p..................................ly to feed the people.
8 Many areas in the tropics have been taken over by vast p..................................s, where products like bananas and pineapples are grown for the Western market.
9 The workers in the fields and factories of the Third World tend to be underpaid and ex..................................
10 Industry in the West depends on developing countries to provide it with cheap r.................................. m..................................s.
11 Unable to support themselves on the land, the rural poor are drifting to the cities, where they live in sh.................................. t..................................s.
12 The ....s they live in lack both fresh drinking water and proper s..................................
13 500 million people in the world today are under-.................................. or, worse, suffering from s..................................
14 If there is a serious d.................................. there may be no food reserves for the poor to fall back on, leading to f..................................
15 Because of problems of distribution, there may be a sh.................................. of food in one region while there is a s.................................. in another.
16 It is difficult for r.................................. a..................................s (such as Oxfam or Caritas) to provide food aid rapidly.
17 In an attempt to attract Western investment in manufacturing, developing countries offer the incentives of cheap l.................................. and low t..................................

→

18 Western (and Eastern) influence in many Third World countries, though less overt than in the 19th century, is still a form of c..............................

19 Surely everyone has a right to good health (freedom from d..............................) and enough to eat (freedom from h..............................).

20 But how many people in the world have the benefit of President Roosevelt's four freedoms: freedom of s.............................., freedom of w.............................., freedom from w.............................. and freedom from f..............................?

In the next five sentences, *one* of the alternatives given is correct and the rest are wrong. Choose the word that fits best in each sentence.

21 Distant as many of us are from the realities of poverty and hunger, it's frighteningly easy to feel ....
complacent contented self-satisfied smug

22 We tend to rely on governments and relief organisations to take on the .... for providing development aid.
response respondence responsibility respondency

23 Knowing that 80% of the world's resources are consumed by 30% of its population gives one a .... feeling.
criminal guilty regretful sinful

24 Grain production in the world is ...., but still millions go hungry.
flying sailing soaring zooming

25 Even though the problems seem to be ...., there must be something every one of us can do.
baffling insoluble ticklish tricky

"Secretly trained by the Americans? That's funny, so were we."

12.2 Liberia *Reading*

Read the article below and then answer the multiple-choice questions that follow.

COUNTRY PROFILE

Liberia

Photo: Wayne Ellwood

Leader Master Sergeant Samuel K. Doe
Economy GNP per capita $520 per year
Monetary unit Liberian dollar and US dollar
Main exports iron ore, rubber, timber, diamonds
People 2 million (1983), about 34% live in towns
Health Life expectancy 54 years
Infant mortality 194 per 1,000 live births
Culture 16 major tribal groups; 93% of population indigenous, 5% descendants of American slaves, others include Lebanese and Asians who control commercial sector. Religion: 75% traditional/animist, 15% Muslim, 10% Christian. Language: Official language English spoken mostly in cities; 20 African dialects used in rural areas.
Source World Development Report 1983.

FRIDAY night in Monrovia and the *McBurger* restaurant is packed with spiffed-up touts drinking Guinness and civil servants lounging over a cheeseburger and Coke.

Liberia is an African curiosity. Tucked between Sierra Leone and Ivory Coast it has been an independent republic since 1847. The idea of Liberia ('land of liberation') was created in America. In the 1820s when the cotton gin reduced the need for slaves in the US south, blacks suddenly became a liability for plantation owners. What better solution than to export them 'home'? Home, of course, was a bit difficult to find after 100 years in America. But West Africa seemed as good a bet as any. So thousands of slaves were repatriated. English-speaking, Christianized and thoroughly American, these blacks were as foreign to local inhabitants as white Europeans. ⟶

Torrential rainfall, no obvious natural resources and a treacherous coastline combined to keep the European colonizers at bay during the 'scramble for Africa' in the 1880s. In Monrovia (named after US president James Monroe) the 'American-Liberians' became the local elite. In the interior, life was much as it had been for generations with tribes growing upland rice in the traditional shifting pattern of 'slash and burn' farmers. The country's precise borders weren't defined until after the Second World War.

In 1926 Harvey Firestone began to carve a rubber plantation out of the forest and Liberia joined the world economy. Harbel Plantation (named after Harvey and his wife Idabelle) became the biggest rubber farm in the world. Rubber soon became the country's major industry, although in the 1950s iron ore replaced it as the number one foreign exchange earner.

But Liberia is best known for its 'flag of convenience' shipping operation. Foreign-owned vessels purchase cut-price Liberian registration and receive reduced taxes and lax safety regulations as part of the deal.

During the recent recession Liberia's economy has scraped bottom. Rubber and iron ore markets died, income plumetted and jobs were slashed. Only Washington's aid dollars keep the country from bankruptcy, and indeed Liberia is the only African nation where US currency is legal tender. In return America's corporate interests are secure, with Liberian bases for Voice of America, a satellite tracking station and the CIA.

In 1979, Master Sergeant Samuel K. Doe kicked out the corrupt regime of President Tolbert and became the first native Liberian descendant to hold power. Great things were promised by his People's Redemption Council. But so far not much has happened, and not much is likely to until the global economy picks up.

In recent years the old elite, the 'Americos', have slowly begun to run the country again. The reality, as Dr Doe soon discovered, is that no one else has the skills. Elections have been promised for 1985, but the decisions that really matter will continue to be made in the boardrooms of foreign corporations.

At a glance

FREEDOM
***

Political prisoners released but strikes and political parties illegal

INCOME DISTRIBUTION
**

Elite dominated by Americo-Liberians and Lebanese controls most wealth

SELF-RELIANCE
*

Dependent on US aid and foreign corporations

POSITION OF WOMEN
***

Strong tribal roles, active in agriculture; female circumcision widely practised

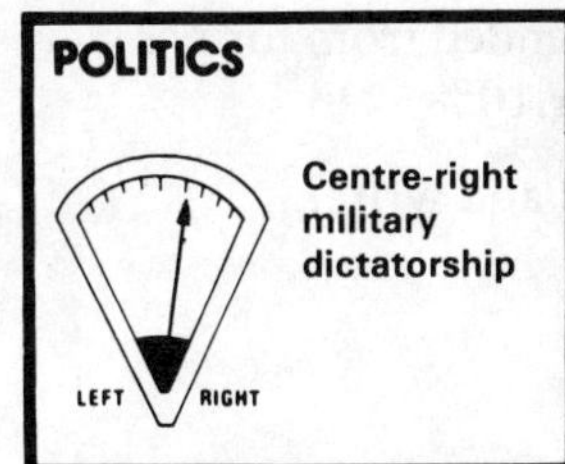

LIFE EXPECTANCY
**
54 years. Health services inadequate, government focus is on Western model

Choose the alternative that best completes each sentence, taking your information from the article on the previous page.

1 In the 1820s former slaves were repatriated because US slave-owners . . .
felt guilty about owning slaves.
were no longer allowed to own slaves.
wanted slaves to go back to their families in Africa.
no longer needed slaves.

2 Liberia had not become a European colony in the 19th century because . . .
the territory belonged to the USA.
the native tribes were hostile.
it didn't seem worth possessing.
European powers couldn't agree on its borders.

3 In recent years . . .
Liberia has grown to depend more and more on rubber.
the rubber market has become more and more buoyant.
the bottom has dropped out of the rubber market.
many Liberian rubber plantations have been chopped down.

4 Liberia could not have survived bankruptcy . . .
without its flourishing export trade.
without the taxes it raises from Liberian-registered shipping.
if the USA hadn't given money.
if it hadn't been a democratic republic.

5 The 'Americos' in Liberia are . . .
US government agents and officials.
employees of US firms.
immigrants from the USA.
descendants of former slaves.

6 Since President Doe seized power he has . . .
been able to replace the 'Americos' in positions of power.
found that only the 'Americos' have the necessary expertise.
reduced the amount of US influence in Liberia.
carried out widespread reforms.

7 Who has the greatest influence on Liberia?
the 'Americos'   President Doe   the US government
big business

→

8 What proportion of the Liberian population are descended from former slaves?
over 90% over 50% under 50% under 10%

9 What proportion of the Liberian population can read and write?
90% 50% 25% 10%

10 What is Liberia's most important export?
diamonds rubber iron ore timber

11 The position of women in Liberian society is described as . . .
'appalling' 'poor' 'fair' 'good'

12 What seem to be the political leanings of the writer?
Left Centre Right none

12.3 Food in one place; need in another *Reading*

Read the editorial from *The Guardian* and decide whether, according to the article, the following statements are true (**T**) or false (**F**).

1 According to *The Guardian*, the Ethiopian government probably knows less about the suffering in Eritrea and Tigre than European television viewers do.
2 Food should be sent directly to the starving people's villages.
3 If the people gather in central distribution points there may be widespread disease.
4 If the people gather in central distribution points this will discourage the planting of subsequent crops and increase dependency on food aid.
5 A disinterested outsider should act as go-between between the Ethiopian government and the rebels.
6 The Ethiopian government has, so far, done its best to provide facilities for relief agencies to distribute food.
7 Even the mountains of food in EEC warehouses are not large enough to feed the millions of starving families in Ethiopia.
8 Famine in Ethiopia has been exacerbated by the state of civil war in the country.
9 Other nations south of the Sahara have been less badly affected by the drought.
10 If the Ethiopian government co-operated more willingly, it would be relatively easy to distribute food to the starving.
11 The Ethiopian government has good reason for opposing the distribution of food directly to villages.
12 The Ethiopian government has good reason to distrust the West for its attitude to the rebels in Eritrea and Tigre.
13 *The Guardian* supports the three-point War on Want proposals.
14 *The Guardian* believes the problems of feeding the people in Ethiopia are insurmountable.

Food in one place; need in another

Without television cameras the famine now ravaging Ethiopia would not have caught the attention of the well-fed world as it has done, with offers of money and other aid flooding in after every programme. European viewers probably know more about what is happening to the starving people of Tigre and Eritrea than the Ethiopian government itself. The chasm between need and help in such a crisis sometimes seems unbridgeable, which is why it is important to choose one practicable means of support instead of letting the obvious concern to do something be dissipated across the board. Such a means was proposed yesterday in the three-point programme put forward by War On Want through its Secretary, Mr George Galloway.

The three requirements are: that the mountains of food, grain especially, available in Europe should be ready for shipment. That food should be distributed to the people where they live instead of going to centralised supply depots, thus reducing the risk of epidemics and encouraging farmers to stay on their land to prepare next year's crop. And that an intermediary between government and insurgents should arrange for the safe passage of food into the famine areas. Willy Brandt was suggested: at any rate someone of his calibre and credentials. Mr Galloway was more forthright than some relief workers are prepared to be in accusing the Ethiopian government of complacency and inertia. It is as well to have that on record. The Ethiopian government has been quick to denounce the paucity of foreign relief (which the United Nations describes as substantial). But only in the last few days has it agreed to allow foreign aircraft to take supplies directly inland, in spite of the notorious port congestion which is delaying delivery of both food and the means of transport. Up to now it has said that if foreign planes were allowed they would be used for espionage.

It goes without saying that there is a very disturbing discrepancy between the 30 million tons of grain which Europe now has in store (thanks to a succession of good harvests, of which the latest has beaten all records) and the 60,000 tons a month which Ethiopia is going to need into next year if hundreds of thousands of people are to stay alive. The discrepancy would be far worse if the grain already delivered to Ethiopia were being put to immediate use. Nor is it enough to single out Ethiopia as the only place of need in Africa. The country's disasters are magnified because civil war and famine have coincided, but all the countries of the Sahel have experienced the drought. The UN estimate is that 6.3 million Africans are suffering its effects today. The Ethiopian famine is only the most conspicuous and certainly the most urgent in terms of numbers; but all round the rim of the Sahara people are dying inconspicuously too.

Although the effects of the Ethiopian famine have been worsened by the government's political preoccupations and by administrative failures the ultimate cause is the drought, which is beyond any government's control. Even in the best of times it would be hard to ensure fair distribution of relief across vast stretches of open and rough terrain. What an intermediary of the kind suggested by War on Want could do would be to ensure that politics do not continue to add yet another dimension of difficulty to some nearly insurmountable physical problems. (The insurgents as well as the government are suspicious when they see truckloads of they know not what entering their territory.) He would also have to convince the government that distribution to villages is essential for the relief to be effective, for in a civil war the government has good reason for wanting people to congregate where it can keep an eye on them. There can be no guarantee that a Willy Brandt style of mediator could overcome the suspicions borne of many years' war—a war, further to complicate matters, in which most Western sympathy has been on the insurgent side. The fact remains that the food is in one place and the need for it in another, and it is worth risking any number of rebuffs to bring the two together.

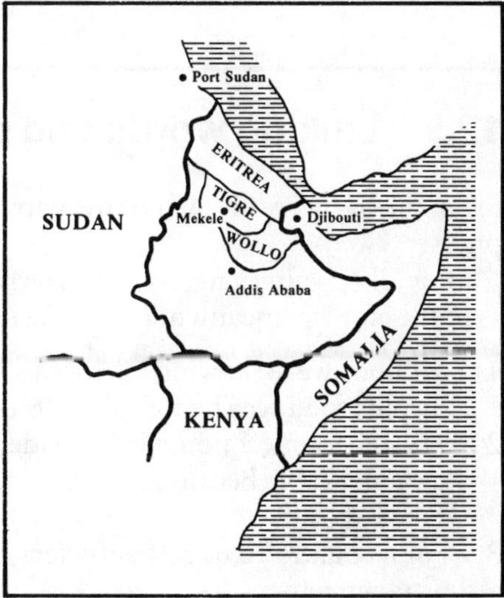

12.4 Reported speech *Use of English*

Rewrite each of the sentences so that its meaning remains unchanged.

1 'It's true that food aid has not been getting through.'
They confirmed that . . .

2 'It might be a good idea if trucks were sent there to help in the distribution of food supplies.'
It was suggested . . .

3 'Western governments have always tended to be too complacent and insular.'
They accused . . .

4 'Donations were received from individuals and organisations.'
According to the report . . .

5 'Over £40 million has been received over the last ten days.'
It was reported . . .

6 'There has been no lack of co-operation with relief workers on the spot.'
It was denied . . .

7 'A rapid increase in the birth rate has turned a crisis into a disaster.'
The speaker insisted . . .

8 'The sooner an agreement is reached the better.'
It was hoped . . .

9 'It is certainly essential to take a long-term view of the situation.'
They agreed . . .

10 'Without the rapid growth in population there would be fewer food shortages.'
He blamed . . .

12.5 Linking words and phrases *Use of English*

From the list here, fill each of the gaps in the sentences with a suitable word or phrase.

after all | alternatively | clearly | evidently | for this reason
in the end | meanwhile | this is why | undoubtedly | unfortunately

1 Millions were starving in Africa's worst famine. ...., in Europe, surplus food was being sold to the Soviet Union.

2 The Liberian economy is dependent on Western development aid but this is not so remarkable because, ..., this is not a unique situation in the Third World.

3 For a country to be self-sufficient it must, ..., use its land resources productively.

4 Economic planning requires taking a long-term view. .... this is becoming less possible in this day and age.
5 Emergency supplies can be brought in by road. ...., they can be transported by sea or by air.
6 Tackling the problems of the Third World is a daunting prospect. .... it is tempting to say that they are insoluble.
7 Those who need help are poor, uneducated and rurally-based. .... there is a massive gulf between them and those who can offer help.
8 The rural poor do not share the same values as educated city-dwellers. .... we must make great efforts to adapt methods to suit their values and ideas.
9 Western economists tend to apply Western theories to the problems of developing countries. .... their proposed solutions are often ineffective.
10 Insuperable though these problems may seem, ... solutions must be found to avert a global catastrophe.

12.6 Letters to the editor *Questions and summary*

The two letters below were written in response to the editorial you read in exercise 12.3. After you have read them through, answer the following questions in writing.

1 Explain the meaning of these words and phrases used in the letters:
key issue (line 4) timely and practicable (line 19) 'safe passage' (line 37) trek (line 84) leader (line 85)

2 According to Stuart Holland, how has the British government acted reprehensibly?
3 What is likely to happen if food aid is flown to Addis Ababa?
4 How can food best be distributed to the areas controlled by the three Liberation fronts?

5 According to Trish Silkin, what was the 'welcome injection of common sense' provided by *The Guardian*'s editorial?
6 What mistake was made in the editorial?
7 How can food be distributed to the people of Eritrea?
8 Write one paragraph summarising the ideas expressed by both writers on getting food to the stricken areas as quickly as possible.

Getting food aid to Eritrea

Sir, — Your editorial (October 26) highlighted what now is the key issue in food aid to Ethiopia. The public response to aid appeals has been phenomenal, raising as much in days as the British government has granted in months.

The response of individual farmers to send grain rather than cash has been welcomed by the voluntary agencies. The archbishops' pressure on the government to make Hercules aircraft available for delivery of grain is both timely and practicable but the Government is only offering two aircraft, when it could give 20, and that is not enough.

But as you ask, where is the grain going and who will get it? If aid is flown to Addis Ababa it may well be weeks or months before it reaches those in need. This is not only bureaucracy, or availability of vehicles. It is the simple fact that the Ethiopian government does not control and cannot distribute aid to the key drought areas unless there is a "safe passage" agreement with the Liberation fronts.

They control up to 85 per cent of Eritrea and Tigray, and nearly half of Wollo. They have made it clear that they will agree to "safe passage" for any vehicles or aircraft with red cross markings. But the government still calls them bandits and refuses to admit that such areas are outside its control.

Last Monday in the Commons I called on Malcolm Rifkind, Minister of State at the Foreign Office, to admit this problem and to recognise that only the Liberation relief associations such as ERA for Eritrea and REST for Tigray can get food quickly to those most in need. So far there has been no response.

Yet if the British Farmers' food aid were to be flown by Hercules to Port Sudan, Mekele and Djibouti direct rather than Addis this could enable the Eritrean, Tigrayan and Wollo liberation agencies to begin distribution within days from now.

Stuart Holland MP.
Shadow Minister of Overseas Development and Cooperation,
House of Commons,
London SW1

Sir, — It is appalling that the media have unquestioningly accepted that the right way to handle the Ethiopian tragedy is to encourage hungry and sick people to trek miles to feeding centres. In this context your leader is a welcome injection of common sense.

You are wrong, however, to suggest that the rebel movement in Eritrea has received more sympathetic support from the West than the Ethiopian government has. After the Second World War Western interests pushed Eritrea into an unworkable federation with Ethiopia and Western governments have never wavered in their opposition to Eritrean independence.

As a result very little of the aid finally being made available to the victims of the current famine will find its way to Eritrea. Ironically, while transport is the major obstacle to getting food to the hungry in Ethiopia, the Eritreans have independent supply routes along the thousands of kilometres of road they have built to bring supplies from Port Sudan into Eritrea.

Some British charities have had the courage of their convictions and are supplying aid through the Eritrean Relief Association which has the capacity to deliver it to 85 per cent of Eritrea. However, with more than a million people wholly dependent on them the ERA needs a level of aid which only governments can provide.

Trish Silkin.
Marquis Road,
London N4.

12.7 Averting calamity

Listening

The interview describes some of the recommendations made by Brian May in *The Third World Calamity* and also by E. F. Schumacher in *Small is Beautiful*. Before you hear the recording for the first time, read through the six points on the left below. Some of the gaps can be filled during your second listening to the recording.

1 ● **No economic activity should be encouraged that does not contain the certain means of absorbing those whom it deprives of their traditional work.**

According to E. F. Schumacher it is better to replace '£.................. jobs' with '£.................. workplaces' in industry, not with '£.................. high technology workplaces.'

Industry in developing countries should be l..................-i.................. and not absorb too much c..................

2 ● **Attempted rural development should mostly be from the village up. Money should be diverted from grandiose, uneconomic projects and devoted to simpler ones.**

Farmers in the Third World's two million ....s should be encouraged to help themselves:

'Give a man a fish and you're helping him for ....; teach him to fish and you help him to help himself for ....; teach him to make his own f.................. t.................. and he'll become self-.................., self-.................. and i..................

Example: Sokoto River scheme – cost of irrigating each hectare of farmland: £..................

3 ● **There should be serious effort to prevent the slightly better off appropriating all the benefits in the incessant battle for a margin above subsistence.**

Workers desperate for work are prepared to take any job and work for s.................. wages. Impossible for employers not to appear to 'e..................' their workers.

4 ● **Special efforts should be made in places of extreme suffering. Organisations like Oxfam and Frères des Hommes are best suited to help.**

But also need to provide gifts of k.................. (not just food) so that people don't become d..................

Food aid sent via governments arrives more ....ly than if it is distributed by relief agencies.

→

5 **● Sales of arms to the Third World should be drastically reduced, even though this would cause a slight reduction in Western living standards.**

eg US military aid to Third World in 1984: $.................... US non-military aid to Third World: $....................

Huge sales of arms to developing countries by both East and West. Even by B...................., S.................... and I....................

Better if Third World governments spent their money not on ....s but on h.................... s....................s.

6 **● World Bank policy should be overhauled in the light of these provisions. Strong pressures should be put on Third World governments to carry out this difficult policy.**

Developing countries should not have to .... more and more to pay their ....s.

Large-scale schemes requiring massive i.................... but of little benefit to the people should be stopped.

12.8 Multinational companies *Listening*

In the recorded conversation you'll hear two people's opinions about the influence of multinationals on the world. As you listen to it for the first time answer questions 1 to 10 below.

1 Saudi Arabia has less economic power than . . .
Switzerland British Petroleum General Motors

2 Greece has less economic power than . . .
BP GM Exxon (Esso)

3 The workers in a South-East Asian free-trade zone . . .
are unreliable are untrained can be dismissed easily

4 In Malaysia and the Philippines silicon chips are assembled by . . .
female workers microscopes robots unskilled girls

5 The people in Third World countries are encouraged to buy . . .
Coca Cola and hamburgers fridges and air conditioners
pineapples and sugar

6 In Africa the sale of powdered milk . . .
caused the deaths of babies endangered the lives of babies
was of no benefit to the population

7 In the UK, multinationals . . .
bribe the government contribute to Conservative Party funds
lobby the government

8 In Iran rapid industrialisation . . .
made the country bankrupt   reduced unemployment
was of no benefit to the people

9 In Japan bribes were taken by . . .
Lockheed employees   the Prime Minister   top officials

10 The 'politicians' in a multinational are more powerful than conventional politicians because they . . .
are more efficient   are not elected   can operate in secrecy

As you hear the recording for the second time, fill the gaps in the sentences below.

11 One third of all world trade is .... multinational companies.

12 The 100 largest economic powers in the world include .... companies.

13 Multinationals can:
– fix their .... to suit themselves
– shift .... from .... countries to .... countries
– avoid .... controls and circumvent ....
– ....profits from developing countries to their mother country

14 A typical factory in a South-East Asian free-trade zone has freedom from:
c.................................. taxes; i.................................. duties; p.................................. taxes;
e.................................. duties

15 In the Third World multinationals can:
– exercise the same control as a c.................................. power
– substitute c.................................. c.................................. (for example: ....,
.... and ....) for food that could feed the people
– encourage sales of s.................................. d.................................., h..................................
t.................................. cigarettes, unsafe d.................................. and j.................................. foods
– interfere in politics by bringing down l..................................-..................................
governments and supporting r..................................-.................................. p..................................
– create a small m.................................. s.................................. of the economy to the detriment of the majority who become ....

16 A large multinational has its own specialists who can l..................................,
b.................................. and form a.................................. with politicians.

12.9 Small is Beautiful *Pronunciation*

Work in pairs. One of you should look at activity 21, the other at 61. You will each have a short extract from *Small is Beautiful* to read and then discuss.

12.10 National income and population

Communication activity

Work in pairs. One of you should look at activity 22, the other at 62. You will see two separate parts of two maps of the world, showing the population and income of different countries.

12.11 Writing an analysis

Composition

Study the notes below carefully and, if possible, discuss the information given in the light of what you have found out in other exercises in this unit. Then write a composition of about 350 words on this topic:

> *'Describe how the patterns of world trade adversely affect the development of Third World countries. What can be done to ameliorate the situation, in your opinion?'*

PRINCIPAL EXPORTS
OF THIRD WORLD COUNTRIES

Sudan: cotton
Uganda: coffee
Barbados: sugar
Ghana: cocoa

Zambia: copper
Liberia: iron ore

Cash crops: staple foods (grain) imported to feed the people

Commodity prices not controlled by exporters

TYPICAL IMPORTS OF
WESTERN COUNTRIES
FROM THIRD WORLD

coffee cocoa
tea tropical fruits
palm oil sugar

minerals

textiles
clothing
manufactured goods

cheap labour

PLUS: DEBT REPAYMENTS TO WESTERN BANKS

TYPICAL IMPORTS
OF THIRD WORLD COUNTRIES

oil
grain (eg US wheat)
luxury consumer goods
machinery

13 History

13.1 Vocabulary

Fill each gap with a suitable word.

1 An important event, such as the foundation of the United Nations in 1945, is a(n) h.................................. event.
2 Any event that is recorded by history is a h.................................. event.
3 Historians are concerned with not simply recording history but also i.................................. it.
4 The cathedral is one of the country's finest examples of Norman a..................................
5 Pottery, jewellery and other a..................................s were found in the burial mound.
6 These remains date back to the I.................................. A..................................
7 The tomb of the king was excavated by an eminent Greek a..................................
8 Visitors come from far and wide to see the s.................................. of the tomb.
9 People often think that life was better in the 'g.................................. o.................................. d..................................s'.
10 It is certainly tempting to feel a certain n.................................. for the past.
11 However, in m.................................. times when everyone owed allegiance to the king, life was probably quite unpleasant for most of the people in Europe.
12 One a.................................. in a recent film was a 'Roman soldier' wearing a digital wristwatch and sunglasses.
13 The Industrial Revolution in England reached its zenith in V.................................. times.
14 Many details of life in years gone by are recorded in ancient m..................................s and c..................................s.
15 Both sides in the war claimed they had right on their side – p.................................. will decide who was right.
16 One of her a..................................s was related by marriage to Napoleon, she claims.
17 His p.................................. as prime minister died in office, but his s.................................. lived to a ripe old age after leaving public life.
18 I've been reading about p..................................-w.................................. British history and was particularly interested to find out about the General Strike in 1926.
19 The old castle was destroyed during a siege in Elizabethan times, but its r.................................. still dominate the town.
20 The standing stones at Stonehenge date back to p.................................. times.

»»→

In the next five sentences, which are quotations about history, decide which word or phrase makes best sense.

21 'History repeats itself; historians repeat ....' (Philip Guedalla)
    history   each other   themselves   dates

22 'No great man lives in vain. The history of the world is but the .... of great men.' (Thomas Carlyle)
    history   biography   achievement   success

23 'History is little more than the register of the crimes, follies and .... of mankind.' (Edward Gibbon)
    achievements   mistakes   events   misfortunes

24 'Our chief interest in the past is as a(n) .... to the future.' (W. R. Inge)
    warning   omen   guide   signpost

25 'What experience and history teach us is this – that people and governments never have .... history, or acted on principles deduced from it.' (Georg Wilhelm Hegel)
    benefited from   forgotten the lessons of   paid attention to
    learnt anything from

Which of the quotations above do you agree with?

"Come along, dear, we're off now."

13.2 Landfall on Tahiti

Reading

Read the passage below and answer the questions on the next page.

CHAPTER ONE

THE LANDFALL

WHEN Cook sailed the *Endeavour* into Matavai Bay on 13 April 1769, it was by no means the first time the Tahitians had encountered white men. Bougainville in *La Boudeuse* had been there, or at any rate a little further round the coast, the year before; Wallis in the *Dolphin* had arrived in 1767, and Quiros was in these seas as early as 1606. But Quiros had long since been forgotten, Bougainville had stayed in Tahiti only thirteen days and Wallis five weeks. Cook was to be here three months, he was to live ashore and make meteorological observations, he was to chart the coast; this landfall was the first great object of his journey.

It might be fairly said, therefore, that with the *Endeavour*'s arrival the penetration of the Pacific was only just beginning. From now on it was going to be no great wonder for the islanders to see a sailing ship beating into land; Cook himself was to return three times, and he was soon to be followed by the Spanish, and Bligh in the *Bounty*, and the English missionaries, and the Nantucket sealers and whalers calling in for 'refreshments' on their way south, and then the French. All these visitors – perhaps intruders is a better word – were going to make their separate contribution to the transformation of the Tahitians, whether by firearms, disease or alcohol, or by imposing an alien code of laws and morals that had nothing to do with the slow, natural rhythm of life on the island as it had been lived up till then.

It was perfectly true that the Europeans were also going to import the antidotes to their poisons and diseases – the doctors, the priests, the administrators and the policemen – but the Tahitians had had no need for these people before; if they had been left undisturbed they might have gone on forever without them, and at the time of Cook's arrival they were probably happier than they were ever to be again.

Naturally neither Cook (at first) nor the Tahitians themselves saw things in this light. Cook was acting under orders from the British Admiralty, and he had no evil designs on these people;

indeed his whole desire was to make friends with them and to interfere as little as possible with their customs. The Tahitians, on their side, were quite unable to stifle their curiosity; they were delighted to greet these fascinating strangers with their great sailing ship, their extraordinary clothes, their wonderful trinkets and gadgets. Even if they had known the evil that was in store for them they would still have welcomed the *Endeavour*.

Thus this early contact between the white-skinned sailors and the dark islanders, this first real shock of recognition, was a momentous occasion, a sharp and irrevocable turn in the history of the Pacific; and it was going to make its impact on Europe as well.

(from *The Fatal Impact* by Alan Moorehead)

1 Before Cook's landfall were Europeans a common sight for Tahitians?
2 How many other places had Cook surveyed in detail before arriving on Tahiti?
3 Did Cook come to Tahiti as a missionary, as a colonist or as a scientist?
4 What had been the Tahitians' reaction to seeing a sailing ship before Cook's landfall?
5 And what was their reaction to seeing a ship after his sojourn?
6 What is meant by 'refreshments' in line 20?
7 What particular 'poison' or 'disease' was each of these the 'antidote' to:
doctors priests administrators policemen?
8 Did Cook ever realise that his stay might have threatened the islanders' happiness?
9 Why were the Tahitians so fascinated by Cook and his crew?
10 What seems to be the writer's attitude to:
the Tahitians Cook the visitors who came after Cook?

13.3 JFK, the knight in not-so-shining armour *Reading*

Read the passage below and answer the questions on the next page.

JFK, the knight in not-so-shining armour

From Alex Brummer in Washington

IT IS OVER 20 years since John Kennedy was martyred at Dallas. The intervening years, with their successive shocks for the presidency, have in many ways strengthened the myth of Camelot.

A recent poll shows that of the last nine occupants of the White House, including F. D. Roosevelt, President Kennedy was the leader who most inspired confidence, had the most appealing personality, could best be trusted in a crisis, and set the highest moral standards.

Despite the botch of the Bay of Pigs, the stumble into Vietnam, and the revelations of the bordello on Pennsylvania Avenue, the nurtured image of a heroic adventurer remains intact.

In recent years, the political literature has painted pathetic images of a drunken Nixon threatening to nuke Vietnam; Johnson accepting envelopes stuffed with cash; Ford lost in the bear garden of White House infighting; and Carter too aloof to wish his secretary Happy Christmas. The more demeaning the revelation, the better the book sales.

There has been a different dimension to the Kennedy literature. The adulatory assessments of Arthur Schlesinger and Theodore Sorensen remain the gospel to the American public. The halo of the New Frontier still glows brightly, surviving even the the efforts of a younger Kennedy to douse it with ineptitude.

The time is plainly right for some authoritative revisionism beyond the pillow-talk of the popular press. The ground was partly broken earlier this year when the Washington Post went ape over the discovery of the Kennedy Tapes. They caused much heart-searching among Washington's journalistic elite, a tug of war between the lustre of Camelot and the squalor of Watergate.

Garry Wills, Professor of American Culture at Northwestern University and a newspaper columnist, strives in a new book, The Kennedy Imprisonment, to blow away the myth and expose the raw Kennedys.

He eschews the sensitivity generally shown them. The mystique is systematically blown away and by the time you reach page 300, the epilogue and the polemical climax, you wonder how the public has remained deceived.

The central theme of the book is that the mistakes of Camelot stem largely from the family attitude toward sex. Camelot was a state of mind —the result of a sustained effort by the family scion, Joseph Kennedy, to create a new breed of American aristocrats, free from the narrow straits of their Irish ancestry and Catholicism.

Professor Wills writes: "A very important and conscious part of the male Kennedy mystique is a pride of womanising . . . The Kennedy boys were expected by their father to undertake a competitive discipline of lust and he let them know he was still in the competition himself."

The sexual history is well aired—Joseph's attempts to seduce his sons' girlfriends; the flaunting of his Hollywood piece, Gloria Swanson, before his wife, Rose, and sons on a ship to Europe. Jack's needs were provided for in the early years by family friends. Among those handed over was Inga Arvad, a European beauty contest winner with Nazi connections.

To Americans John Kennedy is still the heroic adventurer. His latest biographer gives him a rougher ride

Unfortunately, at the time Jack Kennedy was an up-and-coming naval intelligence officer. It soon emerged that the FBI had tapes of Jack Kennedy and Miss Arvad in bed together. It was only through the personal intervention of his father with the then-Naval Secretary, James Forrestal, that he survived in the navy to become a Second World War hero.

In the image creation game anything went. The PT109 incident, which saw the anointing of Jack Kennedy as a war hero, became legendary only after it had been written up in the New Yorker. The account claimed that a fearless Kennedy had gone on the attack after sighting a destroyer.

But Professor Wills, after interviews with other crew members, determined there was no attack. Indeed, an early citation JFK released to biographers, which talked of his personally rescuing three men, had to be toned down because of its hyperbole.

Why should any of this matter if Jack Kennedy was a great President? Professor Wills believes his Presidency was badly flawed by the obsession with "guts" and brains. What Eisenhower, with the help of the CIA, had achieved in Iran and Guatemala —the replacement of an unfriendly regime with a more compliant one—was possible in Havana.

The Bay of Pigs operation attracted the inexpericnced President. It relied on unorthodox channels, avoiding the dull State Department, which he disdained. It put authority in the hands of his brilliant White House recruits, McGeorge Bundy, Walt Rostow, and a dizzying array of academic stars. When faced with doubts from some advisers on the attempted invasion, Kennedy ignored them.

The Camelot mythology says the lessons of restraint learnt during the Bay of Pigs fiasco benefitted the world when the Cuban missile crisis occurred. Professor Wills argues, at his most polemical, to the contrary.

Kennedy could have explained to Americans that the missiles were the answer to his secret war against Castro. He also instantly ruled out the option of open diplomacy. Instead he set up decision-making machinery that was deliberately bold rather than cautious.

He then failed to give the Russians an opportunity to save face. He ensured as risky a response as possible by setting a 24-hour deadline for their reply to his ultimatum calling for the withdrawal of the missiles.

Given the reasonably happy outcome, it has always been hard to dispute Kennedy's handling of the Cuban missile crisis. Indeed, despite the legacy of Vietnam, bestowed by the remnants of the New Frontier on Lyndon Johnson, the American public still rates Kennedy more highly than Roosevelt as the man they would like to handle a crisis.

Poll ratings and public perceptions can change rapidly as President Reagan learns daily. But despite the attacks on Camelot over the last 20 years, nostalgia for Kennedy and the 1960s remains amazingly intact in the public mind.

Given the failure of Teddy to rekindle the flame in 1980, the existence of the Kennedy Tapes, and now Professor Wills' book, the popularity ratings could be due for a change.

---

1 The public image of John F. Kennedy has remained untarnished despite . . .
many books that have revealed his foibles.
his youngest brother's conspicuous incompetence.
the passing years.

2 Most other recent Presidents of the United States . . .
have been exposed on TV.
have had their shortcomings exposed in books about them.
were much worse than John F. Kennedy.

3 Garry Wills' book is about . . .
John F. Kennedy.
the dark side of John F. Kennedy's term of office as President.
the Kennedy family.

4 According to Professor Wills, all three Kennedy brothers . . .
lived in the shadow of their father.
shared their father's taste for womanising.
were less inhibited than their father.

5 John F. Kennedy's first girlfriends were . . .
film stars friends of the Kennedy clan local girls

6 But for Joseph Kennedy's influence, John F. Kennedy's career as a naval officer would have been .... by his liaison with Inga Arvad.
jeopardised ruined unaffected

7 During the Second World War John F. Kennedy . . .
accomplished heroic deeds.
did nothing outstandingly brave.
was hailed in the press as a war hero.

8 The Bay of Pigs operation in Cuba was a . . .
complete success failure partial success

9 In retrospect, John F. Kennedy's handling of the Cuban missile crisis seems to have been . . .
crude masterly rash

10 The writer of the article suggests that, soon, the public's rosy view of John F. Kennedy . . .
is likely to change is unlikely to change will remain unchanged

Explain the meaning of these words and phrases used in the article:
bear garden (line 29) demeaning (line 32) halo (line 39)
went ape (line 47) eschews (line 60) well aired (line 84)
hyperbole (line 119) compliant (line 128) to save face (line 156)
to rekindle the flame in 1980 (line 178)

"Well, that's enough about world domination, now I'd like to talk to you about double glazing . . ."

13.4 Collocations *Use of English*

Fill the gaps in the passage below with any words that make sense in the context. In some cases there may be several possibilities that spring to mind – choose the one you feel sounds best.

Between 1815 and 1914 Europe thrust out into the world, impelled by the force of its own industrialisation. Millions of Europeans poured overseas and into Asiatic Russia, seeking and finding new ......**1**...... in the wider world. Between 1880 and 1900 Africa, a continent four times the ......**2**...... of Europe, was parcelled out among the European powers. And when in 1898 the United States of America, following the European ......**3**...... , annexed Puerto Rico, the Philippines and other islands of the Pacific, and asserted a controlling voice in Latin American affairs, it seemed as though European expansion was turning into the ......**4**...... of the white ......**5**...... over the coloured majority. But expansion carried with it the seeds of its own ......**6**...... . Even before European rivalries plunged the continent into the ......**7**...... of 1914–18, the beginnings of anti-European reaction were ......**8**......in Asia and Africa, and no sooner had the United States occupied the Philippines than they were met by a nationalist ......**9**......under the great Philippine leader, Aguinaldo.

Today, in ......**10**...... , we can see that the age of expansive imperialism was a transient ......**11**...... of history; while it lasted, it left a European ......**12**...... on the world. The world in 1914 was utterly different from the world in 1815, the ......**13**...... of change during the preceding century greater than previously during whole millennia. Though industry in 1914 was only beginning to ......**14**...... beyond Europe and North America, and life in Asia and Africa was still regulated by age-old ......**15**...... , the nineteenth century inaugurated the ......**16**...... of transformation which dethroned agricultural society as it had existed through the ......**17**...... , and replaced it with the urban, industrialised, technocratic ......**18**...... which is spreading – for good or for ......**19**...... – like ......**20**...... through the world today.

(from *The Times Atlas of World History*)

13.5 Idioms with BREAK, BRING and CALL *Use of English*

Rewrite each sentence using the correct form of the verb BREAK:

1 OFF Negotiations between the two sides were discontinued.
2 THROUGH In 1945 Allied forces penetrated the German defences and crossed the Rhine.
3 OUT Fighting started between Hindus and Moslems after the independence of India in 1947.
4 AWAY Bangladesh seceded from West Pakistan in 1971.

Use the correct form of the verb BRING in these sentences:

5 ABOUT The Potato Famine caused the death of a quarter of the population of Ireland between 1845 and 1851.
6 DOWN Germany's defeat in 1918 caused the fall of the Kaiser.
7 BACK Eleven years after the execution of King Charles I in 1649, the monarchy was restored in England under his son.
8 HOME The more I read about history the more it makes me realise how relevant history is for us today.

Use the correct form of the verb CALL to rewrite these sentences:

9 THEIR BLUFF They decided to risk everything by challenging their enemies' supposed power.
10 OFF The attack was cancelled when the winter weather became severe.
11 UP Only unmarried men aged 18 to 41 were drafted into the British army in the First World War – everyone else was a volunteer.
12 TO MIND This reminds me of Henry Ford's remark: 'History is bunk.'

13.6 The Second World War *Questions and summary*

After you have read the passage, answer these questions in writing.

1 Explain the meaning of the following words used in the passage:
clear cut (line 8) formal (line 24) decisive (line 34)
peripheral (line 39) run up (line 51) eclipsed (line 55)
marginal (line 57)
2 What was 'clear cut' about the outbreak of World War I?
3 Why is 1 September 1939 not universally accepted as the start of World War II?
4 Why might April 1932 be considered to be the starting date of World War II?
5 Why does the writer say that the fighting in Europe was virtually over by June 1940?
6 In what way was the First World War not a 'modern' war? »»→

7 In one paragraph of about 50 words, describe how the Second World War repeatedly changed its character and fields of action. Try to avoid quoting directly from the passage as far as you can.

In the first half of the twentieth century mankind experienced two great wars – the first mainly confined to Europe despite being dignified afterwards with the name of world war, the second truly world wide. In both wars Germany and her associates fought roughly the same coalition of Powers. Both wars were bloody and prolonged. In many ways their differences were greater than their similarities.

The outbreak of the First World War was clear cut. At the beginning of July 1914 the Great European Powers were at peace with each other as they had been ever since 1871. A month later all except Italy were at war. There were changes among the participants as the war went on – Italy and the United States joined in, Russia fell out. But no one can doubt that war began on a great scale in August 1914 and continued on much the same scale until November 1918.

But when did the Second World War begin? Many historians, conditioned to think of Europe as the centre of the world, date the war from 1 September 1939 when Germany attacked Poland. This is not an answer that would satisfy the Abyssinians or the Chinese for whom the war began earlier. It would not satisfy the Russians and Americans for whom the war began later. In any case this European war virtually ended in June 1940 with Germany dominating the entire Continent west of Russia. If a formal declaration of war marks the starting point, the Second World War began in April 1932 when Mao Tse-tung and Chou Teh declared war against Japan in the name of the Kiangsi Soviet. (It is a historical curiosity that the Republic of China did not declare war against Japan until after Pearl Harbor.) If we wait until the war was being fought in every continent except the two Americas, the date must be 1942 or even 1944.

The First World War was fought throughout in much the same place and in much the same way. The prospective combatants had long foreseen that the decisive battle would be fought on the plains of Flanders and northeast France. So it was, though four years instead of the expected six weeks were needed to reach the decision. The other campaigns – on the Eastern and Italian fronts, at sea and in Asiatic Turkey – were peripheral to the prolonged battle in France. The methods of war also remained much the same. Though tanks played some part before the end, the outcome depended mainly on masses of infantry flung against each other, much as they had been in the days of Napoleon or the Romans.

The Second World War, though also expected, repeatedly changed its character and field of decisive action while it wore on. A Swiss historian has called it 'one of the most gigantic improvisations in history, far above the usual measure'. Only the British Air Staff had planned their strategy in advance, and this turned out to be irrelevant, for the Royal Air Force long proved incapable of carrying it out. Otherwise every campaign was run up while the war was on. Who could have foretold that the decisive battles of the Second World War would be fought at Stalingrad and Midway Island, El Alamein and Caen? Equally the decisive weapons were not foreseen. Aircraft carriers eclipsed battleships. Mass bombing that had been expected to work wonders made only a marginal contribution to the result. Landing craft and jeeps – instruments that no one had envisaged, at any rate as weapons of war – counted for far more. Tanks certainly played a full part. But few foresaw that, with the coming of the anti-tank gun, the infantry would go in first and the tanks follow, instead of the other way round. The war ended with the explosion of two atomic bombs. Before the war hardly anyone believed that nuclear fission would ever have a practical application.

(from *The Second World War* by A. J. P. Taylor)

13.7 In the year I was born . . . *Listening*

You'll hear two people talking about the events that happened in the world in the years they were born: 1960 and 1965. Look at the events listed here and add the appropriate year beside each one – but be careful because some of them happened in a different year: 1969! Read the list through before you listen to the recording.

WARS India & Pakistan .... Civil war in Congo ....
US bombing of N. Vietnam ....
Honduras & El Salvador after football match ....
Nigerian Civil War ....

POLITICS Independence for Nigeria ....
Independence for French colonies in Africa ....
US blockade of Cuba starts ....
Brasilia becomes new capital of Brazil ....
Summit meeting breaks up after US spy plane shot down ....
US Presidential election won by J. F. Kennedy ....
Willy Brandt elected W. German Chancellor ....
Inauguration of President Nixon ....
de Gaulle wins election in France ....

→

DEMONSTRATIONS Riots in Algiers ....

Demonstrations in Europe against Vietnam war ....

¼ million march in Washington in protest against Vietnam war ....

67 demonstrators killed at Sharpeville by S. African police ....

SCIENCE First man walks on moon ....

A Russian walks in space ....

An American walks in space ....

Maiden flight of Concorde ....

First heart pacemakers developed ....

First Laser constructed ....

Close-up photos of Mars taken ....

ARTS AND ENTERTAINMENT ½ million attend Woodstock rock festival ....

Beatles' 2nd film: 'Help!' ....

Hitchcock's 'Psycho' ....

Pinter's *The Caretaker* ....

OTHER EVENTS Death penalty abolished in UK ....

Massive power cut in USA ....

Charles Manson murders Sharon Tate and four others in California ....

OBITUARY T. S. Eliot ....

Dwight D. Eisenhower ....

Albert Schweitzer ....

Ho Chi Minh ....

Nat 'King' Cole ....

Le Corbusier ....

Boris Pasternak ....

Winston Churchill ....

● What happened in the year *you* were born? Give a short talk to the class or to your group.

13.8 The emigrants *Listening*

Listen to the conversation and answer the questions by filling the gaps or choosing the best alternatives.

1 In the 19th century the emigrants were escaping from:
.... in Ireland; .... in Russia;
.... in industrial areas; .... in agricultural areas.

2 All had one thing in common: they had .... to ....

3 But the streets were not 'paved with ....' – the reality was more often work in the sweat shops of .... or hunger on a barren farm in ....

4 MOVEMENTS OF POPULATIONS – add the nationalities and countries to the map:

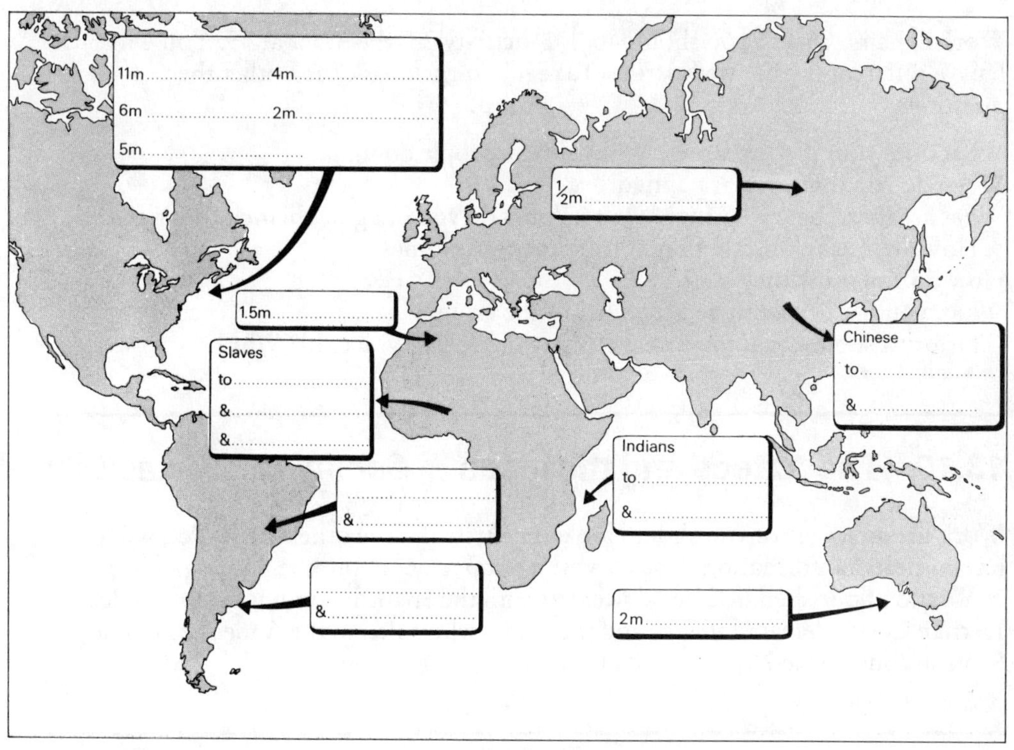

5 The present-day mixture of cultures and races in the New World was established in the . . .
   18th century   19th century   early part of the 20th century

6 The total number of US immigrants between 1821 and 1920 was . . .
   30 million   33 million   130 million   133 million

7 German and Italian are still spoken by South American citizens who . . .
   have recently arrived.
   are the descendants of immigrants.
   cannot speak Portuguese or Spanish.

8 One can deduce the origins of American citizens of European origin by . . .
   noticing their foreign accents.
   looking at the colour of their skin.
   looking through the phone book.

9 The speaker implies that, overall, immigration has contributed to . . .
   the loss of immigrants' cultural heritage.
   prejudice against immigrants.
   a rich mixture of different cultures.

13.9 100 years ago *Picture conversation*

Work in pairs. One of you should look at activity 23, the other at 49. You will each have a different picture to describe. Take it in turns to ask each other these questions:

What does your picture show? What are the people doing?
When do you think it was painted?
What are the people wearing? What colours do you imagine their clothes to be?
How are their clothes different from modern clothes?
How do you think they feel?
What would it be like to be a member of the group?
Is history a subject that interests you or which leaves you cold? Why?

13.10 The Aztecs and the Incas *Communication activity*

Work in pairs. One of you should look at activity 25, the other at 63. You will each have different information to share with your partner about the Aztecs (whose civilisation flourished in Central Mexico until the Spanish *conquistadores* under Hernán Cortés defeated them), and the Incas (who ruled in the Andes before the Spanish conquest led by Francisco Pizarro).

13.11 Writing a 200-word essay *Composition*

In the Proficiency exam you may be asked to write one of the compositions in about 200 words (instead of the more normal 350 words). This may sound as if it's easier, but as you may have found in Units 9 and 10 this kind of shorter essay has to be written in a much more succinct style and should contain no irrelevant information – indeed, you may find that this limit involves omitting a lot of information you would like to include.

Look at the summary of the life of Napoleon Bonaparte below and decide:

1 How you would rearrange it in a more logical, perhaps chronological, order
2 Which of the information you would certainly include and which would have to be omitted in a short essay

When you have made suitable notes, write a composition about Napoleon in answer to the composition topic:

> *'Describe in about 200 words the life and achievements of a famous historical figure.'*

Napoleon

Personal Life

1769 born in Corsica

1796 married Josephine Beauharnais

1810 divorced Josephine as she had borne him no son

1810 married Archduchess Marie Louise of Austria

1811 birth of son

1821 death on remote island of St Helena in Atlantic

Political Life

1799 appointed First Consul of France

1800 reorganised political and educational system in France

1804 Napoleonic legal code introduced (basis of French and many other countries' legal systems, even Japan's)

1804 crowned Emperor of the French

1814 abdicated and sent to Island of Elba

1815 escaped from Elba – ruled again as Emperor for 100 days

1815 exiled to St Helena

Military Victories

1797 against Austrians at Rivoli (N. Italy)

1805 against Russians and Austrians at Austerlitz

1806 against Prussians at Jena

1807 against Russians at Friedland

1809 against Austrians at Wagram

1812 against Russians at Borodino – Moscow taken, but in flames

Military Defeats

*1805** by British at Trafalgar (confirming British naval supremacy)

*1814** by British at Victoria – French driven out of Spain

1812 retreat from Moscow (only 100,000 of the original 600,000 strong army survived)

1813 by Russians, Prussians and Austrians at Leipzig

1814 Paris taken

1815 by British and Prussians at Waterloo

**French forces not personally commanded by Napoleon*

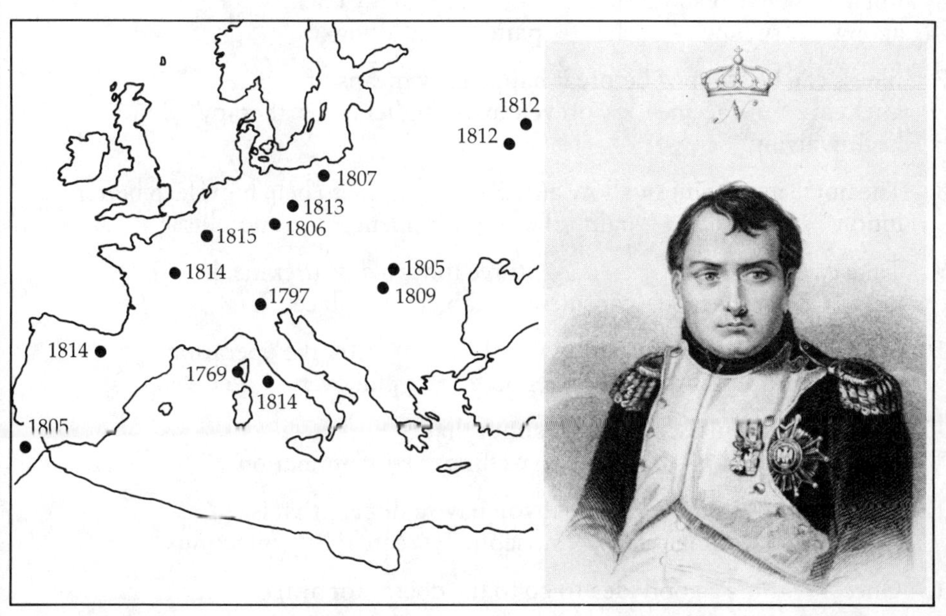

14 Mind and body

14.1 Vocabulary

In the first fifteen sentences, *three* of the alternatives given are correct and *two* are wrong. Choose the correct alternatives.

1 If you still feel ill after taking this treatment, you should see ....
a consultant   a midwife   a specialist   your GP   a quack

2 He will have to go on a diet because he is worried that he is ....
chubby   flabby   buxom   robust   overweight

3 After her illness she started worrying that she was ....
underweight   skinny   slim   thin   slender

4 Many illnesses today are related to ....
grief   stress   tension   worry   suffering

5 What treatment should be given to someone who has ....?
fainted   lost consciousness   passed away   passed out
passed through

6 I'm a bit worried about this .... in my back.
agony   twinge   ache   pain   suffering

7 Illness can be stopped before it happens by means of ....
after care   vaccines   preventative medicine   therapy
healthy living

8 The nurse made him swallow a(n) .... to help him sleep better.
lotion   sedative   pain-killer   ointment   tranquilliser

9 Take two of these .... three times a day after meals.
drugs   lozenges   capsules   tablets   placebos

10 Everyone hoped that he would .... after the operation.
pull out   pull through   get better   pull over   get well

11 I think you should see a doctor about that ....
pimple   rash   blister   swelling   inflammation

12 Keep away from other people if you have a disease that is ....
catching   contagious   antiseptic   catchy   infectious

13 Once a year it's a good idea to go to the doctor for a(n) ....
examination   check-up   operation   post-mortem   medical

14 He had to go to hospital when he ....
had a break   broke up   pulled a muscle   sprained his ankle
fractured his wrist

15 Medical experts have been taking the claims of .... medicine more and more seriously recently.
alternative   complementary   fringe   mainstream   orthodox

In the next ten sentences only *one* of the four alternatives given is correct. Choose the correct alternative and, if possible, explain the meaning of the incorrect alternatives.

16 The doctors examined the patient and decided that he was ....
loony   off his rocker   silly   unbalanced

17 Hayfever is a very common type of ....
antagonism   allergy   therapy   symptom

18 An illness that is caused by the mind is known as a .... illness.
pschyosomatic   pschyosamatic   psychosomatic   psychosamatic

19 Before the operation the patient was given a general ....
anasthetic   anesthaetic   anisthetic   anaesthetic

20 Realising that she was probably pregnant she went to see her ....
pathologist   osteopath   pediatrician   gynaecologist

21 We realised he must be ill when he ....
threw down   threw out   threw in   threw up

22 Malaria is .... by the female anopheles mosquito.
broadcast   sent   transmitted   transported

23 Smallpox, once responsible for millions of deaths, has been virtually ....
exterminated   abolished   erased   eradicated

24 The consultant decided to operate after the patient complained of severe pains in his ....
paunch   tummy   stomach   insides

25 She suffers from a morbid fear of spiders, known to doctors as ....
agoraphobia   claustrophobia   xenophobia   arachnophobia

"There's a man in the bath!"

14.2 Simple secrets

Reading

Answer the multiple-choice questions on the next page about this passage.

Simple secrets and tricks of the trade

BODY AND SOUL

MY thoughts these days are often with those BMA persons who've been chosen to investigate the claims of Alternative Medicine. Almost as often they are with the persons whose alternative practices are being examined.

What happens if their treatments win the BMA seal of approval? With the loss of their claim to be Alternative will they lose their attraction for iconoclastic devotees?

And will the BMA examine some of the practices still indulged in in the name of orthodox medicine? It's not only alternative medicine that attracts venal practitioners prepared to exploit our natural gullibility to make themselves rich.

I suppose it's too late for the BMA to duck out and pass these questions to the new professor of parapsychology in Edinburgh. But it might not be too late to ensure the investigative team includes not just scientists but professional magicians. History suggests they are more effective detectors of fraud than professional scientists.

Gullible scientists told us that Uri Geller had strange psychokinetic powers that could change the physical properties of metal (which he turned to such socially useful purposes as bending teaspoons). Less gullible magicians revealed him as one of their own.

Anyone who, as a child, possessed a Junior Conjuror's Set will have learned two simple lessons about magic. Audiences long to be deceived and are invariably disappointed when they are told how the trick is done.

The Magic Circle adjures its members not to reveal their secrets not just because there is a limited number of "magical" devices but because, when the secret of a trick is revealed, it nearly always disappoints.

The great magicians are those who, using this mundane trickery beneath a camouflage of showmanship and misdirection, can convince an audience it has witnessed something that defies rational understanding.

Conjurors' instruction leaflets first describe The Effect which is what the audience *thinks* it sees happening.

Under The Method they describe what actually does happen — a bit of bare-faced deception from which the audience's attention is diverted, often by exploitation of its longing to be deceived. When scientists examine phenomena that are beyond our comprehension, they tend to concentrate on

The Effect, analysing it, dissecting it, hypothesising about it.

A professional magician, out of habit, goes straight for possible Methods and is unimpressed by anecdotal evidence of Effect. Magicians are also better than scientists at persuading audiences that deception has taken place.

They can reproduce the same Effects as fraudulent operators by using the simple devices of their trade and announce not how the trick was done — which would merely disappoint — but that it was no more magical than the other illusions in their stage acts.

Audiences find these demonstrations more convincing than intellectual arguments. Harry Houdini used them to expose fraudulent "mediums" in the days when seances were more fashionable than they are now. The Amazing Randi still uses them to challenge tricksters more likely to be found on television chat shows than in back rooms in Brooklyn.

A few years ago I learned just how effective the magician's method of exposure can be.

In the days when "psychokinetic metal bending" colonised much time on television and much space in scientific journals, I persuaded one of Britain's best science writers to re-examine his new-found belief in this form of "psychokinesis."

And I persuaded him not by intellectual argument but by performing a mundane card trick that I learned when I was a member of the Magic Circle.

The trick had nothing to do with metal bending or psychokinesis and he still doesn't know how I did it, but the fact that such "magic" could be performed by an ignorant oaf like me re-established the sense of scepticism he had temporarily mislaid. And scepticism is essential when evaluating treatment.

Most people who seek cures are not interested in arguments about schools of thought and logic. They are interested in results. And the most impressive way to present results is in the form of testimonials from satisfied customers.

Yet anyone who's done any sort of service job knows just how easy it is to acquire flattering testimonials. When I was a GP, I had drawersful of grateful letters from patients who had survived my ministrations thanks more to their luck than my judgment. And anyone who treats patients can earn similar tributes thanks to the body's vigorous powers of self-healing.

In conjuror's terms testimonials relate only to The Effect. That's why I hope the BMA will get some magical advice when considering The Method.

Michael O'Donnell

---

1 The writer wonders whether Alternative Medicine practitioners who are approved by the British Medical Association will . . .
attract more patients as a result.
attract fewer patients as a result.
attract patients from orthodox medicine.
stop attracting patients altogether.

2 He suggests that some orthodox doctors . . .
are successful in curing their patients.
are honest with their patients.
deceive their patients.
cannot cure their patients.

3 He suggests recruiting magicians to the BMA investigative team because they . . .
   are less easily deceived than doctors.
   are more scientific than doctors.
   understand alternative medicine better than doctors.
   have been around longer than doctors.

4 Magicians' audiences . . .
   like to discover magicians' secrets.
   do not like to be deceived.
   cannot be easily deceived.
   like to be deceived.

5 Scientists tend to behave in the same way as . . .
   magicians.
   magicians' audiences.
   doctors.
   each other.

6 A real magician is interested in finding out about . . .
   the Effect.
   the Method.
   both the Effect and the Method.
   neither the Effect nor the Method.

7 Audiences will usually believe . . .
   a magician's explanation.
   a magician's demonstration.
   a rational explanation.
   a scientific explanation.

8 In deciding whether medical treatment works one must be . . .
   inexperienced.
   gullible.
   incredible.
   mistrustful.

9 Patients are more likely to believe that a practitioner can cure them if he or she has . . .
   a good bedside manner.
   comfortable consulting rooms.
   letters from cured patients.
   framed qualifications and diplomas.

10 The writer's own patients recovered, he suggests, because . . .
   he cured them.
   they trusted him.
   they were not really ill.
   their own bodies cured them.

11 The writer himself was once a . . .
practitioner of alternative medicine.
magician.
scientist.
scientific writer.

12 The article is written in a . . .
serious style.
sarcastic style.
self-deprecatory style.
light-hearted style.

"I know what you have but I'll be darned if I can remember the name of it."

SLOW FOOD: THE NEW CONCEPT FOR FIGHTING FLAB

Unlike conventional diets, the Constant Energy Diet keeps you satisfied, nourished and energetic while you shed fat. The principles are easy to follow: you merely cut down on some sorts of food and eat the rest in the best combinations.

The basis of the diet is the concept that certain foods can cause an addictive cycle of hunger, fatigue and overeating. What happens is this: when you eat a food that is sweet or starchy, the various carbohydrates in that food are broken down in the gut into glucose and absorbed into the blood to be taken to the brain and other organs which need it. When you eat something sweet, glucose pours into the blood in quantity, and this triggers off a mechanism known as the insulin response. The body counters the sudden flood of glucose by producing insulin to clear the excess glucose from the blood and turn it into glycogen to be stored in the liver and muscles. But when the liver and muscles can hold no more, the surplus glucose is converted to fat deposits.

As the insulin sweeps away the glucose into storage, the level of glucose in the blood naturally drops – sometimes to even lower than it was before, causing a cycle of hunger and fatigue and, in some people, mental symptoms such as anxiety, depression and irritability. It is plain that eating at times when blood sugar is low, particularly eating sweet foods, can perpetuate this cycle. The Constant Energy Diet aims to keep the level of glucose in the blood at a steady level, avoiding the sudden rise that aids the creation of fat deposits.

Apart from causing overweight, this cycle is damaging because it is a physical stress. When blood glucose is low, the brain and other organs cannot work properly so the body pumps adrenalin into the circulation to cope with the emergency. If this happens several times a day, the system is on permanent alert and never gets a chance to wind down.

The Constant Energy Diet breaks this cycle by concentrating on foods that are turned into glucose slowly, so that there is less danger of the system being flooded with an excess that ends up as fat. And it contains some surprises. Foods which had always been thought to be similar, like bread and pasta, have recently been found to break down into sugar at different rates.

These discoveries by doctors in Germany, Britain, Canada and the USA form the basis of the Constant Energy Diet. It tells you which is the best balance of foods to keep your blood sugar properly regulated and hunger at bay.

1. Cut out overload foods

Sweet drinks are banned because they contain liquid sugars which are quickly absorbed into the blood: even pure fruit juice contains quickly absorbed natural sugar and should be diluted, but whole fruit is good because the pulp is broken down slowly and sugars released steadily.

Fatty and sugary foods (sausages, pastries) are banned because they supply too much sugar and saturated animal fat – high in calories and bad for the heart and bowel. Heavily processed carbohydrates (white bread, instant mashed potato) overload the body with refined starch. They are poorer in vitamins, minerals, fibre and protein than the less refined equivalents (porridge oats, wholemeal bread, fresh-boiled potatoes) and cause a faster rise in blood sugar.

2. Eat for energy balance

For slow energy release, it matters not so much that the food is wholemeal (the entire grain ground finely, as in bread) as how near it is to wholegrain (the entire grain ground more coarsely – as in semolina – or not at all). So eat pasta, rice and wholegrain bread.

Adding fibre to your diet by eating bran or wholemeal bread may nourish you and keep you satisfied a little longer, but it is not enough in itself to slow down energy release. And it will not prevent rebound hunger – the pangs you feel when your blood sugar level rises then quickly sinks, as it does after a sugary snack. Wholemeal bread, though more nourishing than white bread, releases its energy into the body just as quickly, according to the findings of David Jenkins and colleagues at Oxford and Toronto universities. Nor does fibre slow down the absorption of sugar in foods such as sweet biscuits.

3. The right combinations

Fats are high in calories and should only be eaten in small amounts, but they do slow down the speed at which food passes out of the stomach into the small intestine and so play an important part in staving off hunger.

Truly satisfying meals contain at least one slow-release food and some fat. But don't be tempted to eat, say, a large hunk of cheese or half an avocado pear at one sitting – fatty foods should always be combined with carbohydrate.

Potatoes are nutritious, and a valuable source of high-quality protein and fibre. They are a fast-release food, and should be eaten with some fat to slow them down. Baked jacket potatoes are best eaten with a modest pat of butter or melted cheese. You can even eat a few roast potatoes or chips, provided they are cut fairly large to soak up less fat.

Fill in the gaps in these flow charts:

a)

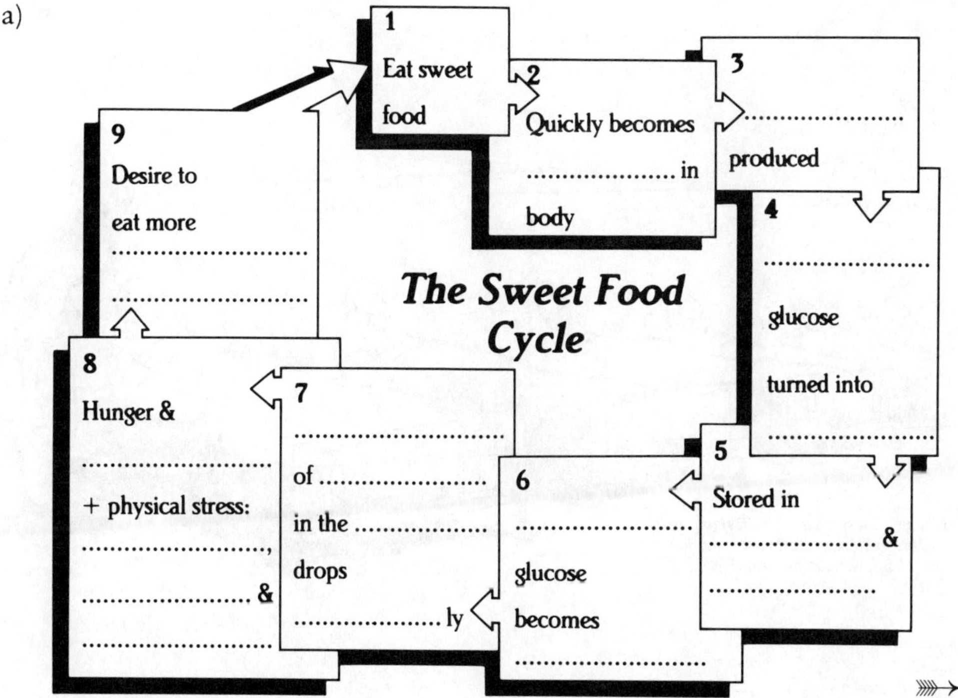

b) 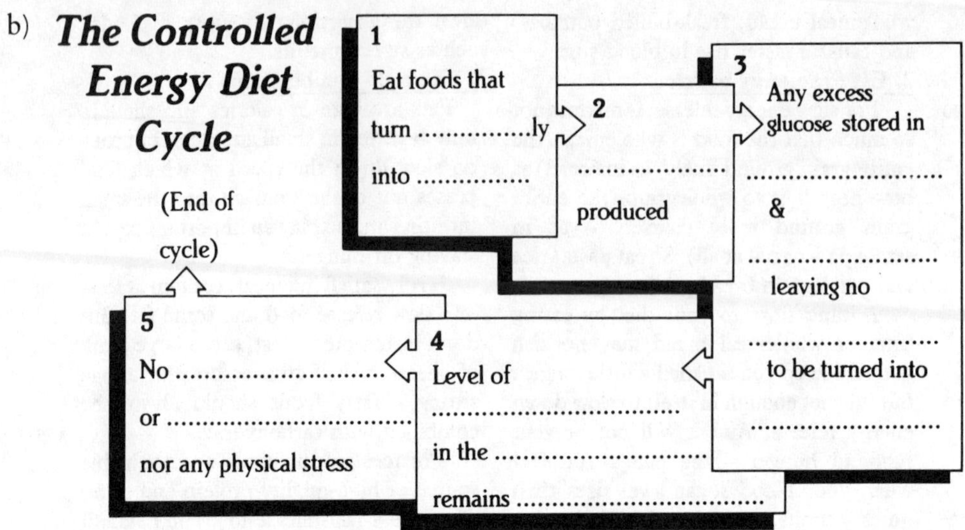
The Controlled Energy Diet Cycle
1
Eat foods that
turn ....ly
into ....
2
....
produced
3
Any excess
glucose stored in
....
&
....
leaving no
....
to be turned into
....
4
Level of
....
in the ....
remains ....
5
No ....
or ....
nor any physical stress
(End of
cycle)

c) Which of the following are 'Slow Energy Release foods'? Tick the ones that are.

apple juice	wholemeal bread	pasta	rice
apples	white bread	oranges	Coca Cola
cakes	wholegrain bread	orange juice	baked potato with butter
chips	semolina	sausages	chocolate

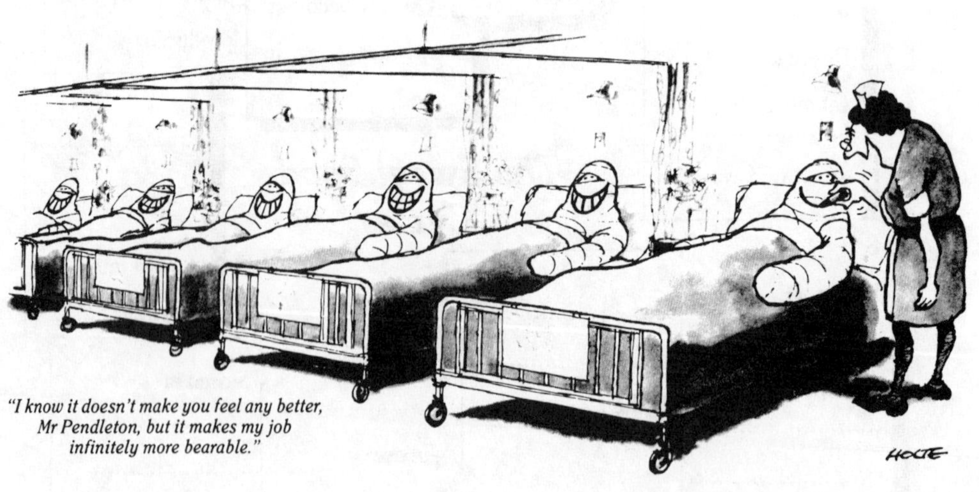
HOLTE
"I know it doesn't make you feel any better, Mr Pendleton, but it makes my job infinitely more bearable."

14.4 Requests and politeness *Use of English*

Rewrite each of the sentences so that its meaning remains unchanged.

1 Next patient, please!
Would . . . *the next patient come in now, please?*

2 Please don't give me an injection.
I'd rather . . .

3 I can't sleep, doctor.
Do you think . . .

4 Can I speak to someone about my problem?
Would it be . . .

5 Smoking is not allowed in the ward.
Would you mind . . .

6 Would you give this to the sister, please?
I hope . . .

7 It seems that I've left my medical card at home.
I don't . . .

8 It'd be nice to have some fresh air in here.
You couldn't . . .

9 I'd like to make a phone call.
I wonder . . .

10 What time do we have to get up in the morning?
Could you . . .

14.5 Uses of the past tense *Use of English*

Fill each gap with suitable words or phrases.

1 I wish I .... so unfit.
2 It's time I .... to get fit.
3 I wish there .... to stop myself feeling depressed.
4 I wish I .... so much beer last night.
5 If only I .... and gone to bed early.
6 I wish he .... so much, the whole room stinks of cigarettes.
7 I'd rather he .... outside to smoke.
8 If you ask me, it's high time he .... smoking altogether.
9 If only she .... crossing the road, she wouldn't be in hospital.
10 Isn't it time you .... in hospital? She must be feeling quite lonely.

Paulette Maisner, with the video programme she uses to help with dieting—picture by E. Hamilton West.

Fighting talk for compulsive eaters

HOW do you spot a compulsive eater in a restaurant? No, it's not the customer who cheerily puts away a great deal more than is wise, and still can't resist great scoops of two or three puds "just to try." That is the sign of the merely greedy, and it's a fair bet that all of us who read this page are *that*.

The serious compulsive eater, according to Paulette Maisner who runs the Maisner Centre for Eating Disorders in Brighton, and has now written a book (with Jenny Pulling) on the subject, is more likely to order an omelette, toy with the food and send it away half eaten. Only then will she rush home (compulsive eaters are women more often than not) to stuff herself silly with anything she can lay her hands on.

Paulette Maisner should know. Now a trim nine stone she was herself a 16-stone compulsive eater until her forties. A typical binge meal as she describes it, "a couple of 1lb Christmas puddings, a packet of mince pies, a tin of condensed milk, packets of biscuits, and muesli," brings the eater no satisfaction. On the contrary, these binges are furtive, joyless affairs, likely to leave the individual lying like a beached whale, exhausted, distended and distressed.

The worst of it is the feeling of a complete inability to choose or to control one's own intake. Indeed, many compulsive eaters talk in Old Testament terms of being "possessed by a demon." Though haunted by thoughts of food, most compulsive eaters sincerely want to be thin. Some achieve thinness, either by fasting between binges, purging themselves with laxatives, or inducing vomiting, ancient Roman style, after eating.

What has gone wrong ? It seems likely that the problem is caused by a complex interaction of physiological and emotional factors. In an ideal world we would eat when hungry, selecting a variety of nourishing foods, and stop eating when we felt full. In this way we would maintain a stable and suitable body weight, and feel good. Unhappily, half the world has not enough food to meet its needs, the other half has eating disorders.

One salient factor might be the unnaturally refined sugary foods available to us. Experimenters have allowed baby rats or recently weaned human infants to choose their own food from a "cafeteria-style" menu to discover whether they will instinctively select a balanced diet (broadly speaking they will). But they know that these experiments are wrecked if sweet foods are included. Both baby rats and baby humans will gorge on sweetness.

Bob Boakes, an experimental psychologist at the University of Sussex who is interested in how we learn an association between flavour and calories, suspects that an innate preference for sweetness may be "hard-wired" into the brain. (For those of you who can't remember, human breast milk tastes sweet.)

An overload of sugar plays havoc with a system not designed for it, leading to a see-saw effect on blood sugar levels, more cravings, and occasionally to what has been called "western malnutrition," where the stodge-fed body craves more food in order to make good deficiences in essential elements.

Add to this the human tendency to lift eating out of its natural context of nourishment, and you have a problem. After all, we first experience food in the highly charged atmosphere of parent-child interaction, and there are several theories about how this could lead to eating disorders later on. The most quoted is that of the clinician, Hilde Bruch, who suggests that the baby offered food for reasons not connected with hunger (as reward, for example, or as antidote to boredom or hurt) might fail to learn to distinguish hunger from other kinds of discomfort. In later life, runs this theory, distress, like hunger, will elicit eating.

There is as yet no hard evidence that this is so. But we do know that consistently inappropriate responses to a baby's needs tend to diminish the child's feeling of competence and control over the environment.

Paulette Maisner has sifted through Bruch and many other theorists, picking out whatever she finds helpful. Her own programme of "re-education" is an eclectic mix of in-depth discussion, relaxation training, 24-hour moral support if necessary, and a regime of sensible mostly whole food eating. Her client bingers cannot, of course, come off food completely to cure their addiction, but they can learn to face up to the problem and to avoid certain "trigger foods".

The aim is to learn to be relaxed about food, and to accept it as a normal part of living. This is not as easy as it sounds, and Mrs Maisner requires considerable commitment in time and money from her clients. After completing an initial seven-page questionnaire, clients fill in daily food and mood charts, and a four-week postal course costs £48, or £90 for 10 sessions at the centre.

Still, if the programme can help relieve the misery and guilt of the compulsive eater, it costs a mere 500 Mars bars.

The Maisner Centre for Eating Disorders, 41 Preston Street, Brighton, East Sussex. Telephone Brighton (0273) 729818, 736905, and 29334.

Feasting And Fasting by Paulette Maisner and Jenny Pulling. Fontana, £1.95.

Catherine Mant

Answer these questions about the passage in writing.

1 Explain the meaning of the following words and phrases used in the passage:
stuff herself silly (line 23) binge (line 30) possessed by a demon (line 44)
fasting (line 49) gorge (line 79) highly charged atmosphere (line 103)
2 What is the difference between greed and compulsive eating?
3 What is paradoxical about Western eating habits and problems?
4 Why do we like sweet foods so much, according to Bob Boakes?
5 What is meant by 'Western malnutrition' in line 95?
6 Why do some adults eat when they are depressed, according to Hilde Bruch?
7 In one paragraph (about 50 words), summarise Paulette Maisner's methods for curing compulsive eaters.

14.7 Homoeopathy *Listening*

Listen to the report on the history and application of homoeopathy and answer the multiple-choice questions about it.

1 Homoeopathy was discovered by Samuel Hahnemann . . .
   early in the 19th century
   late in the 18th century
   in the mid-19th century
   early in the 20th century

2 The 'provers' that Hahnemann used were . . .
   animals
   drugs
   people he knew
   his patients

3 The purpose of 'proving' was to . . .
   test his technique of dosage.
   see the effects of taking different substances on people.
   get doctors to accept his theories.
   cure his patients.

4 Hahnemann found that giving someone a tiny dose of arsenic would . . .
   cure him of arsenic poisoning.
   cure him of vomiting and diarrhoea.
   cause vomiting and diarrhoea.
   have no effect on the patient.

5 In the 'single blind' procedure patients . . .
   are blindfolded.
   are not given any medicine.
   don't know if they have been given the medicine.
   and experimenters don't know who has been given the medicine.

6 The effectiveness of a homoeopathic remedy . . .
   decreases if its strength is reduced.
   does not change if its strength is reduced.
   fluctuates if its strength is reduced.
   increases if its strength is reduced.

7 It is remarkable that even . . .
   dangerous substances can be used in homoeopathy.
   ineffective substances can be used in homoeopathy.
   insoluble substances can be used in homoeopathy.
   unknown substances can be used in homoeopathy.

8 Homoeopathy and vaccination have . . .
   no principles in common.
   one principle in common.
   two principles in common.
   three principles in common.

9 Homoeopathic treatment can be used . . .
   only by qualified doctors.
   only by doctors or specialists.
   only by patients themselves.
   by anyone with a basic knowledge of homoeopathy.

10 A homoeopathic remedy must be suited to . . .
   the patient's personality.
   the patient's illness.
   the patient as well as the illness.
   the patient's medical history.

11 A homoeopathic remedy is . . .
   not as safe as aspirin.
   safer than aspirin.
   more effective than aspirin.
   just as safe as aspirin.

12 Match these homoeopathic remedies to the conditions they treat:
   ACONITE SEPIA SAND GOLD PETROLEUM TOBACCO
   travel sickness migraine a cold fear of failure
   depression lack of confidence

14.8 Was Freud a fraud? *Listening*

In the recording Professor Carl Abrahams is talking about Sigmund Freud. Which of the statements below are true (**T**) and which are false (**F**), according to Prof. Abrahams?

1 Freud was a genius.
2 Freud was a dishonest man.
3 Some patients get worse after psycho-analysis.
4 Professional psychiatrists misunderstand Freud's ideas.
5 Teachers and probation officers apply Freud's ideas to their pupils and clients but this is harmless and amusing.
6 Freud's own patients did recover after he treated them.
7 The 'wolf man' dreamt that he was a werewolf and murdered people at night.
8 Freud's own account of the 'wolf man' case was falsified.
9 Although Freud misdiagnosed the 'wolf man's' illness, his treatment of the patient was a success.
10 Freud was a good writer.
11 Freud asserted that pleasure and sexuality were directly related. ⇝

12 An innocent slip of the tongue is commonly believed to betray a speaker's concealed secret desires.
13 Freud wanted people to think he was undervalued.
14 Freud's books got bad reviews when they first came out.
15 Freud invented the concept of the 'unconscious mind'.
16 Freud's technique of 'free association' was not an original idea.
17 Practically all of the ideas Freud claimed to be original were in fact used by others before him.
18 The popularity of Freud's ideas has hindered progress in research into mental disorders.
19 People who consult Freudian psycho-analysts are being conned (ie tricked) by them.
20 The myths surrounding Freud and his work will soon be discredited.

How would you describe Professor Abrahams' *attitude* during the interview? Write down three descriptive adjectives to characterise your impression of him.

14.9 'Deafness risk' *Pronunciation*

Work in groups of three. One of you should look at activity 27, another at 65 and another at 78. You will each have different paragraphs of the article that appeared under this headline to read and later discuss:

'Deafness risk' in personal hi-fi

14.10 Salt *Communication activity*

According to medical experts, people in the West consume not only too much fat, sugar and alcohol but also too much sodium. An excess of sodium (mostly in the form of sodium chloride – common salt) may be bad for the health and lead to high blood pressure (hypertension) and strokes.

Work in groups of three. One of you should look at activity 29, another at 64 and another at 75. You will each have different information about the amount of sodium present in different foodstuffs.

14.11 Writing a well-balanced essay *Composition*

Use the notes below, together with your own ideas and opinions, as the basis for a 350-word composition on this topic:

> *'We are constantly bombarded with advice from experts on ways of staying healthy and surviving to a ripe old age. Which aspects of their advice do you think it is practicable to follow?'*

Before you start writing discuss your views with a partner, if possible, and then make notes on what you are going to write. Make sure you give some personal examples to make the composition come to life and be of interest to your readers.

DIET

High fibre intake → better digestion + less disease connected with digestion

Reduced salt intake → lower blood pressure

Reduced fat intake → less heart disease

Slow energy release foods → control of weight

Reduced sugar intake → less tooth decay + control of weight

Sufficient vitamins → higher resistance to infection

A well-balanced diet → control of weight

EXERCISE → higher resistance to infection

→ lower susceptibility to heart disease, muscular pains, arthritis, etc.

→ control of appetite

→ feeling of well-being and physical fitness

HABITS

Cigarette smoking → cancer, bronchial disease

Alcohol → liver disease, addiction

Stress at work and at home → heart disease + stress-related illness (migraine, mental illness, depression, etc.)

HEREDITY

Parents' medical history passed on to children

15 War and peace

15.1 Vocabulary

Fill each gap in the first fifteen sentences with a suitable word.

1 There was concern that the situation might develop into a c.................................. war with partisans carrying out a g.................................. war against government forces.
2 A special task force of ....s was sent in to pacify the island.
3 The besieged garrison was relieved when r..................................s arrived.
4 The defending t..................................s were running out of a.................................. and s..................................s.
5 After long and bitter hostilities, a c.................................. was at last called and eventually a peace t.................................. (or a..................................) was signed.
6 The regiment suffered such heavy l..................................s that they had to s..................................
7 In time of war, the army's regular soldiers are strengthened by c..................................s and r..................................s.
8 As part of their training, the troops took part in m..................................s, serving alongside their a..................................s from other countries.
9 Although we are brought up to regard a soldier's life as glamorous, the reality of warfare is simply ....
10 A soldier who fights for any country who will pay him is a m..................................; someone who is not a member of the armed forces is a c..................................; someone who is against fighting and warfare is a p..................................
11 The defence strategies of the West and the East depend on the so-called 'b.................................. of p..................................'.
12 Each side possesses enough I.................................. B.................................. M..................................s to destroy each other ten times over.
13 Although a total freeze on the build-up of arms is unlikely, there have been S.................................. Arms L.................................. T..................................s between the super-powers.
14 The C.................................. for Nuclear D.................................. believes in u.................................. d..................................
15 If nuclear weapons were ever used, life as we know it would be wiped out in the h..................................

Answer the next nine questions by ticking the correct answers – in each case there are *several* right answers and some wrong ones. You must decide how many are correct.

16 Which of the following are officers in the British Army or the US Army or Air Force?
major commodore corporal captain colonel

17 Which of the following are naval officers (in the Royal Navy or US Navy)?
admiral major lieutenant commander brigadier

18 Which of the following are RAF officers?
general squadron leader wing commander aircraftman general

19 Which of these are NCOs (non-commissioned officers)?
private petty officer lieutenant corporal warrant officer

20 Which of these belong to the lowest rank?
seaman private sergeant brigadier aircraftman

21 Which of these are warships?
trawler submarine destroyer aircraft carrier cruiser

22 Which of these are armoured vehicles?
jeep tank fighter armoured car pram

23 Which of these are military weapons?
grenade depth charge torpedo mine missile

24 Which of these would normally be found on a military base?
barracks parade ground bridge guard house periscope

Finally, can you arrange these military units in order of size?

25 6 section or squad (about 10 men) brigade battalion company platoon 1 division (about 20,000 men)

15.2 The end of the war *Reading*

This extract describes the last months of the First World War in 1918, as seen from one young man's point of view. Answer the multiple-choice questions below about the passage.

Nancy's brother, Tony, had also gone to France now, and her mother made herself ill by worrying about him. Early in July he should be due for leave. I was on leave myself at the end of one of the four-months' cadet courses, staying with the rest of Nancy's family at Maesyneuardd, a big Tudor house near Harlech. This was the most haunted house that I have ever been in, though the ghosts, with one exception, were not visible, except occasionally in the mirrors. They would open and shut doors, rap on the oak panels, knock the shades off lamps, and drink the wine from the glasses at our elbows when we were not looking. The house belonged to an officer in the Second Battalion, whose ancestors had most of them died of drink. The visible ghost was a little yellow dog that would appear on the lawn in the early morning to announce deaths. Nancy saw it through the window that time.

The first Spanish influenza epidemic began, and Nancy's mother caught it, but did not want to miss Tony's leave and going to the London theatres with him. So when the doctor came, she took quantities of aspirin, reduced her temperature, and pretended to be all right. But she knew that the ghosts in the mirrors knew the truth. She died in London on July 13th, a few days later. Her chief solace, as she lay dying, was that Tony had got his leave prolonged on her account. I was alarmed at the effect that the shock of her death might have on Nancy's baby. Then I heard that Siegfried had been shot through the head that same day while making a daylight patrol through long grass in No Man's Land; but not killed. And he wrote me a verse-letter from a London hospital (which I cannot quote, though I should like to do so) beginning:

I'd timed my death in action to the minute . . .

It is the most terrible of his war-poems.

Tony was killed in September. I went on mechanically at my cadet-battalion work. The new candidates for commissions were mostly Manchester cotton clerks and Liverpool shipping clerks – men with a good fighting record, quiet and well behaved. To forget about the war, I was writing *Country Sentiment*, a book of romantic poems and ballads.

In November came the Armistice. I heard at the same time of the deaths of Frank Jones-Bateman, who had gone back again just before the end, and Wilfred Owen, who often used to send me poems from France. Armistice-night hysteria did not touch our camp much, though some of the Canadians stationed there went down to Rhyl to celebrate in true overseas style. The news sent me out walking alone along the dyke above the marshes of Rhuddlan (an ancient battlefield, the Flodden of Wales), cursing and sobbing and thinking of the dead.

Siegfried's famous poem celebrating the Armistice began:

Everybody suddenly burst out singing,
And I was filled with such delight
As prisoned birds must find in freedom . . .

But 'everybody' did not include me.

(from *Goodbye to All That* by Robert Graves)

1 According to the writer, the invisible ghosts . . .
really did not exist.
really did exist.
were visible only to Nancy.
were the ghosts of soldiers who had died at the Front.

2 The doctor who came to see Nancy's mother . . .
knew she was dying.
did not realise she was very ill.
gave her tablets to bring down her temperature.
did not examine her thoroughly.

3 The writer mentions the deaths of . . .
five people he knew well.
four people he knew well.
three people he knew well.
two people he knew well.

4 The writer, at the time, was . . .
fighting at the Front.
training new recruits.
training soldiers who wanted to be officers.
training would-be officers, fresh from school.

5 When the Armistice was announced the writer . . .
was overjoyed.
had mixed feelings.
became hysterical.
was overwhelmed with grief.

6 The tone of the writing in the extract seems . . .
emotional.
cynical.
detached.
uncaring.

15.3 Three poems about war *Reading*

Read these poems describing three men's feelings about fighting in a war. Then answer the multiple-choice questions on the next page.

THE SOLDIER

If I should die, think only this of me;
   That there's some corner of a foreign field
That is for ever England. There shall be
   In that rich earth a richer dust concealed;
A dust whom England bore, shaped, made aware,
   Gave, once, her flowers to love, her ways to roam,
A body of England's breathing English air,
   Washed by the rivers, blest by suns of home.

And think, this heart, all evil shed away,
   A pulse in the eternal mind, no less
      Gives somewhere back the thoughts by England given;
Her sights and sounds; dreams happy as her day;
   And laughter, learnt of friends; and gentleness,
      In hearts at peace, under an English heaven.

(by Rupert Brooke)

FUTILITY

Move him into the sun—
Gently its touch awoke him once,
At home, whispering of fields unsown.
Always it woke him, even in France,
Until this morning and this snow.
If anything might rouse him now
The kind old sun will know.

Think how it wakes the seeds,—
Woke, once, the clays of a cold star.
Are limbs, so dear-achieved, are sides,
Full-nerved—still warm—too hard to stir?
Was it for this the clay grew tall?
—O what made fatuous sunbeams toil
To break earth's sleep at all?

(by Wilfred Owen)

THE GENERAL

'Good-morning; good-morning!' the General said
When we met him last week on our way to the Line.
Now the soldiers he smiled at are most of 'em dead,
And we're cursing his staff for incompetent swine.
'He's a cheery old card,' grunted Harry to Jack
As they slogged up to Arras with rifle and pack.

But he did for them both with his plan of attack.

(by Siegfried Sassoon)

1 In Rupert Brooke's *The Soldier*, the poet is praising . . .
England's brave soldiers.
England's free and democratic society.
England's scenery and people.

2 The England described in the poem is England . . .
during peacetime.
in spring or summer.
during the poet's youth.

3 If he dies the poet is sure that . . .
he will be remembered.
England will remain unchanged.
his Englishness is immortal.

4 If the idea of 'England' were replaced in the poem by 'Germany' or another country . . .
the poem would no longer make sense.
the poem would have a different significance.
the poem would still mean the same.

5 The tone of the poem is . . .
sentimental optimistic pessimistic

6 In Wilfred Owen's *Futility*, the soldier described . . .
has only just died.
has been dead for a long time.
is sure to die soon.

7 According to the poem it is pointless that . . .
any man should die in war.
a dead man should be moved into the sun.
a man should grow up to die in this way.

8 The tone of the poem is . . .
resigned sardonic lyrical

9 In Siegfried Sassoon's *The General*, the smiling general is . . .
insincere incompetent happy

10 'Harry and Jack' are . . .
two typical private soldiers.
two now-dead friends of the poet.
two young officers.

11 The soldiers who marched past the general last week . . .
disliked him respected him liked him

12 The tone of the poem is . . .
serious humorous sarcastic

In what way does knowing more biographical information about each poet influence your response to the poems? Ask your teacher to tell you a little about each poet's life and death.

15.4 Gap-filling *Use of English*

In this passage there are 20 missing words, as in the Proficiency exam. Fill each gap with whichever word you think is most suitable.

Army mislays 437 men

By Ian Aitken, Political Editor

The Ministry of Defence conceded yesterday that 437 soldiers serving in West Germany ......1...... disappeared in the past 10 years. It was insisted that there was no ......2...... to believe that ......3...... absentee had defected to the Warsaw Pact, or taken his weapons.

This ......4...... in the Commons last night after an exchange of letters ......5...... Mr Kevin McNamara, Labour MP for Hull South, and Mr John Stanley, the Armed Forces Minister.

Mr McNamara told Mr Stanley that there ......6...... be a quite simple ......7...... to the disappearance of the men, such as ......8...... or domestic tension.

But he added: "The figure does warrant careful examination as to ......9...... there is any pattern of conduct which may have led to their disappearances."

Mr Stanley admitted that any unauthorised absence was obviously a matter for ......10...... The army took all practicable measures to ......11...... the absentees who were reported by units to higher authority after six days.

He went on: " ......12...... a case is reported, all interested authorities are informed ......13...... the relevant UK police force, who pay visits from time to time to addresses known to be connected with the individual concerned. However, there are clearly ......14...... to the resources which the army can ......15...... to tracing individual absentees."

Mr Stanley claimed that the figure of 437 was relatively ....16.... against the 60,000 troops in Germany at any one time as well as the ....17.... of 200,000 troops during the 10 years.

He conceded that the RAF in Germany had no ....18.... absentees during the same period, and that the ....19.... figure for soldiers in Northern Ireland fell a long way ....20.... of the figure for West Germany. Only 38 army absentees remained outstanding in Northern Ireland, he said.

15.5 Idioms with MAKE *Use of English*

Rewrite each sentence so that its meaning remains unchanged, using the words on the left together with the appropriate form of the verb MAKE.

1 PEACE The Austrians ended hostilities with Napoleon in 1809.

2 OUT They couldn't understand what the enemy were trying to say.

3 OUT The sergeant asserted that three men had deserted.

4 A STAND The Russians resisted Napoleon's attack and turned defeat into victory in 1812.

5 THINGS WORSE The onset of winter worsened the situation for the troops.

6 HAIR STAND ON END Seeing the enemy's guns facing him terrified him.

7 MOST OF While they were on leave the sailors exploited their freedom fully.

8 GOOD SHOWING The guards performed creditably in the parade.

9 MOCKERY The indiscriminate killing of civilians makes the treaty seem worthless.

10 NO SECRET I don't conceal my loathing for war.

Treaties Star Wars will break

Sir, — Starting with the nickname Lean Boy for the Hiroshima bomb, the nuclear arms race has thrown up many euphemisms to conceal its full horror. One of the most recent is the term "Star Wars" for President Reagan's Strategic Defence Initiative.

To what extent the enterprise is based on a genuine desire to replace the present race in offensive arms with a system of effective defence, and how much it is stimulated by arms manufacturers, scientists and service personnel, perhaps not even President Reagan himself knows. But what is clear is that SDI is both wasteful and dangerous.

Most physicists outside government circles agree that it would be at most only partially effective. For example, many of the systems envisaged require space stations which would be very vulnerable to counter measures.

There is also a great lack of clarity about the purpose of SDI. Initially presented as a means for population defence, it is now conceded — though not often publicly — that the most that can be hoped for is the defence of specific military sites; perhaps to protect a retaliatory force which could then be more effective in deterring a first strike.

However, even if it could be effective, such a purpose is open to Soviet misinterpretation. SDI might be useful as a bargaining chip in negotiations for arms reductions; but it is already clear that it is having the opposite effect. It is argued that it will create jobs and may have useful non-military spin-offs: both of these aims would be achieved more economically by other means.

And SDI will erode the Anti Ballistic Missile Treaty; signed in recognition of the fact that mutual coexistence is a matter of necessity, it has already helped to retard the arms race. Although the treaty allows research on anti-missile systems, largely because a prohibition on research would be unverifiable, it bans development and testing outside the laboratory.

There are difficulties over precisely what is meant by "development," but it is clear that SDI cannot proceed very far without infringing the provisions of the treaty. In addition some of the developments envisaged would involve breaking the Limited Nuclear Test Ban Treaty and the Outer Space Treaty.

SDI, including research on the scale at present envisaged, is likely to be perceived by the USSR as offensive, providing a counter after an incompletely effective US first strike. It can only lead to counter measures by the Soviet Union and an escalation of the arms race.

At one level the arms race stems from the US desire to be the greatest; its obsessional horror of communism; and the paranoia — to many, more understandable — of the Soviet Union about invasion. And at another level from the complex of industrialists, scientists, and soldiers who pervert political decisions from the common good.

SDI is clearly fed by this same complex and both the enterprise itself and its clear intention to abrogate the ABM Treaty can only further erode trust. Not only that, but the preferred hope that the present situation of mutual deterrence can be superseded by a technological fix inevitably distracts world opinion from the urgent necessity of freezing, reducing, and ultimately abolishing national nuclear stockpiles.

(Prof) **Robert A. Hinde.**
Park Lane,
Madingley,
Cambridge.

Answer these questions about the passage in writing.

1 Explain the meaning of the following words and phrases used in the passage:
euphemisms (line 7) counter measures (line 33)
retaliatory force (line 44) non-military spin-offs (line 58)
counter measures (line 96) stems from (line 101) abrogate (line 116)
superseded (line 122)
2 What motives underlie the Strategic Defence Initiative?
3 How has the presentation of SDI to the public changed?
4 Why is the Soviet Union uneasy about SDI?
5 What are the underlying causes of the nuclear arms race?
6 In one paragraph of 50 to 100 words, summarise the reasons given in the passage that SDI is 'wasteful and dangerous'.

15.7 The invasion of Grenada *Listening*

You'll hear a news report, broadcast on October 27, describing the US invasion of the Caribbean island of Grenada. Fill in the gaps in the captions to the map and answer the multiple-choice questions that follow.

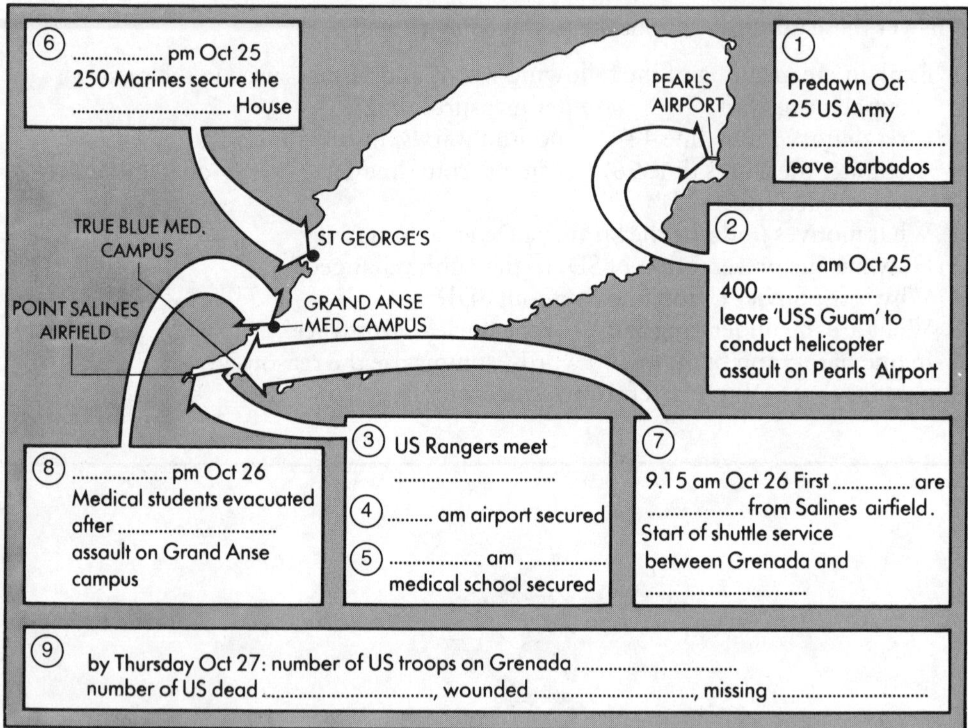

(6) .... pm Oct 25
250 Marines secure the
.... House
PEARLS
AIRPORT
(1) Predawn Oct 25 US Army
....
leave Barbados
TRUE BLUE MED. CAMPUS
ST GEORGE'S
(2) .... am Oct 25
400 ....
leave 'USS Guam' to conduct helicopter assault on Pearls Airport
POINT SALINES AIRFIELD
GRAND ANSE MED. CAMPUS
(3) US Rangers meet
....
(4) .... am airport secured
(5) .... am ....
medical school secured
(7) 9.15 am Oct 26 First .... are
.... from Salines airfield.
Start of shuttle service between Grenada and
....
(8) .... pm Oct 26
Medical students evacuated after ....
assault on Grand Anse campus
(9) by Thursday Oct 27: number of US troops on Grenada ....
number of US dead ...., wounded ...., missing ....

10 At the time of the invasion Grenada was . . .
a British colony   a Marxist state   a democratic republic
an independent state

11 Grenada is the world's No. 1 exporter of . . .
mace   nuts   nutmeg   walnuts

12 The first move in the invasion plan happened . . .
soon after Maurice Bishop came to power.
soon after General Austin's coup.
soon after Cuban forces arrived on Grenada.
a week after General Austin's coup.

13 The US President believes that the Caribbean . . .
is virtually part of the USA.
belongs to the USA.
is a politically unstable area.
is an area under threat from the Soviets.

15.8 The longer Long March *Listening*

Listen to the recording and answer the multiple-choice questions about it.

1 The young officers in Brazil in the 1920s were discontented because . . .
 they were underpaid.
 their equipment was not modern.
 they were despised by politicians.
 (*all three of these reasons*)

2 After the July 1922 revolt in Rio there were . . .
 18 survivors.
 3,000 survivors.
 800 survivors.
 no survivors.

3 Luis Carlos Prestes was sent to Rio Grande do Sul . . .
 as a punishment for participating in the revolt.
 because he was a qualified railway engineer.
 to keep him away from the capital, Rio.
 to recover from his illness.

4 Prestes and his men couldn't reach the troops from São Paulo until . . .
 July 1924.
 October 1924.
 January 1924.
 January 1925.

5 The Prestes Column was made up of soldiers and young officers from . . .
 São Paulo.
 Rio Grande do Sul.
 both São Paulo and Rio Grande do Sul.
 Paraguay.

6 The purpose of Prestes' Long March was to . . .
 get to Rio and overthrow the government.
 support the rebels in São Paulo.
 make it possible for others to overthrow the government.
 reach safety in Bolivia.

7 The Prestes Column did not get to Rio because . . .
 the government mobilised so many forces.
 they were in another part of Brazil.
 Prestes did not intend to attack Rio.
 they were under constant attack from government forces.

8 The march of the Prestes Column ended in October . . .
 1925 1926 1927 1928

»»→

9 When the Prestes Column retreated to Bolivia there were 400 survivors out of an original force of . . .
   1,500   14,000   17,500   20,000

10 While the Prestes Column was on the march, the people of Brazil . . .
   were excited to hear of its exploits.
   were afraid the fighting might get to Rio.
   wanted to know more and more about its victories.
   knew nothing about it.

11 The march of the Prestes Column . . .
   was an important chapter in Brazilian history.
   was forgotten by most Brazilians until recently.
   became well-known all over the world.
   had no effect on Brazilian politics.

12 Subsequently Prestes himself . . .
   retired from politics.
   became President of Brazil.
   rejected capitalism.
   rejected the idea of revolution.

15.9 Attitudes to defence *Picture conversation*

Work in pairs. One of you should look at activity 28, the other at 66. You will be asking each other questions about the pictures there.

15.10 Military spending *Communication activity*

Work in pairs. One of you should look at activity 30, the other at 67. You will be finding out about military spending in various countries.

15.11 Writing a 350-word composition *Composition*

First of all, read this letter and discuss its implications with a partner.

Albert Einstein
Old Grove Rd.
Nassau Point
Peconic, Long Island

August 2nd, 1939

F.D. Roosevelt,
President of the United States,
White House,
Washington, D.C.

Sir:

Some recent work by E. Fermi and L. Szilard, which has been communicated to me in manuscript, leads me to expect that the element uranium may be turned into a new and important source of energy in the immediate future. Certain aspects of the situation which has arisen seem to call for watchfulness and, if necessary, quick action on the part of the Administration. I believe therefore that it is my duty to bring to your attention the following facts and recommendations:

In the course of the last four months it has been made probable - through the work of Joliot in France as well as Fermi and Szilard in America - that it may become possible to set up a nuclear chain reaction in a large mass of uranium, by which vast amounts of power and large quantities of new radium-like elements would be generated. Now it appears almost certain that this could be achieved in the immediate future.

This new phenomenon would also lead to the construction of bombs, and it is conceivable - though much less certain - that extremely powerful bombs of a new type may thus be constructed. A single bomb of this type, carried by boat and exploded in a port, might very well destroy the whole port together with some of the surrounding territory. However, such bombs might very well prove to be too heavy for transportation by air.

You are going to have to write a 350-word composition on this topic:

> *'Describe how the development of nuclear weapons has changed the world, referring to Einstein's letter to President Roosevelt and to what he said shortly before his death in 1955:*
> *"If only I had known, I should have become a watchmaker."'*

But first discuss what you might write in answer to this question with a partner. You may find it hard to limit what you want to say even to 350 words, so your composition must confine itself to the most important points you want to make.

Perhaps you could start by referring to the letter and finish by referring to the quotation? Perhaps you need to do a little research? Make notes on the points you want to make before you start writing.

"Now then, Mrs Oxley, tell us exactly what it is you don't like about our missiles."

16 Science and technology

16.1 Vocabulary

Here, as in the exam, all the questions are multiple-choice and include some questions on grammar or usage. Choose the answer that makes best sense in each context.

1 Technology deals with the .... of science.
appliance application empiricism practicability

2 One of the physical sciences is ....
anatomy botany meteorology palaeontology

3 One of the life sciences is ....
archaeology astronomy astrology zoology

4 One of the social sciences is ....
anthropology geology chemistry physics

5 Many solutions to technical problems are discovered by ....
experience hit and miss rule of thumb trial and error

6 Professor Jones is one of the most brilliant physicists of his ....
class country generation year

7 The highest academic degree that a scientist can be awarded is a(n) ....
BSc DP MSc PhD

8 A scientific hypothesis is tested in a series of .... experiments.
controlled limited supervised theoretical

9 The success of his research was attributed to 10% .... and 90% application.
common sense greed hard work inspiration

10 The government is spending $3 m on .... a new research laboratory.
setting in setting out setting over setting up

11 The budget for R & D has .... by the company's board.
been raised been risen raised risen

12 His ideas are invariably condemned as .... by fellow-scientists.
imaginative impractical ingenious theoretical

→

13 A food processor has become an indispensable piece of .... in the home.
contraption device equipment gadget

14 The designer has applied for a .... for his new invention.
copyright patent royalty trade mark

15 It must have taken a genius to .... this complicated apparatus.
think of think out think through think up

16 Water is a chemical .... made up of hydrogen and oxygen.
compound element mixture solution

17 A substance that causes a chemical reaction is a(n) ....
additive addition catalyst enzyme

18 This contraption has to be plugged into a(n) .... to make it work.
inlet printed circuit plug socket

19 An electrical circuit is protected from overloading by a(n) ....
adaptor flex fuse transformer

20 All the information required to operate the machine is stored in a tiny ....
console control panel dashboard microchip

21 If the warning light should come on, turn the red .... to OFF.
button dial knob lever

22 The amount of fuel remaining in the tank is shown on the petrol ....
indicator gauge pump signal

23 Most motor vehicles have a pressed steel body mounted on a rigid steel ....
axle base chassis undercarriage

24 The person in charge of this construction site is a qualified civil ....
builder engineer mechanic servant

25 You've got to .... – it's a brilliant piece of design!
give it to him hand it to him take it to him take it from him

16.2 The paper clip's grip on history *Reading*

Read the passage below and answer the questions on the next page.

The paper clip's grip on history

Richard Boston with a paean for the nameless

ALDOUS Huxley was a most unfortunate man. When he died in 1963 he must have expired in the confident belief that the event would be given wide coverage in the press the next day. After all, his career had not been without distinction. Where he made his big mistake was in dying on the same day that John F. Kennedy was assassinated. As a result Huxley got about three column inches at the bottom of page 27.

In the same way the death of Victor Farris has gone widely unnoticed because he foolishly shuffled off this mortal coil at the same time as Mr Konstantin Chernenko. Now, as you all know, Victor Farris was the chap who invented the paper clip. The paper milk carton too. And paper clips and milk cartons will be in use long after everyone has forgotten the name of the comrade who came between Andropov and whatever this new bloke is called.

The same goes for the inventor of the supermarket trolley who died in Switzerland a few months ago. Fell off his trolley, so to speak. For all I know, he may be a household name in his own canton and they're putting up a statue of him wheeling his trolley, and are going to commemorate him on one of those ever-so-tasteful Swiss postage stamps we used to collect when we were younger and wiser, but I doubt if his name will be remembered outside the borders of his small country. Personally I forgot it within minutes of reading of his decease.

Not that it matters. Somehow it's hard to imagine things like paper clips and supermarket trollies having had a named inventor. It's like discovering that at a particular moment of history a particular person invented the spoon, or the chair, or socks. One assumes that these everyday objects just happened, or evolved through natural selection.

It ain't necessarily so. I read only the other day that Richard II invented the handkerchief. Almost everything else was invented either by Leonardo da Vinci (scissors, bicycles, helicopters, and probably spoons, socks and the Rubik cube as well) or by Benjamin Franklin (lightning-conductor, rocking-chair, bifocals) or else by Joseph Stalin (television).

It's quite possible that Leonardo or Benjamin Franklin or Stalin also invented the supermarket trolley. Certainly it has been invented more than once. Hardly was Herr Edelweiss (or whatever the Swiss chap was called) in his grave, than news came of the death of Sylvan N. Goodman at the age of 86. Sylvan also invented the supermarket trolley or, as the Los Angeles Times report calls it, the shopping cart.

Apparently the idea came to him in 1937 and it made him more than $200 million. When he first put the trolleys in his shop in Oklahoma nobody used them. This daunted him not at all. He took an advertisement in the Oklahoma City Times in which, lying through his teeth, he announced that shoppers came, saw and said, "It's a wow."

He then hired people to pretend they were shoppers and wheel them about the store. The idea caught on. Sylvan sold his carts to other shops and soon made his first million. Later he designed the luggage trolley for airports and railway stations. There are now reckoned to be more than 25 million supermarket trolleys in use all over the world.

Younger readers probably find it hard to imagine a world without supermarket trolleys. There must be many whose first memory is of being seated in that clever folding bit at the front, with their dear little legs dangling through the

→

holes so thoughtfully provided either by Sylvan or the Swiss gentleman.

What they won't remember is prams, which seem to have vanished. This is a terrible loss. As Osbert Lancaster has memorably written. " For sheer pleasure few methods of progression, one comes gradually to realise, can compare with the perambulator. The motion is agreeable, the range of vision extended and one has always before one's eyes the rewarding spectacle of a grown-up maintaining physical exertion."

How sorry one feels for the modern child in its push-chair, sitting with its back to the engine, its little brain constantly vibrated by those small wheels running over an uneven pavement. With a start in life like that, it's no wonder the younger generation is so strange.

Funnily enough, the chap who invented the folding push-chair also popped off recently, but I've forgotten his name as well. Be that as it may, Herr Edelweiss and Sylvan N. Goodman must have been very clever as well as very rich. The supermarket trolley is very ingenious. Take, for example, the way that the bit folds out to hold your bags, or the little darling.

Or the way you can charge one trolley into the back of another to stack them in neat rows. Or the way that, however hard you push down on the handle, the thing won't tip up. This means you can propel it while bounding after it with both feet together like a kangaroo. Apart from being fun in itself, this has the added advantage of making younger companions blush with embarrassment and take an immediate interest in the shelves of cat food.

Its stability and smooth-running is all the more remarkable when you think how small the wheels are. While in general supporting the proposition that small is beautiful, I have had reservations about this as far as wheels are concerned ever since misguidedly buying one of those bicycles with wheels the size of gramophone records that were so trendy in the Sixties.

At that time I was living in a small village in France where these mini-bikes were unknown. I soon tired of the mirth of the small children who greeted my daily appearance at the baker's to buy a baguette with delighted shrieks about the large monsieur on his *mini-velo*. What was worse was that the thing was so hard to pedal compared with my old BSA with big wheels.

Be that as it may, Herr Edelweiss or Sylvan Goodman, or both, did a grand job and made supermarket shopping far less hellish than it would otherwise be. The next step will be to get the trolleys out of the shops and into the streets. You could put an engine in the front and call it a car. Or give it big wheels and a canopy and call it a pram. The possibilities are endless.

---

1 Match these inventions to the people who (according to the article!) invented them:

handkerchief	Joseph Stalin
supermarket trolley	Leonardo da Vinci
folding pushchair	Victor Farris
bifocal spectacles	Sylvan N. Goodman
television	a Swiss gentleman ('Herr Edelweiss')
milk carton	another man who died recently
paper clip	King Richard II
scissors	Benjamin Franklin
airport luggage trolley	
rocking chair	

2 Who died the same day as the writer Aldous Huxley?

3 Who died the same day as Victor Farris?

4 How many deceased men's names can the writer *not* remember?

5 How did Mr Goodman persuade shoppers to use his 'shopping carts'?
6 Why does the writer disapprove of folding pushchairs?
7 Why does he approve of old-fashioned prams?
8 How many reasons does he give for liking shopping trolleys?
9 Why does he dislike small-wheeled bicycles?
10 How could the shopping trolley be adapted as a vehicle for use on the road or on the pavement?

What did you find to be the most amusing part of the article? Why?
What other recent, simple inventions have become indispensable? Have they made their inventors a million?
What are the most useful, and the most useless, inventions you can think of?

Diesel 46009 proves a £1.6 million nuclear safety point

By David Fairhall

AT 13.19 yesterday British Rail's retired Peaks class diesel locomotive 46009 came from Old Dalby station at about 100mph to strike the nuclear fuel flask the Central Electricity Generating Board had placed across her track.

She was a few minutes late because of anti-nuclear demonstrators on the line, but the tense, waiting spectators knew there was no driver at the controls and no passengers in the three elderly coaches 46009 was pulling.

For a few eerie seconds, I suspect most of us were more concerned with the fate of the train than with the 8ft square yellow-painted steel transport flask whose security this extraordinary event was designed to demonstrate.

Even the board's ebullient chairman, Sir Walter Marshall, admitted to a moment of shock as the 150-ton train struck its target. But he was delighted with the result.

The impact was like a vast bass drum being sounded across the Leicestershire countryside. Then a flash of flame as the locomotive tossed the 50-ton flask aside and leapt over the deliberately derailed wagon that had carried it.

But even though the flask lay on its side so as to give the diesel's protruding draw bar the best chance of prising the heavily-bolted lid open, the flask suffered only superficial damage.

Sir Walter beamed as his engineers connected a pressure meter to the flask's valve and registered a drop through the lid seals of only 0.29 of a pound from the original 100lb per square inch.

"Even better than we expected," he said. "It shows that our calculations were ultra-cautious — which is what we have always known."

Sir Walter openly acknowledged that this expensive crash test, spectacular though it was, was not conducted primarily as a scientific experiment.

The 14-inch-thick forged steel walls of the flask were actually subjected to far more stress last March, when it was dropped from a crane onto concrete.

Yesterday's spectacle — staged at a cost of £1.6 million — Sir Walter said, was to reassure people that the transport of irradiated nuclear power station fuel really was safe from road or rail accidents.

The CEGB's complete four-year programme of full-scale Magnox fuel flask testing is expected to cost £4 million.

Now the board were considering whether to subject the same battered flask to a prolonged fire — another requirement of the international regulations governing nuclear fuel transport from power stations to reprocessing plants like Sellafield (formerly Windscale) in Cumbria.

Locomotive 46009's last run started eight miles back down the British Rail test track towards Nottingham, where a railwayman threw a small external switch to start her moving.

At four miles she could have been stopped by an automatic signal. One mile to go and she passed the point of no return.

The crash was all over in perhaps five seconds, covered for another 10 seconds by the exploding locomotive's smoke.

When the whole train came to rest within about 100 yards, the three carriages were still more or less upright, though most of their wheels, like those of the locomotive, had been torn off.

Only a few windows were smashed. Seats in the rear two carriages were mostly still in place. It was not meant to be the railwaymen's day, but they were quietly just as proud of the way their train had survived as the CEGB engineers were of how their nuclear flask had so passed its test.

On this, a representative for the Welsh anti-nuclear campaign had the last word.

Why, he asks sarcastically at the press de-briefing, if nuclear fuel was so safe on the railways, did the board hand it over to Sellafield where it seemed to be spilt into the Irish sea? An irrelevant question, said the board's spokesman.

Choose the answer that best completes each sentence.

1 The writer reports the time of the crash as 13.19 . . .
to be exact   to give the effect of a timetable   because the test was delayed
because it was lunchtime

2 He refers to the locomotive as 'she' because . . .
it was very old   he loves old trains
this is how railway staff refer to trains   all trains are feminine in English

3 In the test . . .
a nuclear fuel flask was seriously damaged   a train was destroyed
a locomotive was destroyed   a nuclear flask was completely undamaged

4 Sir Walter 'beamed' (line 54) because . . .
he is a jolly sort of fellow   he had been annoyed by the demonstrators
he wanted pressmen to see he was happy
he knew the test had been thoroughly successful

5 After the crash the pressure inside the flask was . . .
99.29 p.s.i.   99.71 p.s.i.   100 p.s.i.   100.29 p.s.i.

6 The locomotive started its final journey . . .
4 miles from the crash point   when Sir Walter pushed a button
in the direction of Nottingham   away from Nottingham

7 A test was carried out in March . . .
to show the public the safety of transporting nuclear fuel by rail
to conform with international regulations
at a similar cost to the one reported in the passage
with a similar fanfare of publicity

8 The phrase 'the board were considering' (line 92) implies that the following information is being reported as . . .
definite fact   conjecture   the writer's opinion   Sir Walter's statement

9 The writer reports the condition of the windows and seats because this is . . .
important information — an integral part of the test
irrelevant but amusing — an interesting by-product of the experiment

10 The tone of the passage suggests that the writer is .... the CEGB.
amused by — hostile to — sceptical of — shocked by

Now look at these letters to the Editor of *The Guardian* about the test:

Sir, — I do not know the full facts about the nuclear safety test carried out on Tuesday and I am not — yet — a qualified scientist because I am still two years from O-level. But two questions worry me.

If there was no radioactive waste in the container used, how can it be tested for radioactive leakage; and will all the containers now be tested in the same way, and at the same great expense?
Alastair Simmons.
London, SW20.

Sir, — The Central Electricity Generating Board has told the Sizewell inquiry that its nuclear power stations can withstand a direct hit from a crashing plane. Can it now arrange for an obsolescent jumbo jet to be flown head-on into the outer containment wall of one such station to demonstrate the point? — Yours truly,
David Ross.
London SE5.

Sir, — I hope the population of the UK can sleep safely now that it's aware that iron bars do not leak from one nuclear waste canister when hit by a train travelling at 100mph. This piece of expensive publicity however fails to reassure me that the CEGB is aware of the statistical necessity of "sample number." — Yours faithfully,
Raymond Dill.
Redhill, Surrey.

Sir, — I'm baffled. The CEGB has spent £1.6 million on testing the strength of one nuclear fuel flask. The redundant train was destined for the scrap-heap in any event. The flask, we are reliably informed, suffered only superficial damage.

What was the £1.6 million spent on? — Yours faithfully,
David Northmore.
Strood, Kent.

Sir,—Will the CEGB now arrange for the Magnox fuel flask to be struck by lightning.—Yours,
H. Horrobin.
Watchet, Somerset.

Which of the writers suggest that . . .

11 the crash was just a costly publicity stunt?
12 fuel flasks are at risk from other dangers than train crashes?
13 every fuel flask should be tested in the same way?
14 the flask should have contained radioactive material?
15 testing just one flask in this way is meaningless?

16.4 The passive and question tags *Use of English*

Rewrite each of the sentences so that its meaning remains unchanged, using a question tag at the end as the example shows.

1 I think Alfred Nobel invented dynamite.
Dynamite . . . *was invented by Alfred Nobel, wasn't it?*

2 I'd say it was impossible that Marconi invented television.
Television couldn't . . . ?

3 One day it's quite possible that robots will do all our housework for us.
All our housework . . . ?

4 The University of Cambridge is going to award Professor Jones an honorary doctorate, I believe.
Professor Jones . . . ?

5 The government is proposing to cut its grants to postgraduate research students, apparently.
Government grants . . . ?

6 Don't you agree that research biologists have carried out some amazing experiments recently?
Some amazing experiments . . . ?

7 I don't think that designers achieved a breakthrough in electric vehicle design until the mid-80s.
A breakthrough . . . ?

8 Technology has not yet found a universally acceptable substitute for the petrol engine, in my view.
No universally acceptable . . . ?

9 It seems that the experts are finding new uses for computers all the time.
New uses . . . ?

10 Surely someone will have patented a 3-D TV by the end of the century?
A 3-D TV . . . ?

16.5 Aspects of the future *Use of English*

Fill each gap with a suitable word or phrase.

1 A cure for cancer is bound .... one of these days.
2 There's no chance .... the common cold in the foreseeable future.
3 By the end of the century most power stations ....
4 Soon all household appliances .... by remote control.
5 I wouldn't be surprised .... a microwave oven eventually.
6 I'm really looking forward .... in a Sinclair C5 vehicle.
7 There .... ever .... substitute for electricity.
8 By the time I .... old, electricity .... lighting.
9 I can't wait .... a personal computer of my own.
10 Astrology .... accepted as a bona fide science.

16.6 The Sinclair C5 *Questions and summary*

Sinclair C5. A new power in personal transport. £399

Plus packing and delivery

■ ***HOW TECHNOLOGY MADE A DREAM A REALITY***

Electric vehicles for personal transport have been a designer's dream for decades. The Sinclair C5 is the first practical realization of that dream.

Though the C5's battery is supremely efficient, delivering its full power in a dramatically different way from a normal car battery, the full weight of Sinclair technology has been deployed to revolutionise body design – ultimately, the secret of success.

The most valuable foundation a vehicle can have is a chassis – so that C5 uses a spinal steel chassis, developed in conjunction with Lotus Cars. But steel is not ideal for a vehicle body. It's heavy, and making it corrosion-resistant is expensive.

So the C5's body is moulded in polypropylene – light, but tough, strong and resilient. Polypropylene does not corrode or fade: the colour is contained in the bodywork, and a wipe restores the finish.

So why doesn't every vehicle use polypropylene? Because large mouldings of polypropylene are exceptionally difficult to make. The C5's body shell is the largest injection-moulded polypropylene assembly ever mass-produced. To produce one is a technical triumph – yet thousands of perfect C5s have been produced.

New tyre technology cuts rolling resistance. But once it's at speed, the aerodynamic shape of a vehicle is even more important than its weight.

The design of the C5's body has been tested and refined in a wind tunnel until it's as near perfect as it can be.

Of course, an advanced vehicle needs much more than a strong chassis, a light body, and plenty of power. Everything about the C5 is the result of endless, painstaking research and development – even the wheels are reinforced nylon. A unique microchip monitors the motor, the driving load and the battery. The process protects the motor and the battery – and provides you with comprehensive information through LED displays on your instrument pod.

Even the steering is new. When you sit in a C5, your hands fall naturally to the steering bars, to give you full control in the most comfortable position.

■ *The C5 and the law*

New government legislation in 1983 opened the way for the C5 – a practical vehicle, with the highest permissible performance at the lowest possible price.

The law allows anyone 14 or over to drive the C5 – with no licence, tax, compulsory insurance or helmet.

And safety organisations have welcomed a new, safe, exciting vehicle for young people.

■ *The C5 and the future*

Electric vehicles are the vehicles of the future. The Sinclair C5 represents the state of the art now – and for some time to come. But the C5 is just the beginning . . . by the early 1990s, Sinclair will have on the roads a range of fast, quiet, astonishingly economical family vehicles.

Order the first of the family – today.

■ *Driving the Sinclair C5*

The C5's 20-mile range (40 miles with a spare battery) and built-in boot make it ideal for shopping trips . . . for getting to the station . . . even for suburban commuting.

Everybody in the family can use it. Can there be a better way for children over fourteen to develop road sense? Cruising at around twice the speed of a bicycle (15mph max.) with drum braking and three wheels, it's far safer than anything on two wheels.

All the controls fall easily to hand. Press the drive button on the steering bars, and you're moving. Release it, squeeze the brake levers, and you've stopped.

If you ever do run out of power, the C5's pedals get you home.

For parking on a gradient, the rear brake lever locks. And for security, there's a key-operated ignition switch.

Technicalities aside, words can't quite describe the sheer fun of driving a C5.

The quiet electric motor buzzes you along – you feel secure, but exhilarated. It's like driving an open-top car, but with none of the noise.

It's unique. We can only suggest that you try one for yourself.

1 Explain the meaning of these words and phrases:

a designer's dream (line 6)	deployed (line 17)	endless (line 48)
the state of the art (line 71)	gradient (line 94)	sheer fun (line 98)

2 What does 'it' refer to in these phrases in the passage?

a) its full power (line 11)
b) It's heavy (line 24)
c) it's at speed (line 40)
d) it's as near perfect (line 43)
e) it's far safer (line 86)
f) Release it (line 90)
g) It's like driving (line 100)
h) It's unique (line 102)

3 How is the C5 technically innovative?

4 How far and how fast can you go in a C5?

5 What is unusual about the steering of a C5?

6 What must a young motor-cyclist have to conform with British law?

7 In one paragraph of about 50 words, assess the suitability of a C5 for a 65-year-old lady with no driving licence, living in a small town.

8 In one paragraph of about 50 words, assess the suitability of a C5 for an 18-year-old man living in a large city.

16.7 Modern airports *Listening*

Listen to the recording and answer the questions.

AIRPORT DESIGN

A What are the two problems that all airports have?

B Add the correct name to each of the airports shown diagrammatically below.
The airports shown are:
ATLANTA FRANKFURT LONDON GATWICK WASHINGTON
PARIS CHARLES DE GAULLE 1 PARIS CHARLES DE GAULLE 2 RIYADH

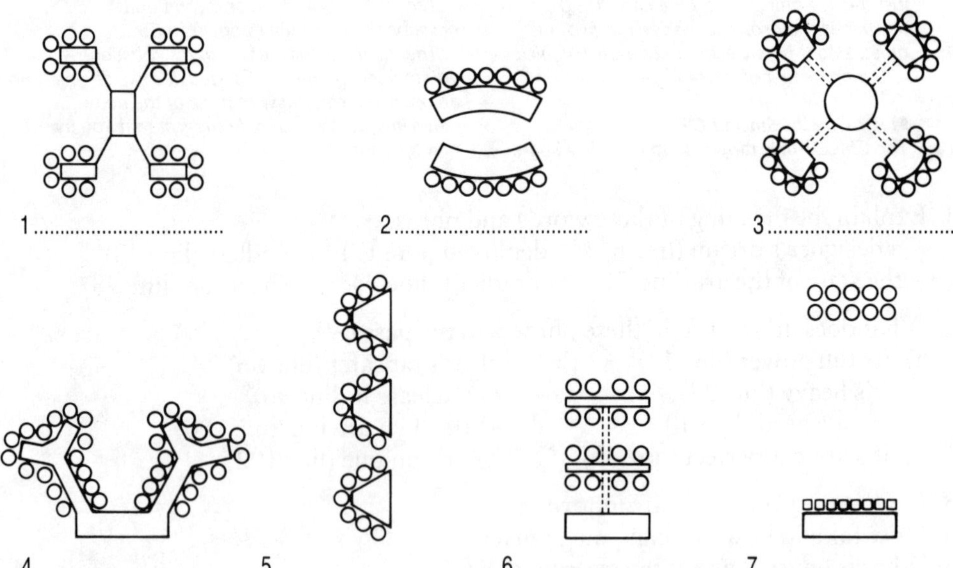

AIRPORT CONVENIENCE

C Match the information given in each column. The first pieces of information are matched already as an example.

Airport	*Distance to city*	*Suggested means of surface transport*
Atlanta	2 km	taxi
Frankfurt ——	10 km	limousine
Gatwick	11 km	30 minutes by rail
Paris	25 km	coach *or* bus and train
Riyadh	45 km	coach
Washington	45 km	frequent rapid trains

(Example: Frankfurt — 10 km — frequent rapid trains)

D Which of the airports mentioned does the speaker like best? ....
Which of them does he dislike most? ....

16.8 Margarine – a triumph of technology *Listening*

You'll hear a description of how margarine is made. Number the diagrams below to show the correct sequence of the manufacturing process. The first and last are already done to help you.

HEAT AND CRUSH PLANT SEEDS

ADD LECITHIN AND MONOGLYCERIDE, COOL AND MIX

REFINE AND DEODORISE, HEAT TO MELTING POINT

RESULT: UNEMULSIFIED MARGARINE INGREDIENTS

RESULT: BLENDED OILS

ADD WATER, SALT, ARTIFICIAL COLOUR AND FLAVOURING, SKIMMED MILK, VITAMINS A + D

AND FULLERS EARTH TO BLEACH OIL

ADD CAUSTIC SODA TO REMOVE ANY WASTE AS SOAP

(STILL CONTAMINATED WITH GUMS AND RESINS)

RESULT: REFINED OIL

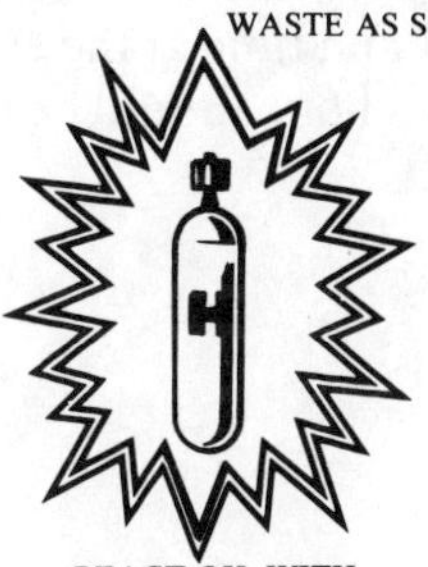

REACT OIL WITH HYDROGEN IN PRESENCE OF NICKEL CATALYST...

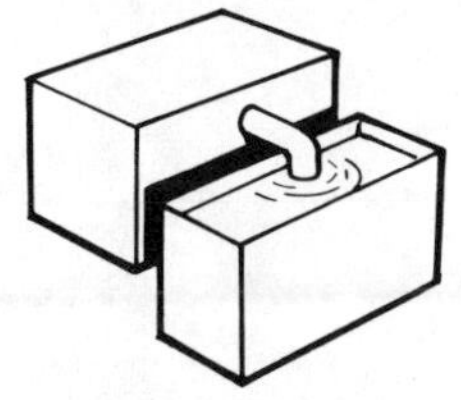

AND PIPE INTO COMPOUNDING TANK **WITH FISH AND ANIMAL OILS**

TO FORM ARTIFICIALLY HARDENED OILS. NOW NEUTRALISE, BLEACH AND FILTER TO REMOVE WASTE PRODUCTS

EXTRUDE INTO PLASTIC TUB ... AND PUT A LID ON IT

16.9 Ionisers *Pronunciation*

Work in pairs. One of you should look at activity 32, the other at 43. You will each have a short passage to read – you will also have to identify the source of the passages and discuss their content.

16.10 Negative ions *Communication activity*

Work in pairs. One of you should look at activity 33, the other at 68. You will each have different information about negative ions to give your partner.

16.11 Writing against the clock *Composition*

Write a 350-word composition on this topic:

> *'Describe the benefits and disadvantages of installing an ioniser in your living room.'*

(Before you start you may need to look at the information given in activities 33 and 68, and possibly in 32 and 43.)

Spend just one hour on this task, including time to make notes on what you want to write – and time at the end to check through your work for mistakes and style. Ideally this hour should be uninterrupted and you should not use a dictionary.

17 Nature

17.1. Vocabulary

Choose the word that best completes each of the sentences.

1 Many species of animals and plants today are ....
endangered in risk risky under danger

2 The indiscriminate use of pesticides has .... many rare species.
devastated extincted cancelled wiped out

3 Modern farm animals and crops are the result of centuries of selective ....
breeding cultivation mating reproduction

4 It took a long time for the theory of evolution to be ....
absorbed accepted acknowledged tolerated

5 Much of our knowledge about evolution comes from the study of ....
artefacts fossils relics ruins

6 My friend is a keen amateur ....
natural historian naturist naturalist naturologist

7 A tropical rain forest, once destroyed can never be ....
recovered regenerated repaired replaced

8 He gets very .... about scientific experiments being carried out on animals.
worked down worked out worked over worked up

9 One of the effects of acid rain is that it causes plants to ....
contract shrink thrive wither

10 Waste paper can be .... instead of being burnt.
decomposed incinerated recycled revamped

11 There are over 850,000 named .... of insects on this planet.
families colonies species varieties

12 Rabbits and mice are ....
amphibians carnivores marsupials rodents

13 Crocodiles and alligators are ....
crustaceans herbivores mammals reptiles

→

14 The oak and the beech are ....
bushes coniferous trees deciduous trees shrubs

15 Crows and vultures are ...., living on carrion.
predators parasites scavengers scroungers

16 The lioness lay in wait for her ....
game prey target victim

17 Rats and mice are usually considered to be ....
pets cuddly vermin weeds

18 Cattle and chickens are .... animals.
domesticated house-broken tame wild

19 Your cat has scratched me with its ....
claws hoofs nails paws

20 We all admired the parrot's beautiful ....
coat bark fleece plumage

21 Many insects, such as wasps and ants, use their .... to touch objects.
aerials antlers feelers horns

22 A .... hatches from an egg laid by a butterfly or moth.
caterpillar chrysalis maggot worm

23 We saw a huge .... of birds through our binoculars.
flock herd pack shoal

24 Those .... could be delicious fried in butter for dinner.
champignons lichens mushrooms toadstools

25 Squirrels and rabbits are .... little creatures.
amiable delicious elegant endearing

17.2 Whales *Reading*

Read this passage and then answer the questions which follow it.

There can be few more depressing stories in the entire history of man's exploitation of nature than the destruction of the unfortunate great whales. The whales have not only suffered untold cruelty but now face total extermination. Already entire populations have been wiped out, and the only reason why no species has yet been finished off is due to the vastness and inaccessibility of the oceans; a pocket or two somewhere has always managed to escape. How ironic if biological extinction were to complete the job.

The basic rule of extinction is very simple: it occurs when a species' mortality is continually greater than its recruitment. There are though, some very special additional factors in the case of whales.

Man does not actually have to kill the last whales of a species with his own hands, as it were, to cause its disappearance. Biological extinction will quickly follow the end of commercial whaling, should that end be due to a shortage of raw material, i.e. of whales. Whalers have long sought to defend their wretched trade by insisting that whales are automatically protected: as soon as they become rare, and therefore uneconomic to pursue, man will have no choice but to stop the hunting. That is a very nice theory, but it is the theory of an accountant and not of a biologist; only an accountant could apply commercial economics to complex biological systems. The reasons for its absurdity are many and varied. In the case of whaling it can be summed up in the following way. When the stock has been reduced below a critical level, a natural, possibly unstoppable downward spiral begins because of three main factors. First, the animals lucky enough to survive the slaughter will be too scattered to locate one another owing to the vastness of the oceans. Secondly, whales being sociable animals probably need the stimulus of sizeable gatherings to induce reproductive behaviour (which has social inferences as well as sexual). It is quite likely that two individuals meeting through chance will not be compatible. (They can hardly be expected to be aware of their own rarity or to realize any need for adjusting their natural inclinations.) This is especially so with polygamous species like the Sperm Whale. Thirdly, and perhaps most important in the long term, even allowing that the whales might still be able to band together in socially acceptable groups (thanks to their undeniably excellent communicative systems), there is a real danger, possibly even a probability, that the whales' gene pools would by then have sunk so low as to be biologically unviable. That is to say, the characteristics possessed by the original population *in toto* would be whittled down to those characters possessed by only the few remaining individuals. The result of such a biological calamity is inbreeding, less ability to adapt to new conditions, and less individual variety. Three words can sum it up: *protracted biological extinction.* The future 'hopes' of these animals are further discussed in the final chapter.

(from *Mammals of the Seas* by Richard Mark Martin)

1 A species becomes extinct when . . .
   too few new animals are born.
   too many animals are wiped out.
   hunting is carried out indiscriminately.
   more animals go on dying than are born.

2 Whalers argue that whales will not become extinct because . . .
   there is much less hunting now than there used to be.
   whaling is now more strictly controlled internationally.
   there are plenty of whales in the oceans.
   the hunting will stop when whales become rare.

3 The writer believes that the whalers' argument is . . .
nice absurd economic biological

4 One reason why the numbers of whales could never recover once whaling has stopped is that surviving whales will be . . .
killed lucky isolated scarce

5 Many species of whales will not breed unless they are . . .
unmolested.
in their established breeding grounds.
in the company of a few other whales.
in the company of many other whales.

6 Even if the surviving whales could band together there would . . .
be renewed risk of hunting if their numbers increased.
be too few of them to breed.
be no guarantee that any of them would breed.
not be enough genetic information available to guarantee their survival.

7 A restricted gene pool prevents a species from . . .
breeding successfully becoming inbred being adaptable
keeping up its numbers

8 The writer considers that protracted biological extinction is . . .
unlikely to happen a distinct possibility unavoidable probable

---

"They've certainly got a lovely view."

17.3 Zoos

Reading

Read the passage below and answer the questions on the next page

I must agree with you (if you are anti-zoo), that not all zoos are perfect. Of the 500 or so zoological collections in the world, a few are excellent, some are inferior and the rest are appalling. Given the premises that zoos can and should be of value scientifically, educationally and from a conservation point of view (thus serving both us and other animal life), then I feel very strongly that one should strive to make them better. I have had, ironically enough, a great many rabid opponents of zoos tell me that they would like all zoos closed down, yet the same people accept with equanimity the proliferation of safari parks, where, by and large, animals are far worse off than in the average zoo. An animal can be just as unhappy, just as ill-treated, in a vast area as in a small one, but the rolling vistas, the ancient trees, obliterate criticism, for this is the only thing that these critics think the animals want.

It is odd how comforted people feel by seeing an animal in a ten acre field. Safari parks were invented purely to make money. No thought of science or conservation sullied their primary conception. Like a rather unpleasant fungus, they have spread now throughout the world. In the main, their treatment of animals is disgraceful and the casualties (generally carefully concealed) appalling. I will not mention the motives, or the qualifications of the men who created them, for they are sufficiently obvious, but I would like to stress that I know it to be totally impossible to run these vast concerns with a knowledgeable and experienced staff, since that number of knowledgeable and experienced staff does not exist. I know, because I am always on the look-out for such rare beasts myself.

I am not against the conception of safari parks. I am against the way that they are at present run. In their present form, they represent a bigger hazard and a bigger drain on wild stocks of animals than any zoo ever has done. Safari parks, properly controlled and scientifically run, could be of immense conservation value for such things as antelope, deer and the larger carnivores. But they have a long way to go before they can be considered anything other than animal abattoirs in a sylvan setting.

I feel, therefore, that one should strive to make zoos and safari parks better, not simply clamour for their dissolution. If Florence Nightingale's sole contribution, when she discovered the appalling conditions in the hospitals of the last century, had been to

»»→

advocate that they should all be closed down, few people in later years would have praised her for her acumen and far-sightedness.

My plan, then, is that all of us, zoo opponents and zoo lovers alike, should endeavour to make them perfect; should make sure that they are a help to animal species and not an additional burden on creatures already too hard-pressed by our unbeatable competition. This can be done by being much more critical of zoos and other animal collections, thus making them more critical of themselves, so that even the few good ones will strive to be better.

(from *The Stationary Ark* by Gerald Durrell)

1 The value of a zoo depends on . . .
the premises it occupies.
the value of its premises.
the number of visitors.
its being much more than a place of entertainment.

2 The writer thinks that people who are anti-zoo . . .
are mad approve of safari parks are probably right
criticise safari parks

3 In most safari parks the animals . . .
are happier than zoo animals.
are well-treated and healthy.
enjoy being able to roam around freely.
frequently become ill.

4 Unlike safari parks, good zoos exist . . .
to make money.
to provide educational facilities.
to keep a lot of animals in a small area.
for the long-term benefit of animals.

5 Safari park staff are . . .
unintelligent inadequate in numbers motivated by greed
inadequately trained

6 Good zoo staff are . . .
two a penny second to none at a premium in the know

7 Safari parks are beautiful places . . .
where scientific research sometimes goes on.
where animals are protected.
where wild animals are killed off.
that benefit both animals and the public.

8 The writer believes that safari parks should be . . .
abolished closed down improved reduced in number

9 Collecting wild animals to keep in zoos can . . .
be cruel preserve them in ideal conditions be dangerous
dangerously reduce their numbers in the wild

10 The writer seems to be a . . .
teacher zoologist zoo lover zoo opponent

17.4 Gap-filling

Use of English

Fill each of the gaps in the passage with one suitable word.

It is not ....1.... to discover an ....2.... animal. Spend a ....3.... in the tropical forest of South America, turning over logs, looking ....4.... bark, sifting through the moist litter of leaves, followed by an ....5...., shining a mercury lamp on a white ....6...., and one way and another you will ....7.... hundreds of different kinds of small ....8..... Moths, caterpillars, spiders, long-nosed bugs, luminous beetles, harmless butterflies disguised ....9.... wasps, wasps shaped ....10.... ants, sticks that walk, leaves that open wings and fly – the variety will be ....11.... and one of these creatures will almost certainly be undescribed by science. The difficulty will be to find specialists who ....12.... enough about the groups concerned to be able to ....13.... out the new one.

No one can say just how many ....14.... of animals there are in these greenhouse-humid dimly lit jungles. They ....15.... the richest and the most varied assemblage of animal and plant life to be found ....16.... on earth. Not only are there many major categories of creatures – monkeys, rodents, spiders, hummingbirds, butterflies – but most of those types ....17.... in many different forms. There are over forty different species of parrot, over seventy different monkeys, three hundred hummingbirds and tens of ....18.... of butterflies. If you are not ....19...., you can even be ....20.... by a hundred different kinds of mosquito.

(from *Life on Earth* by David Attenborough)

17.5 Idioms with RUN and STAND *Use of English*

Write another sentence that means the same as each sentence below, using the words given in bold letters. The words must not be altered in any way.

1 I'll just review some of the reasons why some animals are considered to be pests. **run**
2 They cannot afford to set up a nature reserve on this site. **run**
3 Could you photocopy this magnificent picture of a lion for me? **run**
4 The zoo met with a lot of difficulty in getting the pandas to mate. **ran**
5 There's not much time left if we want to save the whales. **running**
6 As animals can't speak in their own defence, we must support them. **stand**
7 Do you know what the abbreviation RSPCA means? **stands**
8 It's high time that the government declared itself opposed to hunting. **stood**
9 When it comes to poisoning dear little creatures like mice, it's hard to be objective about the issue. **stand**
10 It's absolutely obvious that rare species of animals and plants need protection. **stands**

17.6 Charles Darwin *Questions and summary*

Read the passage and answer the questions in writing. Do the whole exercise in no longer than 50 minutes and try to do it without the aid of a dictionary.

In 1832 a young Englishman, Charles Darwin, twenty-four years old and naturalist on HMS *Beagle*, a brig sent by the Admiralty of London on a surveying voyage round the world, came to a forest outside Rio de Janeiro. In one day, in one small area, he collected sixty-eight different species of small beetle. That there should be such a variety of species of one kind of creature astounded him. He had not been searching specially for them so that, as he wrote in his journal, 'It is sufficient to disturb the composure of an entomologist's mind to look forward to the future dimensions of a complete catalogue'. The conventional view of his time was that all species were immutable and that each had been individually and separately created by God. Darwin was far from being an atheist – he had, after all, taken a degree in divinity in Cambridge – but he was deeply puzzled by this enormous multiplicity of forms.

During the next three years, the *Beagle* sailed down the east coast of South America, rounded Cape Horn and came north again up the coast of Chile. The expedition then sailed out into the Pacific until, 600 miles from the mainland, they came to the lonely archipelago of the Galapagos. Here Darwin's questions about the creation of species recurred, for in these islands he found fresh variety. He was fascinated to discover that the Galapagos animals bore a general resemblance to those he had seen on the mainland, but different from them in detail.

The English Vice-Governor of the Galapagos told Darwin that even within the archipelago, there was variety: the tortoises on each island were slightly different, so that it was possible to tell which island they came from. Those that lived on relatively well-watered islands where there was ground vegetation to be cropped, had a gently curving front edge to their shells just above the neck. But those that came from arid islands and had to crane their necks in order to reach branches of cactus or leaves of trees, had much longer necks and a high peak to the front of their shells that enabled them to stretch their necks almost vertically upwards.

The suspicion grew in Darwin's mind that species were not fixed for ever. Perhaps one could change into another. Maybe, thousands of years ago, birds and reptiles from continental South America had reached the Galapagos, ferried on the rafts of vegetation that float down the rivers and out to sea. Once there, they had changed, as generation succeeded generation, to suit their new homes until they became their present species.

The differences between them and their mainland cousins were only small, but if such changes had taken place, was it not possible that over many millions of years, the cumulative effects on a dynasty of animals could be so great that they could bring about major transformations? Maybe fish had developed muscular fins and crawled on to land to become amphibians; maybe amphibians in their turn had developed water-tight skins and become reptiles; maybe, even, some ape-like creatures had stood upright and become the ancestors of man.

In truth the idea was not a wholly new one. Many others before Darwin had suggested that all life on earth was interrelated. Darwin's revolutionary insight was to perceive the mechanism that brought these changes about. By doing so he replaced a philosophical speculation with a detailed description of a process, supported by an abundance of evidence, that could be tested and verified; and the reality of evolution could no longer be denied.

Put briefly, his argument was this. All individuals of the same species are not identical. In one clutch of eggs from, for example, a giant tortoise, there will be some hatchlings which, because of their genetic constitution, will develop longer necks than others. In times of drought they will be able to reach leaves and so survive.Their brothers and sisters, with shorter necks, will starve and die. So those best fitted to their surroundings will be selected and be able to transmit their characteristics to their offspring. After a great number of generations, tortoises on the arid islands will have longer necks than those on the watered islands. And so one species will have given rise to another.

This concept did not become clear in Darwin's mind until long after he had left the Galapagos. For twenty-five years he painstakingly amassed evidence to support it. Not until 1859, when he was forty eight years old, did he publish it and even then he was driven to do so only because another younger naturalist, Alfred Wallace, working in South East Asia, had formulated the same idea. He called the book in which he set out his theory in detail, *The Origin of Species by Means of Natural Selection or the Preservation of Favoured Races in the Struggle for Life.*

Since that time, the theory of natural selection has been debated and tested, refined, qualified and elaborated. Later discoveries about genetics, molecular biology, population dynamics and behaviour have given it new dimensions. It remains the key to our understanding of the natural world and it enables us to recognise that life has a long and continuous history during which organisms, both plant and animal, have changed, generation by generation, as they colonised all parts of the world.

(from *Life on Earth* by David Attenborough)

1 What was the purpose of the HMS Beagle's journey?
2 What was Darwin's reaction to his unexpected discovery of so many species of beetle in Brazil?
3 What is the meaning of 'immutable' in line 9?
4 What is meant by 'Darwin was far from being an atheist' in line 10?
5 What first intrigued Darwin about the Galapagos animals?
6 What is meant by 'recurred' in line 16?
7 How did the tortoises on each Galapagos island differ?
8 How did the animals on the Galapagos find their way there, according to Darwin's speculation?
9 What is the meaning of 'insight' in line 41?
10 What was revolutionary about Darwin's ideas?
11 What are 'hatchlings' (line 48)?
12 How quickly did Darwin publish his theory?
13 What made him publish his book when he did?
14 How have modern discoveries changed ideas on natural selection?
15 In one paragraph of 70–100 words, summarise Darwin's innovative description of the process of natural selection.

17.7 When dinosaurs ruled the earth *Listening*

A Match the silhouettes to the dinosaurs named in the recorded discussion.

Silhouette number	*Name*	*Length or wingspan*
	Brontosaurus	
	Diplodocus	
	Ichthyosaurus	
	Procomsognathus	
	Plesiosaurus	
	Pterodactylus	
	Pteranodon	
	Stegosaurus	
	Triceratops	
	Tyrannosaurus	

B Add the appropriate dimensions in the right-hand column.

C Answer these multiple-choice questions:

1 The largest dinosaurs were . . .
sea-based land-based predators amphibious

2 The most intelligent dinosaur was . . .
carniverous fish-eating herbivorous omniverous ⋙→

3 The fiercest dinosaur mentioned is . . .
Pteranodon   Stegosaurus   Triceratops   Tyrannosaurus

4 Dinosaurs probably became extinct because . . .
temperatures rose   temperatures fell   of a global catastrophe
modern reptiles live in water or holes

17.8 Worm technology *Listening*

Listen to the recording and answer these questions. Your teacher will play the recording twice.

1 The world's longest earthworms are .... metres long.
3   6   30   60

2 Which of these sketches best shows the appearance of an earthworm's skin?

a)

b)

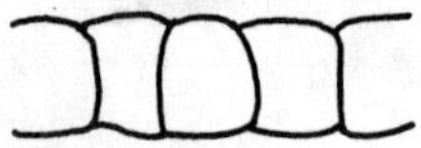

c)

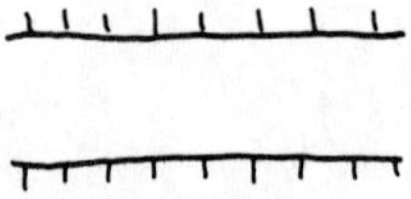

d)

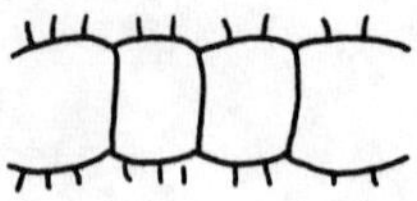

3 Earthworms are .... in cultivation.
a nuisance   indispensable   harmful   helpful

4 Earthworms live on . . .
living plants and roots   decaying plant matter   plants and soil   soil

5 Earthworms .... soil.
clean   create   mix   stabilise

6 How many ways are mentioned that describe how earthworms keep soil in good condition?
3   4   5   6

7 Quantities of earthworms can be added to soil after . . .
it has been demolished.
it has been poisoned by chemicals.
its nutrients have become exhausted.
land reclamation from the sea.

8 Which of these processes can be performed by worms? *Tick one or more boxes.*

- high quality paper manufacture ☐
- low quality paper manufacture ☐
- making a kind of bread for animals to eat ☐
- printing ☐
- producing bacteria ☐
- producing artificial fertiliser ☐

9 Worms are not used in hamburgers because . . .
worms are poisonous to humans.
worm meat is contaminated with harmful bacteria.
beef is cheaper.
no humans could ever face eating worms.

10 You may find worms on the menu in . . .
California Korea Japan many countries

17.9 Are you an animal lover? *Picture conversation*

Work in pairs. One of you should look at activity 35, the other at 70. You will have questions to ask each other, playing the roles of examiner and candidate.

"We don't know what it is but it eats table scraps and hums."

17.10 The jungle *Communication activity*

Work in pairs. One of you should look at activity 34, the other at 69. You will be given some ideas for a discussion about the destruction of the world's tropical rain forests.

17.11 Practice under exam conditions *Composition*

Write **one** of these composition exercises, allowing yourself one hour only. This time includes preparation of notes and ideas and, afterwards, time to check your work through for mistakes.

1 Describe a visit to *either* a zoo *or* a circus *or* a safari park *or* an oceanarium. (About 350 words)
2 What do you think can be done to conserve nature and protect endangered species from the destructive forces of man? (About 350 words)
3 Basing your answer on your reading of the prescribed text you have studied: Describe the scene or section of the book that impressed you most. Compare this part of the book with another part that you did *not* enjoy. (About 350 words)

Checking through Look carefully for any mistakes or slips of the pen you may have made, like the ones illustrated here:

Its important to emphasise that	Rarely it is possible to
Perhaps it should pointed out	I decided to do a long journey
Wild animalls should be free	We enjoied the performace

By now you're probably familiar with the kind of 'silly mistakes' you make yourself when you're writing quickly. As long as these are spotted and corrected before your work is handed in, there's nothing to worry about – but you *must* allow yourself enough time to check through!

18 Living in society

18.1 Vocabulary and usage

Mixed in among the vocabulary questions there are a number of questions on grammar and usage, similar to the kind you may meet in the exam.

1 Every member of the community has their own personal .... to make.
announcement contribution donation endowment

2 In this very poor neighbourhood many youths belong to ....
bands gangs groups packs

3 At the end of the match the .... went wild with excitement.
audience congregation mob spectators

4 We're looking for new blood to join our dynamic ....
circle clique set team

5 Let's .... after work and thrash this out between us.
come together gather together get together meet together

6 Someone who prefers not to join in with everyone else is a(n) ....
deviant individual loner pervert

7 I didn't take up his recommendation, as he sounded so .... about it.
half-baked half-hearted half-timbered half-witted

8 A good education is an asset you can .... for the rest of your life.
boast about call upon fall over resort to

9 To enter a skilled trade a new recruit may have to serve a(n) ....
apprenticeship education initiation training

10 He turned to a life of crime .... he had had a normal, happy childhood.
as long as despite even though provided that

11 Society .... laws to regulate the behaviour of its anti-social members.
depends of depends upon is depended of is depending on

12 If you .... a crime being committed, you should report it to the police.
are seeing had seen should see were to have seen

→

13 Technically speaking, anyone who .... the law is a criminal.
could have broken   has been breaking   has broken   may have broken

14 Even if you kill someone in self-defence you may be charged with ....
bumping him off   homicide   lynching   manslaughter

15 The salesman told me that reading this book would make me more intelligent but I think I've been ....
blackmailed   conned   libelled   slandered

16 Our well-respected police force can be relied upon to .... the law.
administer   bend   enforce   flout

17 The scoundrels who mugged two old ladies have been convicted of ....
arson   assault   looting   vandalism

18 A prisoner serving a life sentence may eventually be released on ....
bail   leave   parole   probation

19 The defendant was found guilty by the jury and given a suspended ....
conviction   fine   sentence   verdict

20 Some people say that all violent criminals should be ....
detained   locked in   locked out   put away

21 The judge .... the witness for his frivolous attitude.
abused   commended   prosecuted   reprimanded

22 Most members of society are perfectly .... citizens like me.
law-abiding   legal   legitimate   obedient

23 Don't give in to the .... of cheating in an exam – you may get caught!
allure   inducement   provocation   temptation

24 In a multiple-choice exercise it's sometimes easier to .... the wrong answers before choosing the correct one.
eliminate   exclude   obliterate   omit

25 And it's always better to make an educated .... than to leave a blank.
attempt   endeavour   chance   guess

18.2 Reading comprehension

Here, as in the exam, there are three passages with 15 questions altogether. Try to do all three within 30 minutes.

FIRST PASSAGE

There is nothing that man fears more than the touch of the unknown. He wants to *see* what is reaching towards him, and to be able to recognize or at least classify it. Man always tends to avoid physical contact with anything strange. In the dark, the fear of an unexpected touch can mount to panic. Even clothes give insufficient security: it is easy to tear them and pierce through to the naked, smooth, defenceless flesh of the victim.

All the distances which men create round themselves are dictated by this fear. They shut themselves in houses which no one may enter, and only there feel some measure of security. The fear of burglars is not only the fear of being robbed, but also the fear of a sudden and unexpected clutch out of the darkness.

The repugnance to being touched remains with us when we go about among people; the way we move in a busy street, in restaurants, trains or buses, is governed by it. Even when we are standing next to them and are able to watch and examine them closely, we avoid actual contact if we can. If we do not avoid it, it is because we feel attracted to someone; and then it is we who make the approach.

The promptness with which apology is offered for an unintentional contact, the tension with which it is awaited, our violent and sometimes even physical reaction when it is not forthcoming, the antipathy and hatred we feel for the offender, even when we cannot be certain who it is – the whole knot of shifting and intensely sensitive reactions to an alien touch – proves that we are dealing here with a human propensity as deep-seated as it is alert and insidious; something which never leaves a man when he has once established the boundaries of his personality. Even in sleep, when he is far more unguarded, he can all too easily be disturbed by a touch.

It is only in a crowd that man can become free of this fear of being touched. That is the only situation in which the fear changes into its opposite. The crowd he needs is the dense crowd, in which body is pressed to body; a crowd, too, whose physical constitution is also dense, or compact, so that he no longer notices who it is that presses against him. As soon as a man has surrendered himself to the crowd, he ceases to fear its touch. Ideally, all are equal there; no distinctions count, not even that of sex. The man pressed against him is the same as himself. He feels him as he feels himself. Suddenly it is as though →

everything were happening in one and the same body. This is perhaps one of the reasons why a crowd seeks to close in on itself: it wants to rid each individual as completely as possible of the fear of being touched. The more fiercely people press together, the more certain they feel that they do not fear each other. This reversal of the fear of being touched belongs to the nature of crowds. The feeling of relief is most striking where the density of the crowd is greatest.

(from *Crowds and Power* by Elias Canetti)

Choose the answer that *best* reflects the meaning of the passage.

1 People fear burglars because . . .
   they arrive suddenly and unexpectedly.
   they attack people in the assumed safety of their homes.
   they grab you in the dark.
   they steal your most treasured personal possessions.

2 In public, according to the writer, we . . .
   always avoid contact with people.
   do not object to someone attractive touching us.
   feel most vulnerable.
   try not to be touched.

3 If, by chance, someone does touch us we feel . . .
   disgusted by this.
   hostile to them.
   shocked by this.
   surprised by this.

4 The way we feel when in a crowd is presented as a(n) . . .
   absurdity   logical conclusion   opposite   paradox

5 Once formed, crowds always tend to . . .
   become uncomfortable   contract   expand   split up

SECOND PASSAGE

DREAMS. Now and again I have had horrible dreams, but not enough of them to make me lose my delight in dreams. To begin with, I like the idea of dreaming, of going to bed and lying still and then, by some queer magic, wandering into another kind of existence. As a child I could never understand why grownups took dreaming so calmly when they could make such a fuss about any holiday. This still puzzles me. I am mystified by people who say they never dream and appear to have no interest in the subject. It is much more astonishing than if they said they never went out for a walk. Most people – or at least most Western Europeans – do not seem to accept dreaming as part of their lives. They appear to see it as an irritating little habit, like sneezing or yawning. I have never understood this. My dream life does not seem as important as my waking life, if only because there is far less of it, but to me it *is* important. As if there were at least two extra continents added to the world, and lightning excursions running to them at any moment between midnight and breakfast. Then again, the dream life, though queer and bewildering and unsatisfactory in many respects, has its own advantages. The dead are there, smiling and talking. The past is there, sometimes all broken and confused but occasionally as fresh as a daisy. And perhaps, the future is there too, winking at us. This dream life is often overshadowed by huge mysterious anxieties, with luggage that cannot be packed and trains that refuse to be caught; and both persons and scenes there are not as dependable and solid as they are in waking life, so that Brown and Smith merge into one person while Robinson splits into two, and there are thick woods outside the bathroom door and the dining-room is somehow part of a theatre balcony; and there are moments of desolation or terror in the dream world that are worse than anything we have known under the sun. Yet this other life has its interests, its gaieties, its satisfactions, and, at certain rare intervals, a serene glow or a sudden ecstasy, like glimpses of another form of existence altogether, that we cannot match with open eyes. Daft or wise, terrible or exquisite, it is a further helping of experience, a bonus after dark, another slice of life cut differently for which, it seems to me, we are never sufficiently grateful. Only a dream! Why *only*? It was there, and you had it. 'If there were dreams to sell,' Beddoes inquires, 'what would you buy?' I cannot say offhand, but certainly rather more than I could afford.

(from *Delight* by J. B. Priestley)

6 The writer's parents . . .
became very anxious at holiday times.
couldn't understand his dreams.
spoke calmly about their dreams.
weren't interested in hearing about his dreams.

7 Most people the writer knows . . .
are irritated by their dreams.
do not enjoy their dreams.
are bored by hearing about his dreams.
wish they didn't dream.

8 Brown, Smith and Robinson are . . .
dead friends of the writer.
living friends of the writer.
people you or I might know.
people who were well-known when the essay was written.

9 In our dreams we experience . . .
deeper anxiety and unhappiness than in our waking lives.
greater fear, despair and joy than in our waking lives.
more interesting events than in our waking lives.
premonitions of future events.

10 The writer reproaches people who belittle dreams because . . .
they are daft and don't understand how important dreams are.
they think dreams are less important than their waking lives.
they don't agree that dreams are just as important as being awake.
each dream is a tangible part of our experience.

THIRD PASSAGE

By Martin Wainwright

The Old Bailey listened spellbound yesterday to the tale of a pensioner's doomed attempt to hold hostages at a London bank and rob it of £85,000. Mrs Peggy Barlow, aged 70, of West Kensington, skipped her weekly bridge party to carry out the raid, travelling on her bus pass and armed with a perfume spray which she pretended was a gun.

She grabbed a customer at the bank and bundled her into the manager's office, pressing the perfume canister into her side in a style she had noticed on a TV film about Chicago gangsters. Then she ordered everyone to keep quiet and demanded all the money in the bank, modifying this to £85,000 after a delay which led her to shout: "Hurry up, I'm desperate!"

Mrs Barlow, who walks with the help of a stick and is a bank manager's widow herself, admitted demanding the money with menaces from Mr David Ball, manager of the National Westminster Bank in Kensington High Street.

Her counsel, Mr Brian Barker, said that the story was almost beyond belief and involved an "extraordinary aberration" brought on by threats of bankruptcy. Mrs Barlow who has two grown-up children, had debts of £70,000 and faced daily demands from creditors in the weeks before her raid.

"A younger person may have been able to take this desperate financial situation in their stride but it worried this lady so much that she turned bandit," said Mr Barker.

The court heard that Mrs Barlow had put herself in some danger, with armed police wearing bullet-proof jackets sent to the bank after staff pressed a panic button. Although her planning was sophisticated she reckoned without her hostage, Mrs Julien Watkins.

Mr Peter Doyle, prosecuting, said that Mrs Watkins had suddenly decided to have a go and had pinned Mrs Barlow to the wall with the help of the bank manager. Three policemen then arrived and arrested Mrs Barlow.

The Recorder of London, Sir James Miskin QC, said that the raid had been doomed from the start but has still led to a lot of trouble. He added that before the offence Mrs Barlow had led a "socially splendid and responsible" life and had been too proud to ask for help with her finances (which have since been resolved by the sale of her cottage). Sentencing her to nine months' imprisonment, suspended for a year, he warned her not to do anything idiotic again.

Mrs Barlow thanked him and left the court to have a glass of Scotch and describe how she had planned a " kind and gentle " raid in contrast to the ones she saw on television.

" I must have had a brainstorm. I'm normally a very placid and timid person," she said. " Mercifully, everyone has been very kind and understanding and I've promised not to break the law again."

11 People in the courtroom found Mrs Barlow's case . . .
fascinating ludicrous stupid scandalous

12 Mrs Barlow attempted the robbery because . . .
her late husband had worked in a bank.
she was confident of success.
she was irresponsible.
she was worried sick.

13 The robbery was foiled when . . .
armed police arrived.
her hostage grabbed her.
she realised she could not succeed.
the bank manager grabbed her.

14 Mrs Barlow might well have . . .
been shot herself.
got away with the money.
injured someone.
shot her hostage in panic.

15 Mrs Barlow is now . . .
bankrupt in jail solvent unrepentant

"Whenever I visit you. Fred, it's difficult not to think of you still at the bank."

18.3 Transformations *Use of English*

Rewrite each sentence so that its meaning remains unchanged.

1 We'll always remember these days together at our meetings in the future.
Whenever . . .

2 I admire her achievements a great deal but as a person I loathe her.
Much . . .

3 It's because he was reprimanded that he is feeling so upset.
If . . .

4 You should admit that you're to blame, not try to conceal it.
I'd rather . . .

5 The realisation that I had been conned came later.
Only . . .

6 The police are advising vigilance as there have been more robberies lately.
Due to . . .

7 It is fairly unlikely that he will be convicted of the offence.
There . . .

8 When a policeman appeared at the door I was pretty taken aback.
Imagine . . .

9 The prosecution have a very weak case since they cannot produce sufficient evidence.
Unless . . .

10 He said he was delighted but he sounded much too half-hearted to me.
I wish . . .

18.4 Fill the gaps *Use of English*

Fill each gap with a suitable phrase or word.

1 Difficult .... I was able to answer most of the questions.

2 She was afraid to scream .... waking the neighbours.

3 'Your parents wanted you to become rich and famous, didn't they?'
'Yes, and it's been impossible to .... their expectations.'

4 'She said she'd kill me!'
'My word, she .... awfully upset then.'

5 We look forward to receiving your donation, ... it may be.

6 'He's now made a complete confession of the crime.'
'But only yesterday he denied .... it.'

7 Never in my life .... such a monstrous crime!

8 The murderer was locked up in a top security prison. .... he succeeded .... from it.

9 'So you both found it hard to get used .... in a foreign country?'
'No, not at all. I didn't find it at all difficult and .... my friend.'

10 It seems to me that examinations are .... proficiency in a language.

18.5 Questions and summary *Use of English*

Read the passage and answer the questions that follow. Try to do the whole exercise in 50 minutes, including time for checking through your work at the end for mistakes and slips of the pen.

My lessons in the classroom

"You must be mad!" was the general comment of family, friends and colleagues. "Giving up a teaching post now, when there isn't much chance of finding another one, ever!

"And what about all that lovely money you're earning, and all those long holidays!"

But I had already come to my lonely decision, after months of concealed suffering. The demon of unemployment should be enough to make those of us fortunate to have a job pull up the drawbridge behind us, and yet here was I, prepared to join the clamouring horde on the opposite bank.

But I knew I could no longer continue in the teaching profession. To wake in the morning with a fear of the day ahead, to force a hasty breakfast down an unwilling throat, and then set off for work with pounding heart and frozen face had become habitual, and I had turned to tranquillizers to help me along.

It had not always been as bad as this. Ten years ago I managed well enough, and the holidays for rest and recuperation used to come round just in time.

But I, in common with most other teachers, am enormously self-critical, and I knew now that I was no longer "managing". My classes were noisy, the children were not learning very much, my attempts to cope with changing teaching methods were patchy, I had run out of enjoyment and enthusiasm. It was time to stop.

But was it all my own failure? In fairness to myself, I don't think it was. I had plenty of ideas, I loved my subject, and, by and large, I liked children.

I had been idealistic. But the reality I faced was bored children, over-stimulated by video-watching the night before and tired out by a late bedtime. They were children who were given the wrong food at the wrong time, who came breakfast-less to school and then stuffed themselves with gum, crisps and sweets bought on the way; who were "high" with hunger in the lesson before lunchtime and giggled restlessly as the smell of chips from the school kitchen came wafting to all floors.

There were children who ⟶

absorbed all the smutty side of sex before they were 10, and were constantly teasing and titillating each other ; bright, hard-working little girls who changed, under the pressures of peer group and advertising, into assertive, screeching empty-heads, with a tube of mascara in their pencil cases and "My Guy" concealed on their desks.

Then there were the ones from difficult homes, such as Simon, whose parents had split up after many years together and who was not wanted by either—his tired eyes flickered all round when I tried to remonstrate with him privately, and his pale face never stopped twitching. But he could bring chaos to my lessons with his sniggerings and mutterings.

The rudeness I had to put up with, and the bad language, appalled me. I had no redress, as the only form of punishment available was a detention, which meant keeping myself in too.

Sometimes parents could be contacted, and their help sought, but frequently they were as bewildered and incapacitated as we ourselves.

A frequent image came before me, as I lay in bed after an early wakening—the maths room, after a "wet break", chairs turned over, books and orange peel on the floor.

The fourth year are due for their English lesson, so I come in and attempt to assert myself and restore order. Jeremy is telling jokes. Donna is cackling. Andrew is standing on a desk and yelling out of the window.

At one time my very presence in the doorway would be enough to ensure a partial silence. Now they give a vague "Hello, Miss", and carry on.

I distribute the work sheets, expensively photocopied, and we try to start, but two slow girls are making noises : "Miss, I can't understand this !" And James is quietly reading his football magazine, Jeremy continues to tell jokes, more quietly now, and Michèle bares her gum-filled teeth and urges Paul to shut his face.

I have been trying to create the basic conditions in which teaching becomes possible, but I have failed, and no longer have the stomach for the job. And that is why I'm giving up.

Anne Bonsall

1 Why were the writer's friends and family taken by surprise?
2 Who are the 'clamouring horde on the opposite bank' in line 22?
3 Why was the writer's heart pounding as she set off for work?
4 How well had she managed to adapt to new teaching methods during her ten years' teaching?
5 What is the meaning of 'wafting' in line 68?
6 Why did the hard-working little girls change?
7 What do you think 'My Guy' (line 79) is?
8 What is the meaning of 'remonstrate' in line 87?
9 Why was the writer unwilling to punish pupils who misbehaved?
10 Who are referred to as 'we ourselves' in line 101?
11 How do the 4th year English class react to the writer's entry into the room?
12 What do you think is meant by a 'wet break' in line 105?
13 What is meant by 'the stomach for the job' in line 134?
14 In one paragraph of 50–100 words, summarise the reasons why the writer does not blame her failure on her own shortcomings.

18.6 Listening comprehension

Here, as in the exam, there are four listening texts for you to listen to and answer questions about.
(Your teacher will play each recording twice, with a pause between each playing.)

FIRST PART: The English pub

1 According to David Rees, most beer sold in the UK is made by . . .
companies belonging to a large conglomerate.
companies with various business interests.
companies with no real interest in pubs.
specialist brewing firms.

2 When you buy a pint of beer you can, according to David Rees, . . .
eat a good meal.
meet strangers in quiet corners.
take part in a game.
talk to friends at the bar.

3 When he describes British lager, David Rees sounds . . .
angry
amused
proud
scornful

4 Pubs are being modernised in order to . . .
attract younger customers.
attract customers of all ages who have money.
exclude older, poorer customers.
make them seem more trendy.

5 A traditional pub has . . .
both young and old customers.
fewer customers than a modern one.
less space than a modern one.
mainly older customers.

6 A 'theme pub' is one which . . .
has been completely modernised.
is decorated in a style suggested by its name.
is decorated in the worst possible taste.
looks like every other modern-style pub.

7 The modern trend is for pubs to be under the management of . . .
a freelance manager.
an employee of the brewery.
a landlord.
a tenant.

»»→

8 The speaker prefers landlords because they . . .
   are independent of the brewery.
   are interested in the local community.
   are more friendly to customers.
   pay the brewery a rent.

9 Which of these qualities of a country pub does the speaker value *most*?
   Its log fire in winter.
   The quality of the traditional beer it serves.
   Its picturesque, old-fashioned appearance.
   The fact that it's a second home for everyone in the village.

10 Which of these qualities of a town pub does the speaker value most?
   The noise and smoke.
   The welcoming atmosphere.
   The good conversation.
   The arguments and stories you can overhear.

SECOND PART: Looking for a job?

Tick (✓) *only* the advice and information given by the speakers.

APPLICATION FORM

1 Photocopy it and practise filling in the copy. ☐

2 Write your final version neatly and clearly. ☐

3 Use a separate sheet for any extra information you want to give. ☐

4 Personnel officers read application forms very carefully. ☐

5 Use words that show you want to be successful in business. ☐

6 Mention any unusual hobbies or jobs. ☐

THE INTERVIEW

7 Be confident. ☐

8 Avoid answering questions about your leisure interests. ☐

9 Ask the interviewer what his company does. ☐

10 Find out about the companies that are in competition with his. ☐

11 You may have to have lunch with the interviewer. ☐

12 The interviewer may insult you. ☐

13 Remain calm whatever happens. ☐

14 Expect to be surprised. ☐

15 Arrange to participate in some mock interviews beforehand. ☐

16 Tell the interviewer that you are sensitive and clever. ☐

'CREATIVE JOB SEARCHING'

17 This technique is better than conventional application for jobs. ☐

18 Get in touch with employees working in companies in your chosen field. ☐

19 You will get a job if you are persistent enough. ☐

20 It helps to be personally known to the management of a company. ☐

THIRD PART: Rules and values

Listen to the interview with a sociologist and answer the questions.

1 Rules are different from laws in that . . .
- there is no threat of punishment involved.
- rules are more powerful.
- rules are not understood by people.
- rules are not recorded.

2 Society has rules in order to . . .
- control how people spend their time.
- give guidance on how to behave.
- maintain political stability.
- regulate people's behaviour.

3 An adult playing the role of parent or teacher is in a similar position to that of a . . .
- chess player
- criminal
- judge
- policeman

4 Most of us would never break the law because we . . .
- are afraid of being caught.
- are afraid of being punished.
- fear disapproval.
- want to be the same as everyone else.

5 If the members of a society did not share the same set of rules . . .
- a new set of rules would evolve naturally.
- there would be more crime.
- there would be social harmony.
- no one would know how to behave.

→

6 Our circle of friends consists of people who . . .
   like what we like.
   obey the same rules.
   share the same values.
   think the same way as we do.

7 In the United States many people drop out of society because . . .
   they are black or Hispanic.
   they cannot be successful.
   they don't share the same values as the majority of society.
   they take drugs.

8 When a society's values are challenged 'positively' by rebels . . .
   a social revolution may follow.
   criminal values may be substituted.
   society may disapprove strongly.
   society's rules and values may change.

FOURTH PART: **Attitudes**

You will hear the same text spoken in five different ways, each conveying a different attitude. Select *one* adjective to describe each attitude:

angry depressed diffident disappointed impressed
half-hearted heart-broken hysterical sarcastic

1:
2:
3:
4:
5:

18.7 Interview

In the examination the examiner will be awarding marks for:
FLUENCY and GRAMMATICAL ACCURACY,
PRONUNCIATION OF INDIVIDUAL SOUNDS and SENTENCES (stress and intonation),
INTERACTIVE COMMUNICATIVE ABILITY and VOCABULARY RESOURCE.

Try to give a good impression of your spoken English. Don't just wait to be asked questions – behave and speak as you would in a real conversation.

Photograph

Work in pairs, with one of you looking at activity 36 and the other at 72. Take it in turns to play the roles of 'examiner' and 'candidate'.

Reading passage

Work in pairs. One of you should look at activity 24, the other at 41. You will each have a short reading passage to discuss.

Communication activity

Work in pairs or groups of three. Before you start, look at the information below.

One of the problems about being successful in society is that you may become rich and famous and thus become a target for kidnappers, who may take you hostage and demand an enormous ransom for your release.

Decide together which of the measures listed here are **do's** and which are **don'ts** for rich people who want to stay safe. Give your reasons too.

HOW NOT TO BE KIDNAPPED

TRAVEL IN ISOLATED AREAS
KEEP TO A SET ROUTINE AT WORK OR ON HOLIDAY
KEEP A LOW PROFILE
MAKE RESERVATIONS IN YOUR OWN NAME
CARRY IDENTIFICATION DOCUMENTS AND MEDICAL DETAILS
PARK IN PROTECTED AREAS
CARRY LUGGAGE WITH YOUR NAME AND ADDRESS ON IT
STOP AT THE SAME BAR/RESTAURANT/PARK ON YOUR WAY HOME
TELL FAMILY AND FRIENDS WHERE YOU ARE GOING
VARY YOUR ROUTE TO AND FROM THE OFFICE
ARRIVE EARLY FOR APPOINTMENTS
ARRIVE EXACTLY ON TIME AT AIRPORTS AND STATIONS
ARRANGE COVERT SIGNALS TO USE WITH FAMILY ON PHONE/ IN LETTERS/FACE TO FACE
BE SUSPICIOUS OF EVERYBODY YOU DON'T KNOW
THINK IT COULD NEVER HAPPEN TO YOU
FIND OUT ABOUT THE POLITICS OF ANY COUNTRY YOU VISIT
IGNORE THE POSSIBILITY OF DANGER TO YOUR FAMILY

Just supposing you or a member of your family were kidnapped and the criminals/bandits/terrorists demanded far more money than you could possibly pay, what would you and your partner(s) do?

What punishment would you recommend for a convicted kidnapper?

How can would-be kidnappers be deterred from perpetrating such a crime?

18.8 Composition

Write *two* of the following composition exercises in 2 hours. Allow enough time to check your work through before you hand it in – and do <u>**please**</u> make notes before you start writing each composition.

1 Describe *either* a social conformist *or* a social non-conformist of your acquaintance. (About 350 words)

2 'The punishment should fit the crime.' To what extent do you agree with this well-known cliché? (About 350 words)

3 You have been sent the following cutting from a newspaper in your country. Prepare a suitable document that can be handed out to visitors arriving at the airport or frontier. (About 150 words)

Reports in the Foreign Press

THERE have been a growing number of reports in newspapers abroad that there is a " crime wave " in this country. The Minister of Tourism fears that this may cause concern among foreign visitors, who may assume they are likely to be robbed once they set foot in the country.

What is needed is a short, persuasive handout warning tourists of the dangers of pickpockets and thieves but which does *not* alarm them unduly. It should offer advice on how to minimise the risks by taking the right precautions.

A prize will be given to the originator of the handout used.

4 Write a letter giving advice to a friend who is determined to drop out of college and start work on a building site. (About 350 words)

5 Basing your answer on your reading of the prescribed text you have studied, answer *one* of the following: (About 350 words)

Describe and give examples of the way in which the writer builds up a sense of excitement and tension as the plot unfolds.

What makes the text stand out as a 'work of literature' above the common run of popular fiction (or drama).

'Any good work of fiction has just the same ingredients as a detective story.' To what extent is this view applicable to the text you have read?

"Is this your first manhunt, Potts?"

Communication activities

1

It's your turn first to answer your partner's questions about this photograph. Don't let your partner see the photograph while you're answering the questions.

Next, ask your partner the questions on page 12 about his or her photograph.

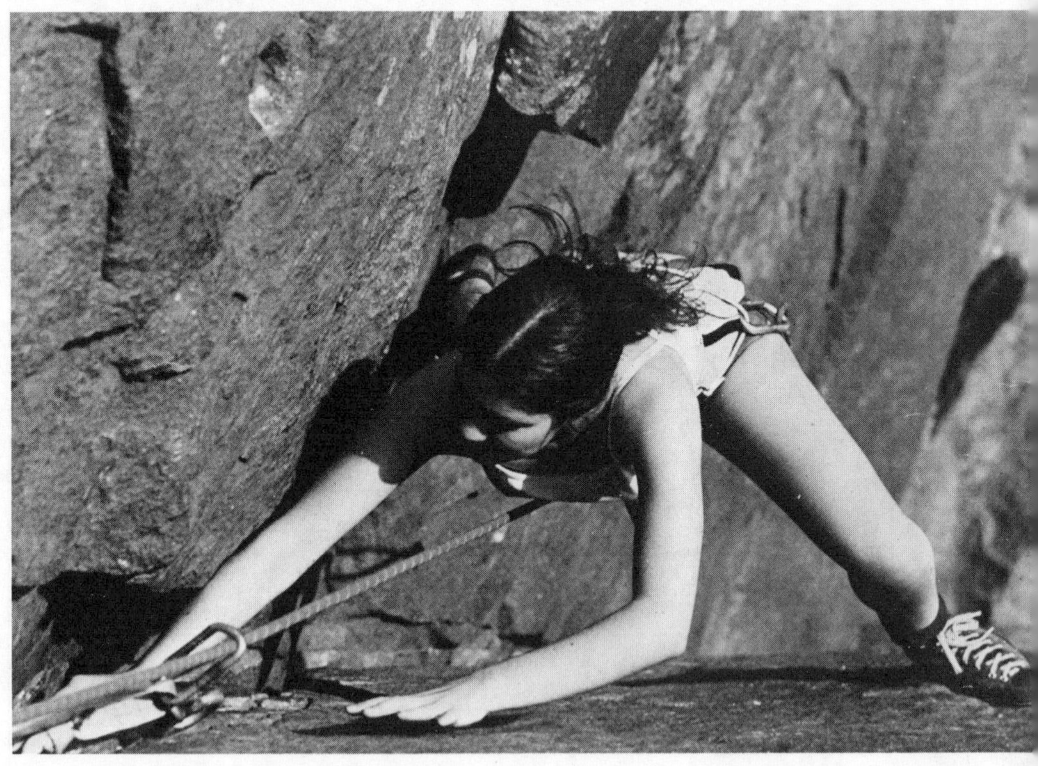

2 This passage is part of the 'blurb' on the dustjacket of a well-known dictionary. Your partner has a different blurb – read yours aloud and then listen to your partner's reading.

To make it easier to read, it is reprinted beneath in 'breath-sized chunks' with *stressed syll*ables in it*al*ics. When reading from this version, pause briefly at the end of each line to draw breath and only let your voice fall sharply where there is a full stop.

The LONGMAN DICTIONARY OF CONTEMPORARY ENGLISH is a completely new dictionary prepared mainly for teachers and students of English, which will also prove stimulating to all those interested in language.

The dictionary documents the English language as it is used throughout the world today, with particular emphasis on Britain and the United States. Its aim is to analyse the meaning and grammatical behaviour of each word as clearly and accurately as possible. A

The *Long*man *Dic*tionary of Con*tem*porary *Eng*lish
is a com*plete*ly *new dic*tionary
pre*pared main*ly for *teach*ers and *stu*dents of *Eng*lish,
which will *al*so prove *stim*ulating to *all* those *in*terested in *lan*guage.

The *dic*tionary *doc*uments the *Eng*lish *lan*guage
as it is *used* through*out* the *world* to*day*,
with par*tic*ular *em*phasis on *Brit*ain and the U*nit*ed *States*.
Its *aim* is to *an*alyse the *mean*ing and gram*mat*ical be*hav*iour of *each word*
as *clear*ly and *acc*urately as *poss*ible.

● Decide which blurb is more likely to persuade you to buy the dictionary.

3 Begin by asking your partner the questions on page 38. Then answer your partner's questions about this photograph.

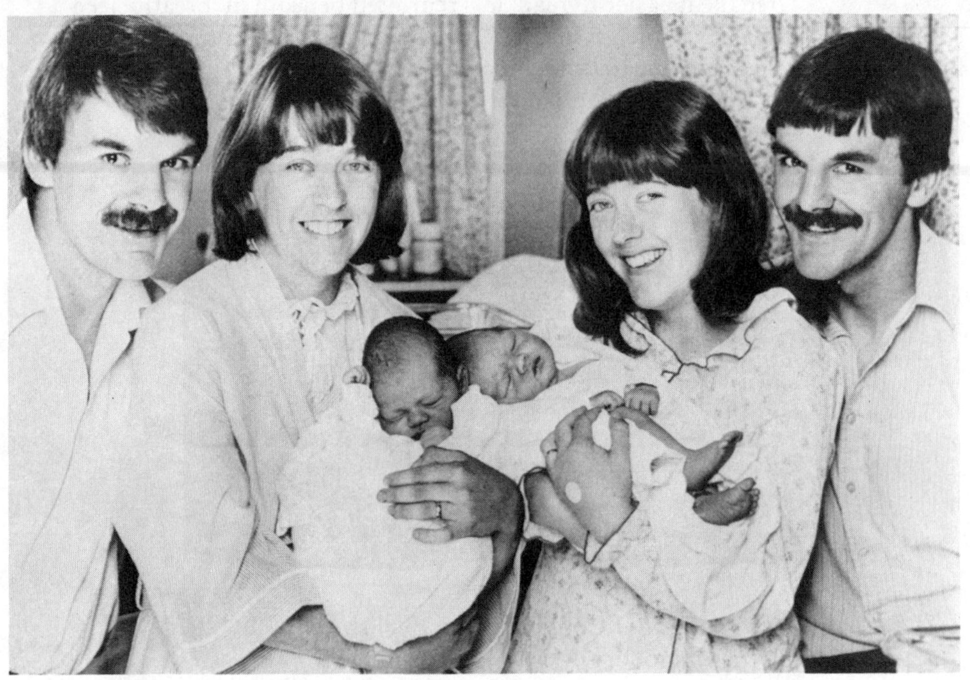

4 To make it easier to read the passage, the version beneath is printed in 'breath-sized chunks' and has the *catenation* marked.

Read your description *first*.

LYNTON AND LYNMOUTH, Devon

Lynton is poised on a cliff 600ft above Lynmouth, amidst superb Exmoor scenery including the magnificent Valley of the Rocks and restful woodland walks beside the East Lyn River. Once the centre of a prosperous herring industry, Lynmouth became a popular resort during the Napoleonic wars. Lynton was 'discovered' by the poets Shelley, Wordsworth and Coleridge in the 19th century, and there is still a working water-powered cliff lift connecting the villages.

/lɪntən/ /lɪnməθ/

Lynton is poised on a cliff six hundred feet above Lynmouth,
amidst superb Exmoor scenery
including the magnificent Valley of the Rocks
and restful woodland walks beside the East Lyn River.
Once the centre of a prosperous herring industry,
Lynmouth became a popular resort during the Napoleonic wars.
Lynton was 'discovered' by the poets Shelley, Wordsworth and Coleridge
in the 19th century,
and there is still a working water-powered cliff lift connecting the villages.

● Where do you think each text was taken from? What details of the style and content reveal the origin of the passages?

5

Below are definitions of some of the words on page 26 – your partner has definitions of the others. Work out together the differences between the words by explaining your own information. **Do not** read the definitions aloud: try to summarise them in your own words.

antonym a word opposite in meaning to another word: *'Pain' is the antonym of 'pleasure'.*

collocation an arrangement of words which sounds natural: *'Strong coffee' is an English collocation but 'powerful coffee' is not.*

dialect [C; U] a variety of a language, spoken in one part of a country, which is different in some words, grammar, or pronunciation from other forms of the same language: *He speaks the Yorkshire dialect of English. This is a poem written in Scottish dialect.*

grin a smile which shows the teeth; a smile which seems almost to be laughing, esp a very wide smile, which may sometimes also be an expression of suffering: *He didn't understand; he just stood there with a silly grin on his face.*

irony [U;C] **1** a way of speaking which expresses by its manner the opposite of what the words say: *The irony in his words was unmistakable.* **2** the sort of event or result which is just the opposite of what one would hope for or meant to happen, or the state when this happens: *The irony lay in the fact that he was there all the time, although I didn't see him.*

phrasal verb a group of words acting as a verb and usu consisting of a verb with an adverbial or prepositional particle [⇨ G272]: *'Get up' and 'get by' are phrasal verbs.*

scowl 1 [IØ (*at*)] to make an angry or threatening expression; to frown angrily: *The teacher scowled at his noisy class. What a scowling face you have!* **2** [T1] to express in this way: *He scowled his displeasure.*

slang [U] language that is not usu acceptable in serious speech or writing, including words, expressions, etc regarded as very informal or not polite and those used among particular groups of people (marked *sl* in this book): *There are lots of slang words for money, like 'bread' and 'dough'. He likes to use army/schoolboy slang. Slang often goes in and out of fashion quickly.*

6

Look at this reproduction of a Victorian 'narrative painting'. Tell your partners what you think is the story behind this picture. Your partners' paintings show different parts of the same story. Then see if you can work out how the three scenes fit together and what must have happened in between.

Decide on suitable titles for the three paintings and for the whole story.

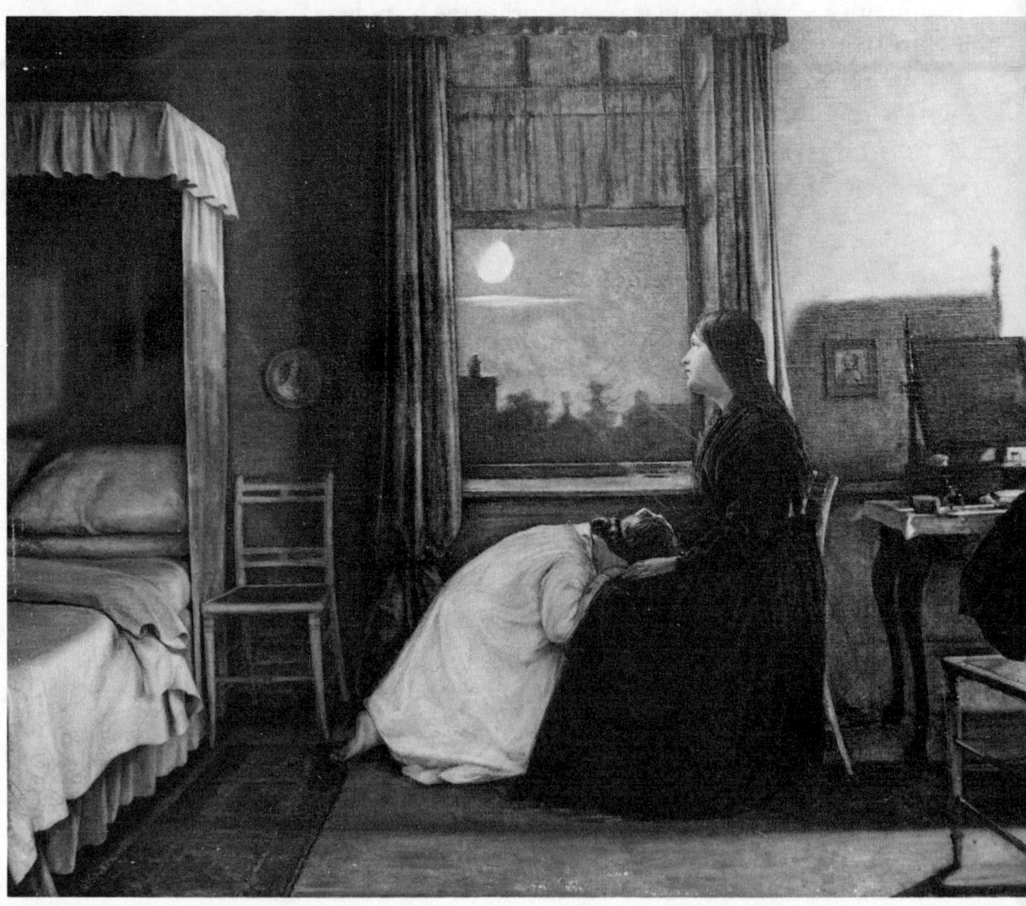

7

Your partner has the details of the second half of the voyage shown below. Tell your partner about the first half of the voyage and then find out about the second half, marking the route Naomi James took on the map.

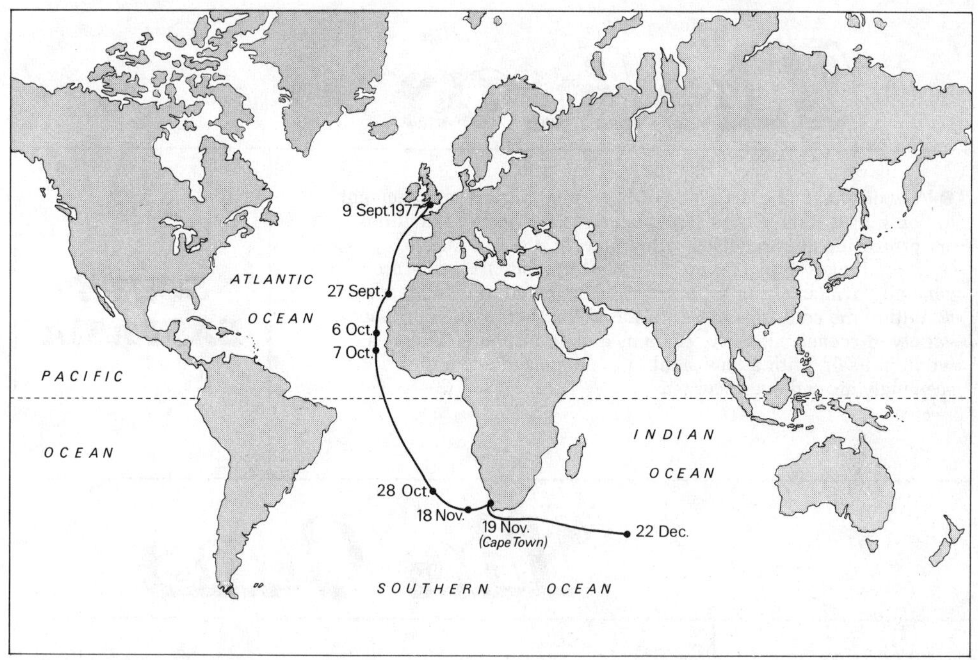

9 Sept 1977: With only 2 years' sailing experience, set off from Dartmouth in 'Express Crusader' (sponsored by *Daily Express*). Age 28, just married to Rob James (experienced sailor). Only Boris, her kitten, for company.
27 Sept: Rendezvous off Canary Islands for spare parts and photos
6 Oct: Sunstroke
7 Oct: Radio broke down
28 Oct: Boris fell overboard and drowned
18 Nov: Self-steering broke
19 Nov: Put in to Cape Town for urgent repairs
22 Dec: Fell into ocean . . .

8 Look at the information given below about the advantages and disadvantages of spending a holiday in some exotic parts of the world. Use it as the starting point for a discussion with your partners, who have more information about the same places.

The Pros

● A widespread characteristic of hotel and tourism management in South East Asia is their high standards. Service and facilities are professionally organised, often more so than in Europe. Cuisine of every type and origin – Western and Oriental – are generally available in most areas. This is the gourmet's Mecca. ● Within the countries of South East Asia there's an enormous variety of scenery, history, customs and atmosphere. This is a world in itself, with a new sight, an unexpected encounter seemingly around every corner.	**SOUTH EAST ASIA**

The Cons

SRI LANKA	● Definitely not for the swinging or the sophisticated wanting 'luxury', haute cuisine and every comfort. The hotels tend to be simpler in standards, the people relaxed in their lifestyle. ● Technology is not one of Sri Lanka's greatest assets. Electricity and water supplies can break down more often than they should – meaning discomfort. It's the sort of thing you should be prepared for. To expect international city standards is unrealistic. ● Entertainment can be limited, and government controls may mean simple catering. ● The 'monsoon' periods can produce heavy rain, poor (even dangerous) sea bathing and generally reduced hotel facilities.
SOUTH PACIFIC	

9

Before you start talking, make some notes in answer to the questions below. Then ask your partner the questions and give your own answers. Your partner has different questions to ask you.

Who are your favourite painters?
  Why do you enjoy / not enjoy looking at paintings?
What are your favourite operas?
  Why do you enjoy / not enjoy opera?
What are your favourite pieces of classical music?
  Why do you enjoy / not enjoy listening to classical music?
Who are your favourite popular singers or groups?
  Why do you enjoy / not enjoy pop or rock music?
Who are your favourite film stars?
  Why do you enjoy / not enjoy the cinema?
What are your favourite TV programmes?
  Why do you enjoy / not enjoy watching television?

10

The rearranged version below of the news item should help you to read it more fluently.

Rat à l'orange

THE only way to fight China's growing rat pest problem is to open rat meat restaurants and promote the rodents as a gourmet dish, according to the Economic Information newspaper. An estimated three to four billion rats eat 15 million tonnes of grain a year in China and annual pest-control drives have failed to stop the damage, it said in an article quoted by China Daily. — Reuter.

Rat à l'orange /ræt æ lɒrɒnʒ/
The only way to fight China's growing rat pest problem
is to open rat meat restaurants
and to promote the rodents as a gourmet dish,
according to the Economic Information newspaper.
An estimated three to four billion rats
eat fifteen million tonnes of grain a year in China
and annual pest-control drives have failed to stop the damage,
it said in an article quoted by China Daily.

11

1 In your own words, tell your partner about the first part of the article. Answer any questions he or she may have.
2 Find out about the second part of the article from your partner.
3 Tell your partner about the third part of the article.

First part

But now in these days of devaluation of the once proud Mexican peso, the time for at least partial revenge may have arrived. The US is being paid back in kind — short changed.

Less than 10 years ago the peso stood at a solid 12.50 to the dollar. When Mexico's financial crisis struck in 1982 it had slipped to 70, and since has slumped to 250 with experts expecting another devaluation before the autumn.

Suddenly last year, there was a surprising shortage of the now near worthless old one peso coin (about the same size as the old British half-crown) and the police discovered tons were being smuggled across the US border. Melted down, the metal in the coins was worth several times their face value.

The government, therefore, recently struck a new, much smaller and cheaper one peso. The only problem is that the coins are still flowing across the border in their millions, though this time in the pockets of individual Mexicans rather than metal dealers.

Third part

But on the border itself, the new peso has come as a further blow to an area already hit disastrously by Mexico's deep crisis of the last three years. Many of the US border cities are isolated by hundreds of miles from other major US centres and depend on Mexican commerce for much of their existence.

Since the 1982 devaluation Mexican shoppers have stayed away in their droves. US border unemployment rates have shot up — Laredo in Texas, for instance, now has a rate of 27.4 per cent, while in Calexico, California, unemployment is as high as 37 per cent.

Small and medium shop owners in El Paso, Texas, have reported an 80 per cent drop in sales. Even huge supermarkets like Safeways and Sears on the border have had to close their doors.

The new peso coin, therefore, has sparked a wave of angry protests. One leading Texan Senator, inundated by letters from constituents, has asked the State Department to intervene and persuade the Mexican government to do something.

12

Ask your partners the following questions:

1 How much reading do you do? How much time do you spend each week reading books, and how much time reading newspapers or magazines? How much do you read in English, rather than in your own language?
2 What kinds of books do you enjoy reading? Do you choose different sorts of books for different occasions (journeys, holidays, bed, etc.)?
3 If you could choose between reading a book or seeing the same story as a film in the cinema or serialised on TV, which would you prefer?
4 Who are your favourite authors? Describe the kinds of books they write.
5 Describe one book you have particularly enjoyed reading recently. What did you like about it? What were its faults?
6 Are there any books you'd like to re-read (or have re-read)? What are the qualities of such a book?
7 Is there any particular book you'd recommend to your partners? What do you think they'd enjoy about it?

13

FLIGHT DELAYED...

CONNECTION MISSED...

BAGGAGE LOST...

AND YOU FORGOT
YOUR WIFE'S BIRTHDAY.

A Answer your partner's questions about the pictures above.

B Then ask your partner the following:

1. What does your picture show? Describe it in detail.
2. What might it be advertising, do you think? Can you suggest several possible types of service or product?
3. If I told you it was part of an advertisement for Radiopaging, what questions would you ask me?

(Explain how the text below fits with the picture your partner has been describing to you.)

Every day thousands of hard working, reliable men and women walk out of their offices and simply vanish.

And every day thousands more hard working, reliable men and women waste countless hours trying to track them down.

In the process tempers are frayed, business lost, opportunities missed.

It's a crime.

Because wherever you are, whatever you're doing, now you have the freedom to keep in touch with every business opportunity simply by using a British Telecom Radiopager.

With a Radiopager anyone can be contacted virtually anywhere in the country.

So when someone has a message for you, your secretary can simply dial your personal Radiopager number.

Your Radiopager will then 'bleep' to tell you that the office is trying to get in touch.

Dial 100 now and ask for "Freefone Radiopaging" or send the coupon.

To: Angela Humpston, Radiopaging Product Manager, Ref. RG. 112, British Telecom Radiopaging, FREEPOST 5, London W1E 4LH. Please provide me with full details of British Telecom Radiopaging Services.

Name__________

Position__________

Address__________

__________ Postcode__________

Tel. No__________

Type of business__________

British TELECOM Radiopaging

TELECOM Radiopaging

Make efficiency work for you.

14

The newspaper article below is incomplete. Your partner has the missing paragraphs. Take it in turns to tell each part of the story in your own words.

Roll on Christmas in Moscow

From UPI in Moscow

Lucky Muscovites have found the perfect Christmas gift for the friend who has nothing: a toilet paper subscription.

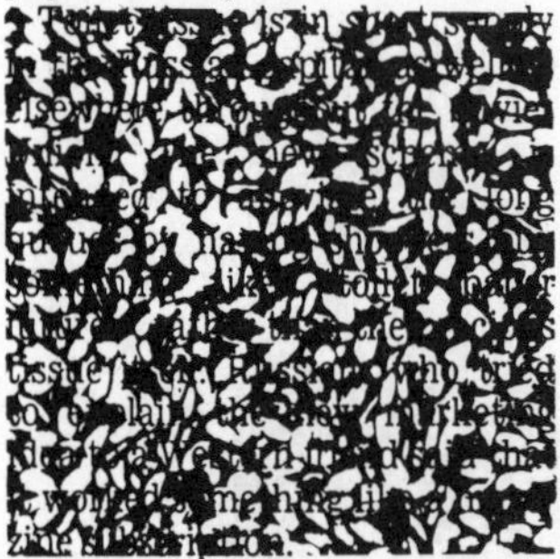

"You go to the store and fill out a form—a postcard, actually," one man said. "This postcard will be mailed back to you whenever the store gets a fresh supply of toilet paper, and only those with postcards will be allowed to buy it." The postcards cost 3 kopecks (about 2p)—cheap enough, but there is no guarantee about when the purchase contract will be fulfilled.

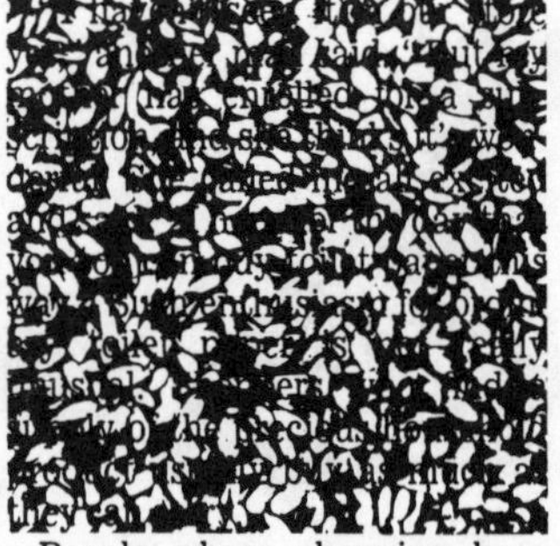

People whose shopping bags are overflowing with toilet paper usually lace up the rest and hang it around their necks. The sight of a happy Russian who has scored such a coup always generates excitement among other shoppers.

This year's pre-Christmas shopping season has been no exception, hence the new postcard subscription plan. But shortage-weary Muscovites already have spotted a flaw in that, too. "It seems there's a shortage of postcards," said the man whose mother managed to snare one. "That means we still have to hang on to our old copies of Pravda and Izvestia."

15

This amusing extract comes from *Up the Garden Path* by Sue Limb. Your partners have different extracts from the same book.

Read your extract out to your partners first. Concentrate on conveying the mood of the passage – it's a kind of internal monologue expressing Izzy's midwinter disgruntlement.

I

/ɪzi/ Izzy pressed her nose to the glass: the whirling snow had blotted out Earl's Court. Unfortunately the effect would only be temporary. New Year. Time for a little resolution. All right, then, but where to begin? The body, perhaps. Izzy had been feeling so fat recently that it was like having somebody else in bed with her. She would have to shape up. But alas, so far her idea of exercise was reaching for the chocolates.

Then there was the untidiness. Izzy looked about her. It was only a one-bedroom flat, with a double bed for the vice and a bookcase for the versa, but Izzy had acquired dirty habits early and practice had made perfect. Izzy's mother had got up at the crack of dawn to scrub the farmyard and fold the cows, but the infant Izzy had ignored this example and played vile games behind the barn in the mud with little John Wilson, her partner in grime. Start as you mean to go on.

● When all three extracts have been read, discuss what connections there are between them and what the novel they come from is about. What have you found out about the plot and the characters?

16

Answer your partner's questions about this photograph:

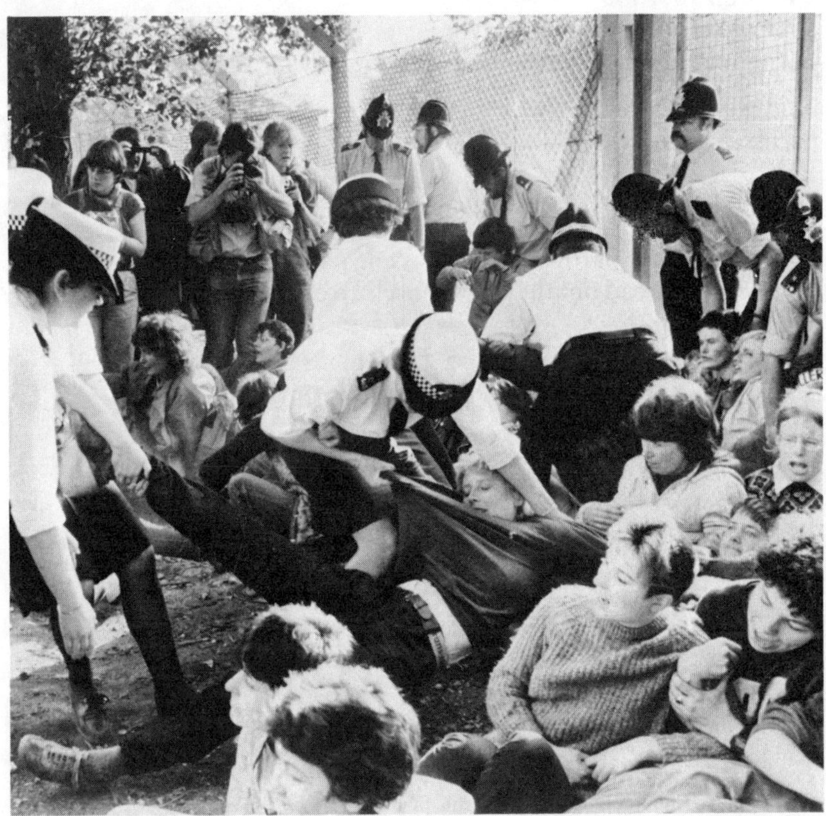

Ask your partner the following questions about his or her picture:

What's happening in your picture?
How is it different from the one I described to you?
What kind of people are they? How are they feeling?
Have you ever taken part in a political rally or demonstration? What was it like and how did you feel?
How can members of the public make their views known to the government?
How can a government explain and justify its policies to the public?
Thinking of your own country's present government, is there any particular policy that you support very strongly?

17

Find out your partner's views on the following issues, which concern individual freedoms and State control.

Do you think individuals should be free to decide whether or not to:

- join any political party (including the Communists or Fascists)
- drink alcohol at any age
- drive at 150 kph
- wear seat belts in cars
- do military service
- take drugs
- have an abortion
- immigrate into your country

or should the State control these activities, by means of laws?

Find out which of the above are, in fact, controlled by the State in your partner's country.

18

Your partner has the missing paragraphs of this article. Take it in turns to read out the whole article to each other.

On a wing and a paper clip

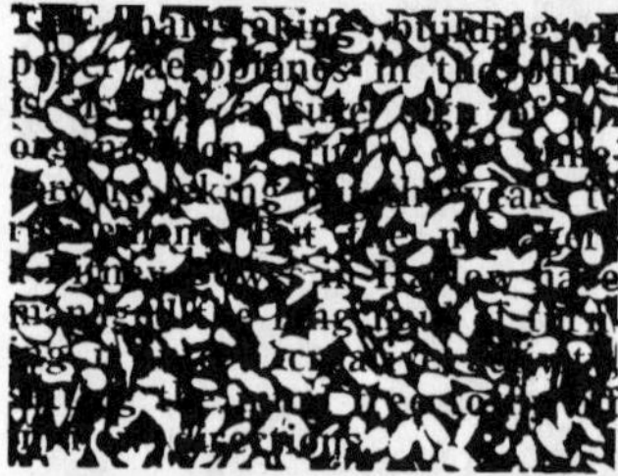

Test flights took place in the table tennis room of the firm's sports and social club. The 25 managers and supervisors taking part in the project were asked to design and fly 60 planes in an hour, after being given paper, weights, scissors and rough job specifications.

In a practical sense the exercise was a disaster. The teams managed to construct only three planes, and all those were rejected because they failed to fly the specified distance laid down by the organisers.

Paper is Pitney Bowes' business, in the sense that the machines they make take the sweat out of office correspondence. This bizarre use of their stock-in-trade was part of a company-wide plan to involve their supervisors more in the company's achievement.

● Find out what your partner's views are on this method of management training.

19

Begin by asking your partner these questions about his or her picture.

What does your photograph show?
Describe the people in the picture and what they're doing.
What do you think they are saying to one another?
Could this kind of thing *really* happen in the future?
What kinds of robots and machines will be common in, say, 20 years' time?
Do you enjoy science fiction books and films like 'Star Wars'? Give your reasons.
Describe one science fiction book or film that particularly impressed you.

Then answer your partner's questions about this picture:

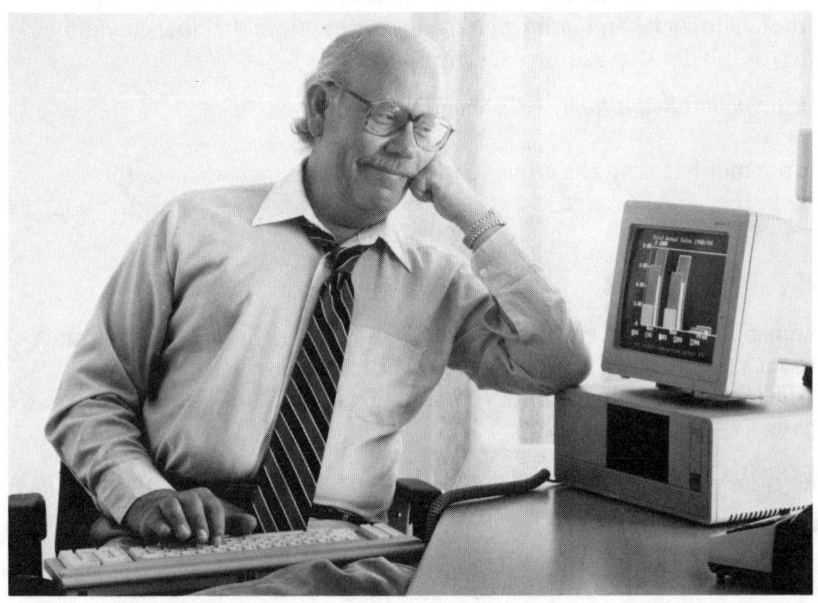

20

Look at the predictions below and, in your own words, tell your partner about them. Your partner has some other predictions. Discuss the effects each event might have on people's lives. Would you dread or look forward to each prediction coming true?

by 1995: You'll be able to enjoy three dimensional television by means of laser holography projectors.
by 1998: There will be automated highways, centrally controlled, making greater traffic density and speeds possible.
by 2000: A medicine will be in use to control your metabolic rate and stop you getting fat.
by 2010: Every home will have a computer that will understand and speak your language and with which you'll be able to have conversations.
by 2015: You will be able to drive across the Atlantic Ocean on a bridge.
by 2020: Honeymoons on the moon will be fashionable.
by 2030: You will be able to trade in your used body parts for replacements.

21 Read this passage out to your partner.

One of the unhealthy and disruptive tendencies in virtually all the developing countries is the emergence, in an ever more accentuated form, of the 'dual economy', in which there are two different patterns of living as widely separated from each other as two different worlds. It is not a matter of some people being rich and others being poor, both being united by a common way of life: it is a matter of two ways of life existing side by side in such a manner that even the humblest member of the one disposes of a daily income which is a high multiple of the income accruing to even the hardest working member of the other. The social and political tensions arising from the dual economy are too obvious to require description.

(from *Small is Beautiful* by E. F. Schumacher)

- When your partner has read the continuation of this passage, discuss the points made in the two extracts.

22 Your partner has the other half of these two 'cartograms'. Find out about your partner's information by asking questions.

Discuss what conclusions you reach from studying the information given.

NATIONAL INCOME (the larger the area, the higher the share of total world GNP)

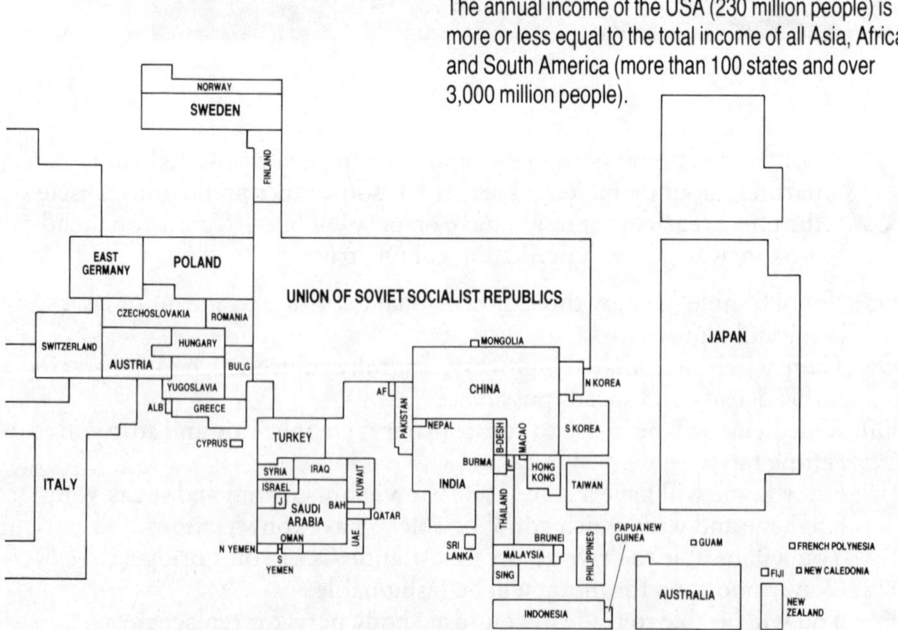

POPULATION (the larger the area, the greater the share of world population)

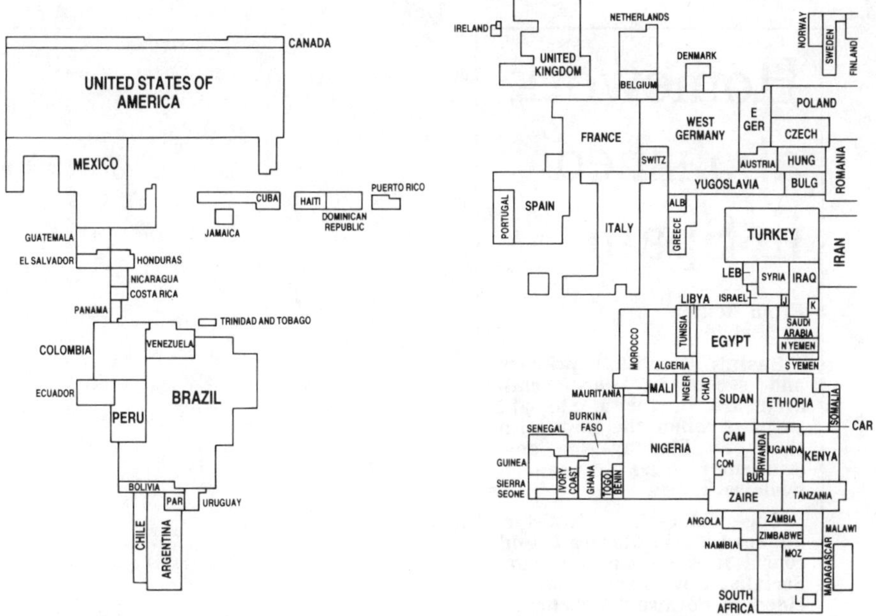

23

Answer your partner's questions about this picture.

Then find out about your partner's picture by asking the questions on page 178.

24

Begin by reading this passage to your partner. Your partner has the second half of the same newspaper article.

> # Homework abolished in Spain
>
> **From Reuter in Madrid**
>
> **Spain's 6 million primary and secondary school children are in for a pleasant surprise when the new term starts on Monday—the government has banned homework.**
>
> **The Education Minister, Mr Jose Maria Maravall, told reporters yesterday that the Socialist Government had decided to do away with homework and official exams in state and private schools for pupils between ages six to 14.**

Find out your partner's opinion of this newspaper article. Is it genuine?

25

THE INCAS

Largest extent of Inca empire (1532): whole of east coast of South America and the Andes from Ecuador to Chile.

Capital city: Cuzco, high in the Andes.

16,000 km of roads covered the empire. Runners carried oral messages or coded messages (knots in coloured cords).

Totalitarian (but fairly benign) organisation of subjects' lives. All produce was owned by the state.

Highly developed welfare system: widows, orphans and invalids cared for by the state; pensions for the over-50s.

Highly developed agriculture (potatoes originate from this area); complex irrigation systems.

Suspension bridges; sophisticated surgical techniques (even brain surgery).

They did not have writing, the wheel or gunpowder (unlike the Spaniards).

They worshipped the Sun – believed Pizarro to be 'son of Viracocha', their white-skinned god.

Last king, Atahualpa, executed by Pizarro in 1533. Inca civilisation destroyed.

26

Study this reproduction in silence for a few moments. Then describe it *in detail* to your partner. Describe what appears to be happening, what might have happened earlier and might happen later. Explain exactly what you like and dislike about it.

Afterwards, have a look at your partner's picture and give your own views on it.

Think of another painting you particularly like, or which you remember well, and describe it to your partner.

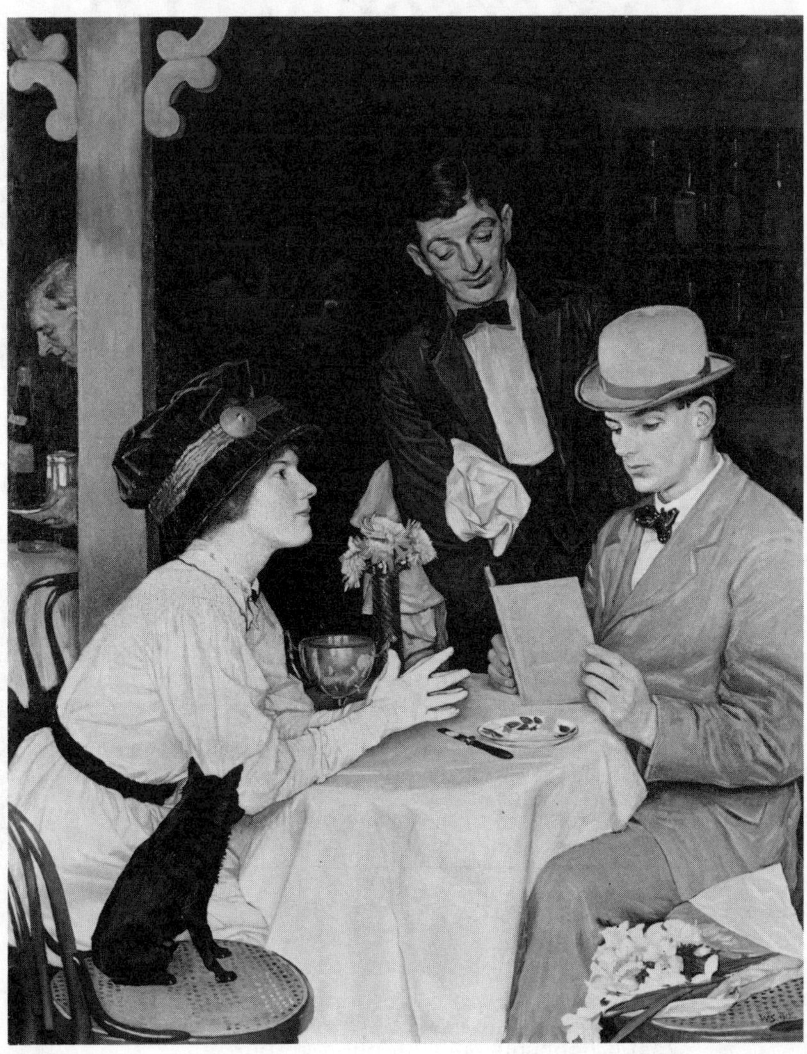

27

Read your parts of this article out to your partners. They have the missing paragraphs.

When you have finished, discuss your reactions to the article.

'Deafness risk' in personal hi-fi

By Andrew Veitch

1 A thousand people a year risked becoming partially deaf as a result of using personal hi-fi, environmental health specialists were warned yesterday.

2

3

4 The Walkman cassette system produced only 20 milliwatts of power per channel.

5 However, each milliwatt produced sound levels at the rate of 90-105dB(A)—units of sound measurement weighted to correspond to the response of the human ear.

6
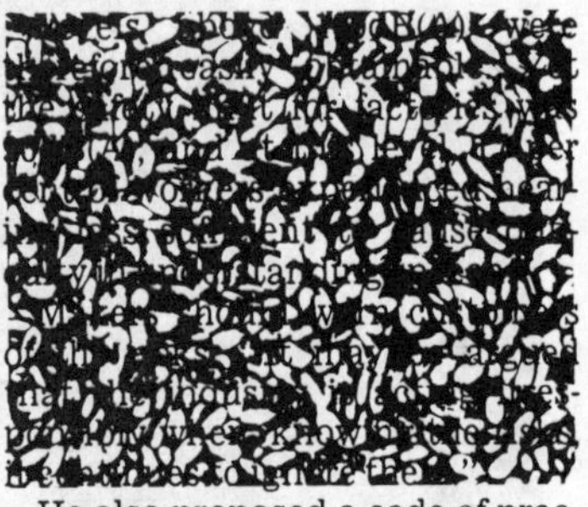

7

8 He also proposed a code of practice limiting sound levels in discotheques, and obliging owners to post notices warning customers of the health risks and indicating the sound level on the dance floor.

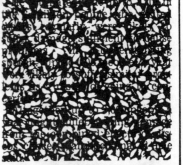

9

10

28

Ask your partner these questions about his or her photograph:

What is happening in your photograph?

Who are the people in the picture? What do you think they're talking about?

What would it be like to be a submariner? What kind of person would be a good one?

What is the purpose of submarines armed with nuclear missiles?

What is the role of a 'conventionally armed' submarine in this day and age?

Describe your own country's defence policy.

Answer your partner's questions about this photograph:

29

The chart shows how many milligrams of sodium are present in various foods. Your partners have complementary information. Find out what your partners know and discuss the implications of this on your own diets.

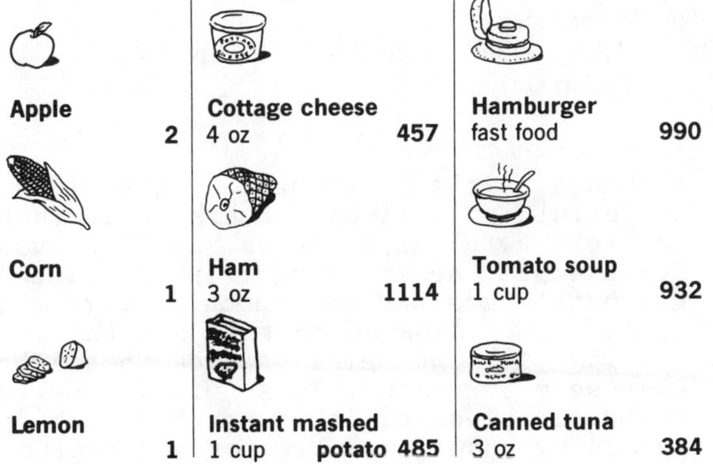

Apple
2
Cottage cheese
4 oz
457
Hamburger
fast food
990
Corn
1
Ham
3 oz
1114
Tomato soup
1 cup
932
Lemon
1
Instant mashed
1 cup
potato
485
Canned tuna
3 oz
384

30 Compare your partner's information with the information shown on your half of this 'cartogram'

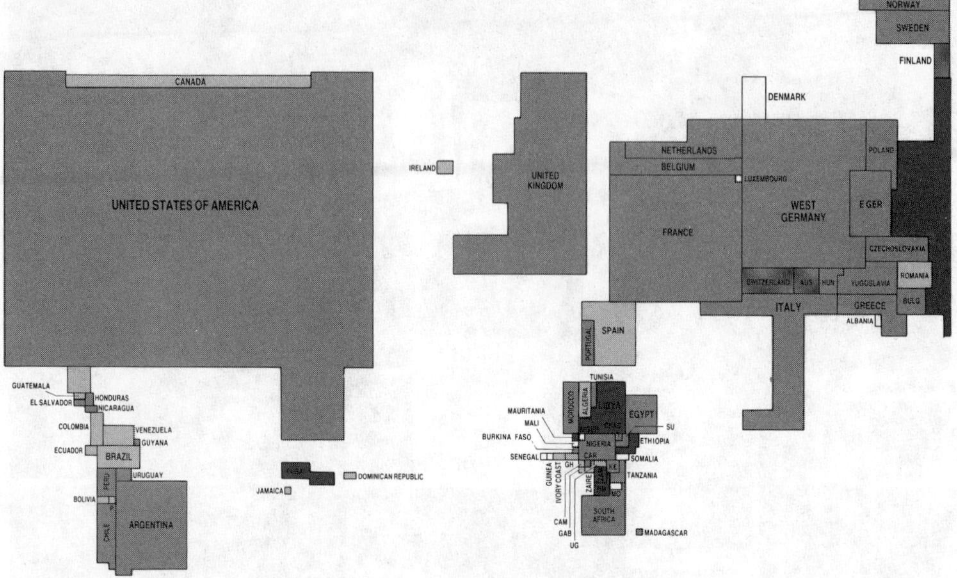

The larger the area the greater the share of world military spending.
The darker the tone the higher the proportion of GNP devoted to military spending.

- There are about 26 million people in the world's military forces and about 52 million workers keeping them supplied.
- Military aircraft, vehicles and ships as well as arms are exported to the majority of countries in the world by arms-producing countries.

Share of world arms sales
USSR 36%   USA 34%   France 10%   Italy 4%
UK 4%   W. Germany 3%

31 Although he claims to have 'the world's most wonderful job', Michael Buerk seems to have had some awful experiences. In El Salvador, for example, he was caught in the middle of a gun battle and had to crouch in terror in a ditch . . . compared to this a night in a Turkish jail and being seasick in a lobster boat seem luxurious. Worst of all, he says, was a sleepless night in northern Ethiopia searching unsuccessfully for a scorpion in his room. In Ethiopia, again, he witnessed terrible human suffering – an experience which changed his way of looking at the world. (100 words)

32

Look at this passage and read it to your partner. Discuss with your partner where you think this passage originally appeared. What is your partner's opinion about the content of each passage?

Anyone who has suffered from the effects of an impending thunderstorm will need no introduction to ions and their action upon the human system. Lethargy, dizziness, headache and even bouts of depression can all have their origin in these tiny invisible electrical particles that are always present in the atmosphere. On a more prosaic level, modern furnishing fabrics, air-conditioning and the increasing use of high technology electronic equipment all help to create a high level of positively-charged ions in an office environment.

33

Begin by studying the information below. Your partner has more information on the same theme and should be able to answer these questions:

What do negative (–ve) ions do?
How effective is an ioniser?
Does everyone feel a benefit from using one?
What do negative ions do to the brain?
Can negative ions help plants to grow?
How can we increase the number of negative ions?

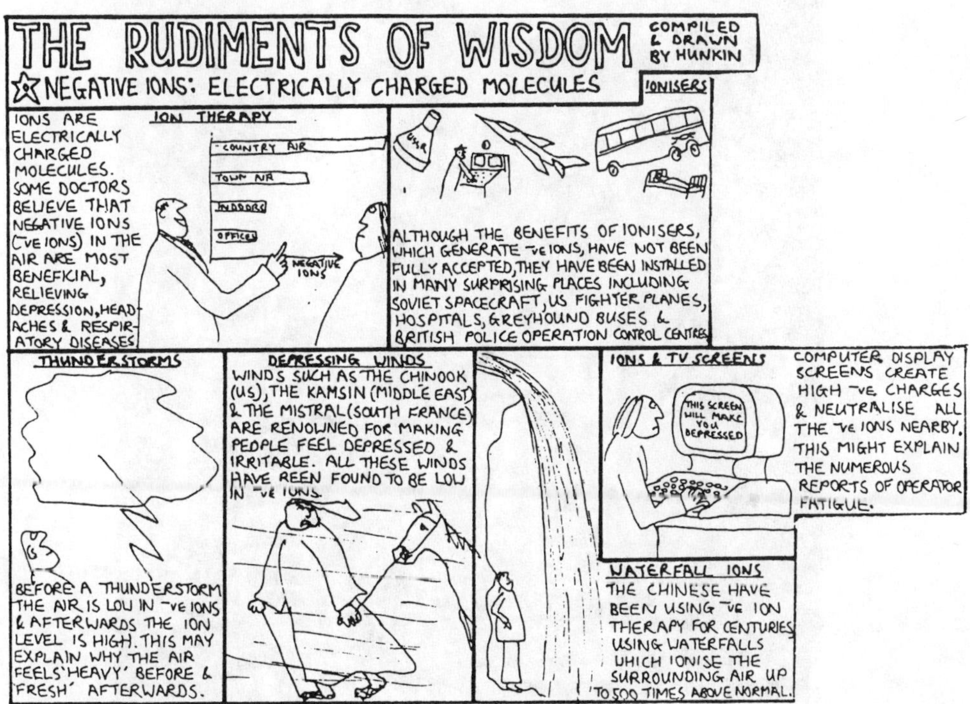

34 Tropical rain forests occupy only 6% of the world's land surface, yet they contain over half the world's plant and animal species. Here are some facts and ideas to use in a discussion with your partner. Study them *before* you start. Begin like this: 'Did you realise that . . .'

- This year a tropical rain forest 3 times the size of Switzerland is being destroyed.
- In 25 years the vast forests of Malaysia and Indonesia will have ceased to exist.
- A tropical rain forest contains an ecological system supporting an enormous variety of plants and animals, mostly unrecorded by science.
- The original native inhabitants, who understand the forests and the uses of their plants, are being eliminated or displaced.
- Farmers cut and burn the trees to plant crops. For a few years they get harvests but then the nutrients are used up and erosion begins. The farmers move on, leaving behind a wasteland that can never be replanted as forest.
- One cause of the destruction is shortsightedness – seeing only a short-term profit and ignoring the long-term effects.
- There is no hope of stopping the destruction if we remain blind to the rate of destruction and if governments continue to support the headlong exploitation of natural resources.

35 Answer your partner's questions about this picture before you ask him or her the questions below.

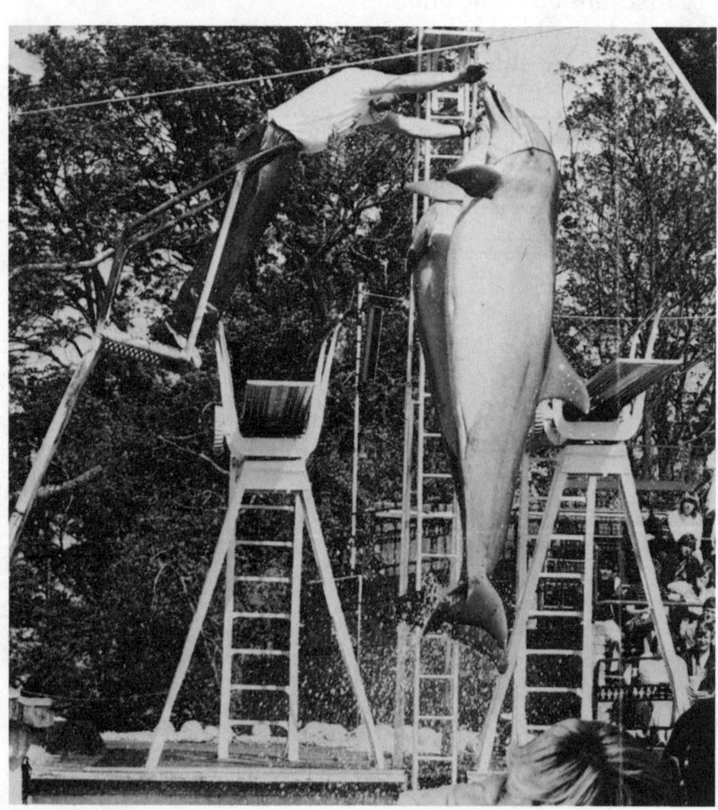

What does your picture show?
When do you think it was painted?
What is the boy going to do and why?
What is your reaction to this picture?
Why could a similar scene not occur today in your own country?
How does the view of nature depicted here differ from your own?
Are you an 'animal lover'? Why (not)?
What can we learn from studying animals?

36

Begin by asking your partner (the 'candidate') these questions about his or her photo, which shows an elderly couple dozing in the sun:

What's happening in your picture?
Why is the man's hand on the bag?
What kind of people are they? How old are they?
Where do you think the picture was taken?
Could it have been taken in your country? Why not?
What would it be like to be the same age as the couple in the photo?
What facilities and services are available to the very old in your country? Are the old cared for, or neglected?

Afterwards, answer your partner's questions about this picture:

37 It's your turn first to ask your partner questions about his or her photograph, so look at page 12 and ask the questions shown there.
After that, answer your partner's questions about this photo:

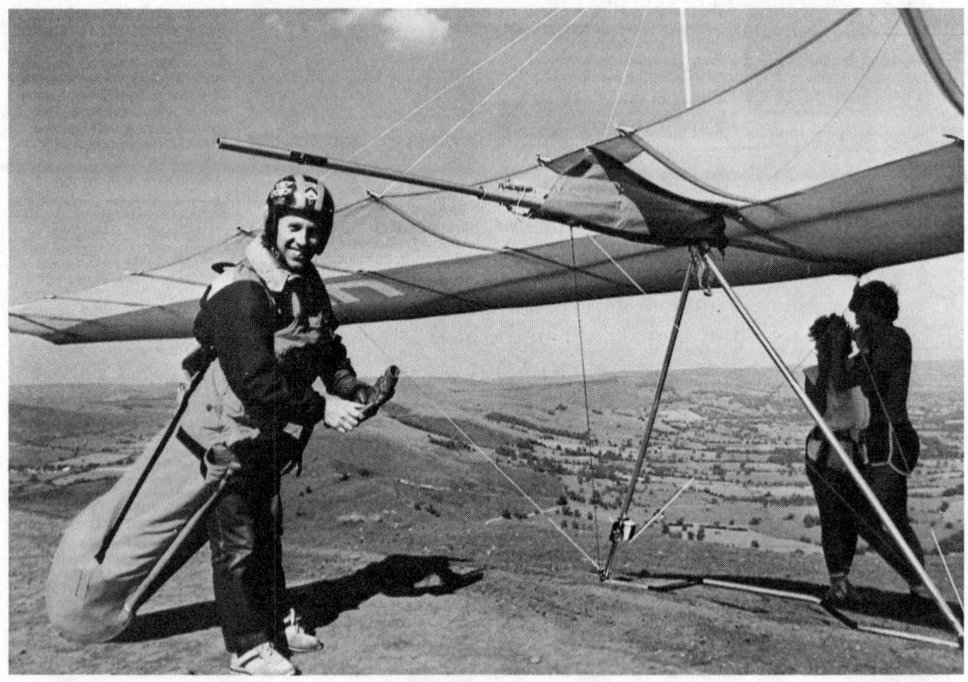

38 Below are definitions of some of the words on page 26 – your partner has definitions of the others. Work out together what the difference is between the words by explaining your own information but **not** by reading it aloud – try to summarise the information in your own words.

accent [C; (U)] a particular way of speaking, usu connected with a country, area, or class: *He speaks with a German accent. There are many accents in the English-speaking world. She studies different types of accent.*

frown 1 [IØ] to draw the hair-covered parts above the eyes (**the eyebrows**) together in anger or effort, to show disapproval, or to protect the eyes against strong light, causing lines to appear on the forehead: *She frowned when the sun got in her eyes. 'The boys are late,' he said, frowning anxiously at the clock. The teacher frowned at the noisy class.* **2** [T1] to express by doing this: *The teacher frowned his disapproval at the noisy class.* **3** [IØ] (*fig*) (of a thing) to have a dangerous or frightening appearance when seen from below: *The mountains frowned down on the plains.*

jargon [U; C] *often derog* language that is hard to understand, esp because it is full of special words known only to members of a certain group: *He spoke in a meaningless jargon. The jargon of scientists isn't easy to understand. The explanations in a dictionary must be kept as free of jargon as possible.*

sarcasm [U] speaking or writing which tries to hurt someone's feelings, esp by expressions which clearly mean the opposite to what is felt: *'Thank you for bringing back my bicycle so quickly; you've only had it six months,' he said with heavy sarcasm.*

synonym a word with the same or nearly the same meaning as another word in the same language: *'Sad' and 'unhappy' are synonyms.*

prepositional verb *also* **fused phrasal verb** a phrasal verb formed from a verb and a preposition, as in the sentence *'I came across* (= met) *an old friend last week'*.

chuckle a quiet laugh: *He gave a chuckle as he read her letter.*

idiom 1 a phrase which means something different from the meanings of its separate words: *'To be hard up' is an English idiom meaning 'to lack money'*. **2** the way of expression typical of a person or a people in their use of language: *The French and the English idioms have very different characters. Each writer has his own idiom, some more difficult to understand than others.*

39

Your partner has the details of the first half of the voyage shown below. Find out about it and mark the route Naomi James took on the map. Then tell your partner about the second half of the voyage.

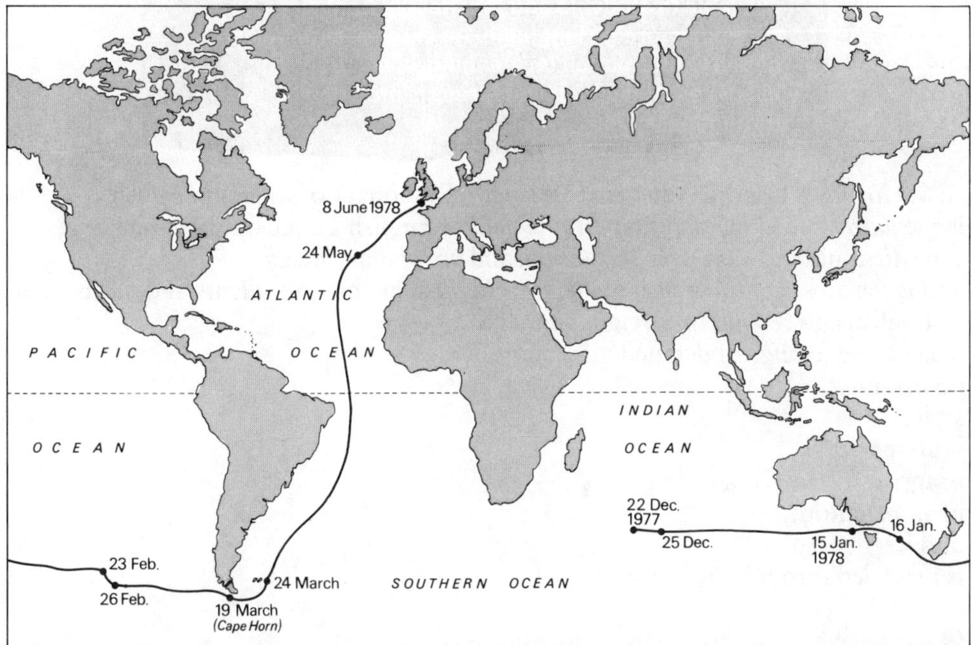

22 Dec 1977: . . . nearly drowned
25 Dec: Christmas dinner – roast chicken, artichokes, asparagus, white wine
15 Jan: Rendezvous off Tasmania for spare parts and food supplies
16 Jan: Terrible storm – waves 15 m high
23 Feb: Mast damaged in another storm
26 Feb: CAPSIZED
19 March: Rounded Cape Horn with icebergs visible to starboard
24 March: Stopped at Falkland Islands (Malvinas) for repairs
24 May: Rendezvous at sea off the Azores – saw Rob again for first time this year
8 June 1978: Arrived back in Dartmouth. First woman to sail single-handed round world. Fastest ever time for the voyage – 262 days.

40

This passage is part of the 'blurb' on the dustjacket of a well-known dictionary. Your partner has the blurb from another dictionary. Listen to your partner's reading and then read yours aloud to your partner.

To make it easier to read, it is reprinted beneath in 'breath-sized chunks' with *stressed syll*ables in *ital*ics. When reading from this version, pause briefly at the end of each line to draw breath and only let your voice fall sharply where there is a full stop.

A S Hornby's Oxford Advanced Learner's Dictionary of Current English is the world's leading dictionary in the field of English Language Teaching.
This dictionary covers over 60 000 vocabulary items and is the most comprehensive reference book available to students and teachers of English as a second or foreign language. An extensive range of detailed information on meaning, style, grammar, usage, pronunciation and stress is provided throughout.

*A. S. Horn*by's Oxford Ad*vanced Lear*ner's *Dic*tionary of C*ur*rent *Eng*lish
is the *world's lead*ing *dic*tionary in the *field* of English *Lan*guage *Teach*ing.
This *dic*tionary, *co*vers over *six*ty *thous*and voc*ab*ulary *i*tems
and is the most compre*hen*sive *ref*erence *book* a*vail*able to *stu*dents and *tea*chers of *Eng*lish as a *sec*ond or *for*eign *lan*guage.
An ex*ten*sive *range* of *de*tailed infor*ma*tion
on *mea*ning,
style,
*gram*mar,
*us*age,
pro*nun*ciation,
and *stress*
is pro*vid*ed through*out*.

● Decide which of the blurbs is more persuasive.

41

Begin by listening to your partner reading the first half of a newspaper article. Then read this passage, the continuation of the same article, to your partner.

Pupils would be assessed by teachers' observations and other criteria, he said, and the decision would lead to higher standards of education.

Mr Miguel Basanta, secretary of a Madrid Parents' Association, supported the move: " A child must study . . but what we are opposed to is that they should be given such a weight of work after school that it keeps them busy until they go to bed.

" They've got to have time to play and meet other children," he said.

Find out your partner's opinion about this item, which appeared in *The Guardian*.

42 Begin by answering your partner's questions about this photograph. Then ask your partner the questions on page 38.

43 Look at this passage and read it to your partner. Discuss with your partner where you think this passage originally appeared. What is your partner's opinion about the content of each passage?

The afternoon 'Office Blues' may not always be due to lunchtime activities! Similar conditions in the home can be aggravated by cigarette smoke, pollen and dust in suspension in the air. The Davis Ionisers are designed to restore the atmospheric 'balance' by emitting a constant stream of negatively-charged ions which both attract and neutralise their counterparts to produce an environment more conducive to alertness and well-being. Similarly, cigarette smoke, pollen and dust particles are neutralised and tend to be carried floorwards rather than remaining suspended.

44 Study this reproduction in silence for a few moments, so that you can describe it *in detail* to your partner. Describe what appears to be happening, what might have happened earlier and what might happen later. Explain what it is you like and dislike about it.

But first, find out about your partner's picture.

Afterwards, have a look at your partner's picture and give your own views on it.

Think of another painting that you particularly like, or which you remember well, and describe it to your partner.

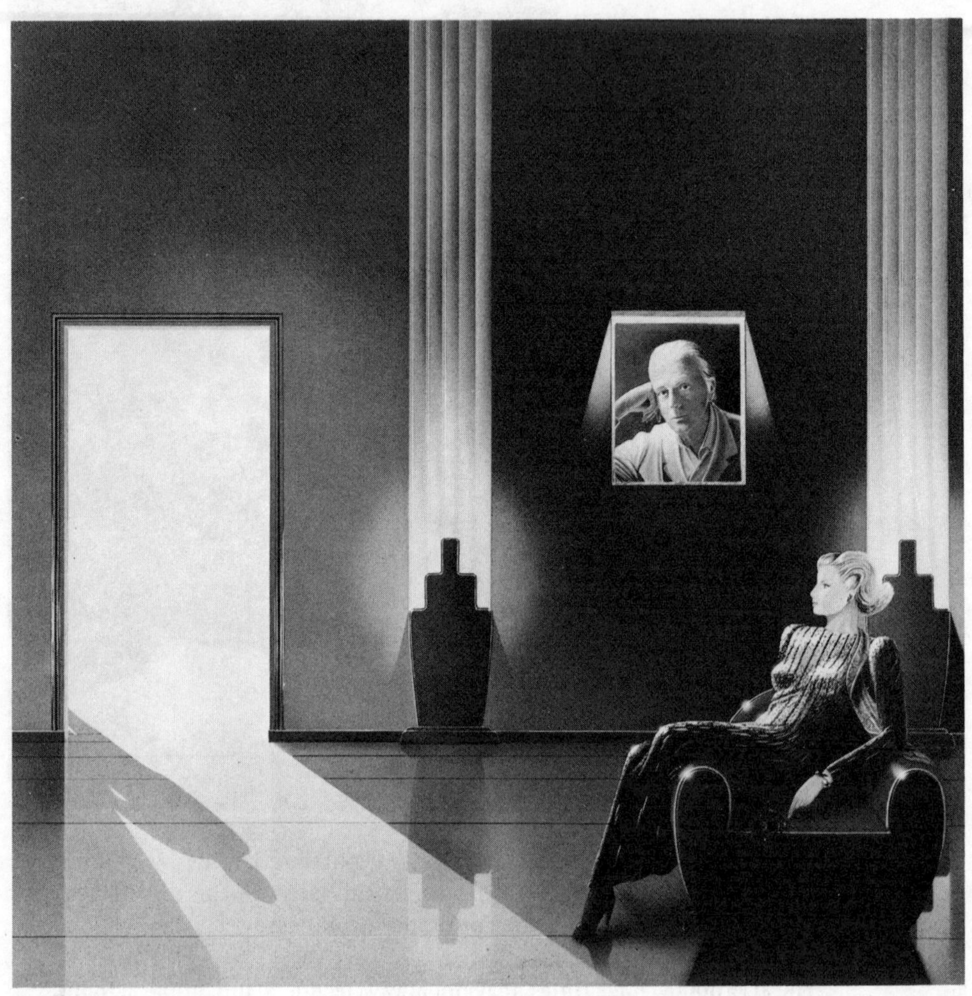

Parfums Givenchy

45

To make it easier to read the passage, the version beneath is printed in 'breath-sized chunks' and has the *catenation* marked.
Read your description *second.*

> **FOWEY, Cornwall**
>
> **Fowey has been a busy port since the Middle Ages. It is a delightful old town with narrow streets running steeply down to quays where pirates and smugglers once unloaded their cargoes. Nowadays the harbour is full of fishing boats and pleasure craft, though ocean-going ships still use the port to take on china clay. Across the wide harbour is the village of Polruan, connected to Fowey by a passenger ferry. Fowey today is a yachtsman's paradise and nearby sandy beaches and spectacular cliff-top walks make it an ideal centre for visitors.**

/fɔɪ/

Fowey has been a busy port since the Middle Ages.
It is a delightful old town
with narrow streets running steeply down to quays
where pirates and smugglers once unloaded their cargoes.
Nowadays the harbour is full of fishing boats and pleasure craft,
though ocean-going ships still use the port to take on china clay.
Across the wide harbour is the village of Polruan, /pɒlruːən/
connected to Fowey by a passenger ferry.
Fowey today is a yachtsman's paradise
and nearby sandy beaches and spectacular cliff-top walks
make it an ideal centre for visitors.

- Where do you think each text was taken from? What details of the style and content reveal the origin of the passages?

46

Before you start talking, make some notes in answer to the questions below. Then ask your partner the questions and give your own answers. Your partner has different questions to ask *you.*

Who are your favourite composers?
Why do you enjoy / not enjoy classical music?
Who are your favourite stage actors?
Why do you enjoy / not enjoy going to the theatre?
Who are your favourite film directors?
Why do you enjoy / not enjoy the cinema?
What are your favourite musical shows?
Why do you enjoy / not enjoy musicals?
What are your favourite ballets?
Why do you enjoy / not enjoy ballet and dance?
Who are your favourite sportsmen and women?
Why do you enjoy / not enjoy watching sports?

47

Look at the information given below about the advantages and disadvantages of spending a holiday in some exotic parts of the world. Use it as the starting point for a discussion with your partners, who have more information about the same places.

The Pros

● Scenically a really beautiful island for the imaginative traveller – unspoilt and relatively little developed. Try to explore the island before leaving – you won't regret it! ● An Indian Ocean island rich in history and culture, far more so than, for example, Seychelles, Mauritius or the West Indies. ● Generally predictable seasonal weather patterns – 'monsoons' during February – March and July – September. ● The friendliness of the island people is a delightful and unforgettable 'bonus'. ● Local prices tend to offer excellent value – both for 'extras' and souvenirs.	**SRI LANKA**

The Cons

SOUTH PACIFIC	● Some of the islands have an isolated location and involve long and sometimes complex flying arrangements. ● Although costs of meals and such like are reasonable in the South Pacific, 'extras' in French Polynesia tend to be expensive due to the high cost of living. ● Weather is an important factor, December through to April being the months when violent tropical storms occur, however they are usually infrequent and tend to be of brief duration. ● The arrival and departure times of the international flights tend to be in the small hours.
SOUTH EAST ASIA	

48

The rearranged version of the news item should help you to read it more fluently.

Bird brained

A YEAR-long search by a British naturalist, Dick Watling, in Fiji for a bird thought to be extinct ended when it crashed on his head. The bird, known as MacGillivray's petrel, was recorded for the first and last time 129 years ago. Mr Watling lured one in at night from the sea using flashlights and recordings. It crashed on his head and after examining the bird he let it go.—Reuter.

Bird brained

A year-long search by a British naturalist, Dick Watling, in Fiji
for a bird thought to be extinct
ended when it crashed on his head.
The bird,
known as MacGillivray's petrel, /məgɪlɪvreɪz petrəl/
was recorded for the first and last time a hundred and twenty-nine years ago.
Mr Watling lured one in at night from the sea
using flashlights and recordings.
It crashed on his head
and after examining the bird he let it go.

49

Find out about your partner's picture by asking the questions on page 178.

Then answer your partner's questions about this picture.

50

Your partner has the first and third parts of the article.

1 Find out about the first part of the article from your partner.

2 In your own words, tell your partner about the second part of the article. Answer any questions he or she may have.

5 Find out about the third part of the article from your partner.

Second part

It took the wily Mexican no time at all to discover that the new one peso was the same size as the US quarter, yet was less than one fiftieth its value. The result is that US coin machine operators across the length of the 2,000-mile border are screaming.

In a consumer society where a coin in the slot will buy almost everything from a fluffy toy to a car-wash, the Mexicans are cashing in. "We've lost thousands of dollars," said a spokesman for a vending machine company in Dallas, referring only to the fate suffered over a short period of time by his bubble-gum machines.

Many slot-machine traders are refusing to speak to the press in the hope that the word will not spread. Too late, however, since it is already common knowledge among the millions of Mexicans who come across the border each year — many of them illegally, searching for work — that a week's laundry can be done for two new pesos (less than one English penny) and four pesos (about 1½p) will get you a packet of cigarettes.

Texas has been the worst-hit state, but the new peso, like the Mexicans, is migrating northwards. Poetic justice has already seen many turn up in Louisiana, while millions might be expected soon in Chicago, which, after Mexico City and Guadalajara, rates as the city with the third largest Mexican population in the world.

51

DON'T WORRY. THIS'LL DO NICELY.

The good news was I'd charged the air-tickets to the American Express Card. When you do this, American Express automatically arrange insurance at no extra charge, which, subject to the conditions of the cover, takes care not only of accidents but flight delays and lost luggage as well. It means you can spend up to £100 on meals and refreshments each time you're delayed four hours or more – which certainly eased the pain in Edmonton and Amsterdam.

As for the luggage … if it's still missing after 48 hours, they let you spend up to £200 replacing your things, and that's on top of the £100 luggage delay insurance. How many cards give you that kind of cover!

I even managed an eleventh-hour reprieve on the birthday fiasco. I phoned the theatre and booked two seats on the Card for that evening. Maybe that's why they say you get more than just a card with American Express.

DON'T LEAVE HOME WITHOUT US.

A The text on the previous page accompanied the pictures that your partner is looking at. Ask your partner the following:

1 What do your pictures show? Describe them in detail.
2 What might they be advertising, do you think? Can you suggest several possible types of product or service?
3 If I told you they were part of an advertisement for American Express, what questions would you ask me?

(Explain how the text above fits with the pictures your partner has been describing to you.)

B Then answer your partner's questions about the picture below:

MISSING

52

The newspaper article below is incomplete. Your partner has the missing paragraphs. Retell the story between you, in your own words, taking it in turns with each of the missing paragraphs.

Roll on Christmas in Moscow

From UPI in Moscow

Toilet tissue is in short supply in the Russian capital, as well as elsewhere throughout the Soviet Union. The new scheme is intended to alleviate the long queues by having shoppers buy something like "toilet paper futures" rather than the precious tissue itself. Russians who tried to explain the new marketing idea to a Western friend said that it worked something like a magazine subscription.

"I haven't seen it in our store yet," another man said. "But my mother has enrolled for a subscription, and she thinks it's wonderful. She called me all excited and said: "I hope for the day that you too can buy toilet paper this way." Such enthusiasm for ordinary toilet paper is not really unusual. Shoppers who find a supply of the precious household product usually buy as much as they can carry.

Once the word spreads about a store stocked with toilet paper, either by word of mouth or as a result of spotters' reports of toilet-paper necklaces moving along the avenues, the shelves are soon bare.

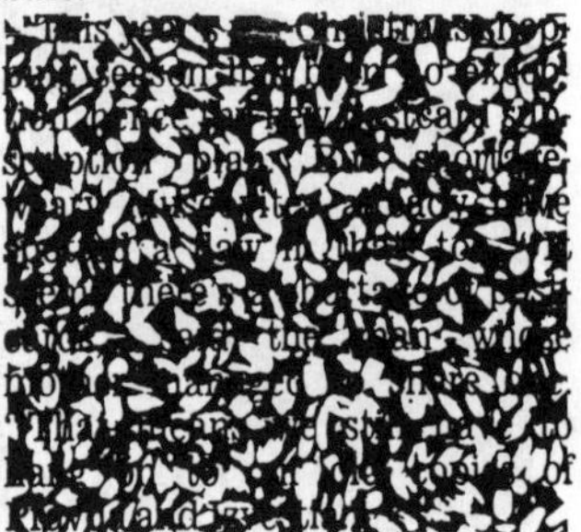

53

This amusing extract comes from *Up the Garden Path* by Sue Limb. Your partners have different extracts from the same book.

Read your extract out to your partners. Concentrate on conveying the wryly humorous tone of the passage.

4

All good things must come to an end: and so, sometimes, must the bad ones. The appalling Christmas holidays gave way, in the end, to the mis-named Spring Term. That term in which the sixty-two varieties of flu rage, the Deputy Head contemplates suicide and the earth seems sunk for ever in its iron sleep. Izzy and Maria taught in Islington. Izzy got the tube to /ɪzlɪŋtən/
Notting Hill, where Maria picked her up and drove with her usual horrifying dash down—or rather against—the Euston /ju:stən/
Road. One of the disadvantages of teaching in Islington was that the sun was in your eyes both on your way to school and your way home. Maria greeted this as a sign of the hostility of

the universe; for Izzy it was an excuse for exotic sunglasses. In January, of course, there was more often than not no sun at all, only a kind of dismal veil of fog and fumes.

● When all three extracts have been read, discuss what connections there are between them and what the novel they come from is about. What have you discovered about the characters and the plot?

54

Answer your partner's questions about this picture.

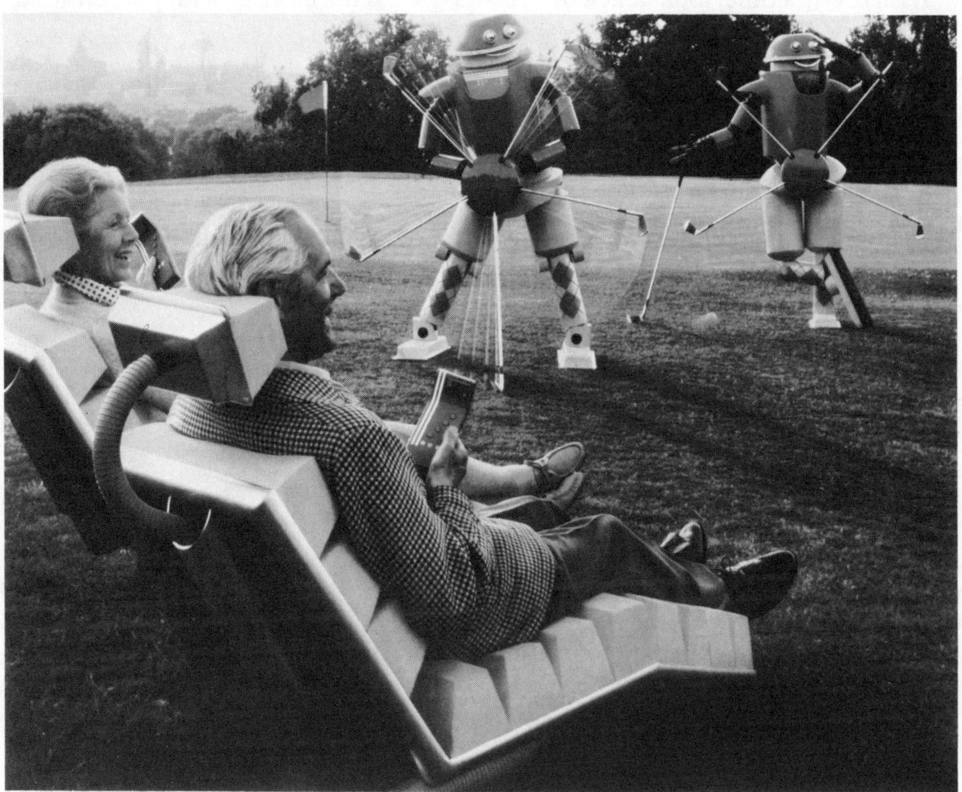

Then ask your partner these questions about his or her picture:

What does your photograph show?
How is the man feeling?
Why do you think he feels so pleased?
Would you be so happy if you were in his shoes?
What do you think he's just been doing and what's he going to do next?
Do you enjoy using computers? Or do you find them intimidating?
Describe your first experiences of using a computer.
How do/would you feel about using a computer regularly in your job or studies?

55

Ask your partners the following questions:

1 What is your impression so far of the prescribed book you're reading? What do you find appealing about it?
What do you find difficult about it?
2 Is it the kind of book you'd normally read for pleasure?
Is it a book that you 'can't put down', or is it heavy going?
3 How relevant does it seem to your own tastes, experiences and concerns?
4 What are your reactions to its style? And to its plot? And to its characters?
5 Can you think of a specific example of something you've found particularly interesting, moving or amusing? Read out an extract to show what you mean, if possible.
6 If there's still time, look at activity 12 and discuss the more general points raised there.

56

Find out your partner's views on the following issues, which concern individual freedoms and State control.

Do you think State corporations should control the following services and industries:

- radio and television
- railways
- buses and long-distance coaches
- the telephone system
- electricity and gas supplies
- oil and petrol
- the steel manufacturing industry
- airlines
- motorways
- hospitals and medical services
- banking

or should they be operated by competing commercial companies?

Find out which of the above are, in fact, nationalised State-run industries in your partner's country.

57 Your partner has the missing paragraphs of this article. Take it in turns to read out the whole article to each other.

On a wing and a paper clip

THE painstaking building of paper aeroplanes in the office is usually a sure sign of an organisation full of time-servers, eking out the years to retirement. But the managers at Pitney Bowes in Harlow have managed the long haul of turning it into a creative activity, setting the mind free to fly off in new directions.

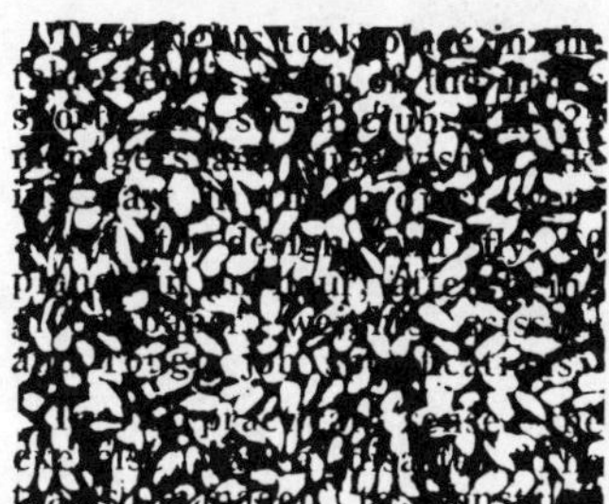

The benefits came elsewhere. "It did us a whole lot of good," said Pitney Bowes' managing director Ron Williams, second from left in the picture above. "It stimulated lateral thinking and innovation, and made us question everything we do in production, design and organisation."

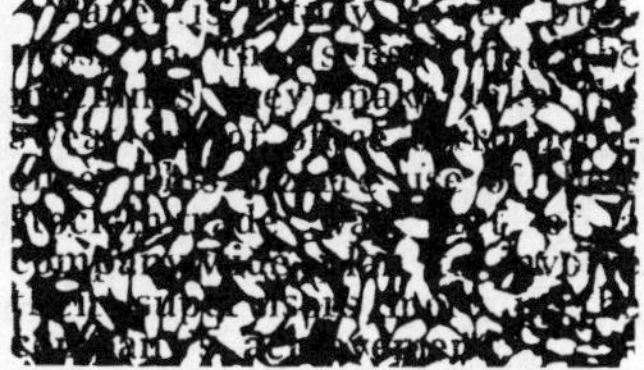

● Find out what your partner's views are on this method of management training.

58 El Salvador; gun battle, crouching in ditch, terrified
Turkish jail (one night)
Seasickness in lobster boat
Northern Ethiopia: sleepless night searching unsuccessfully for scorpion
Ethiopia: terrible human suffering – changed his way of looking at the world

59

Ask your partner these questions:

What does your picture show?
What kind of people are they?
What are they protesting about, do you think?
What other methods could they use to show their views?
What methods are common in your country to show people's opposition to government policies?
How can a government react to protests from the people?
Is there any particular policy of your country's present government that you feel strongly about?

Answer your partner's questions about this photograph:

60

Look at the predictions below and, in your own words, tell your partner about them. Your partner has other predictions to tell you about. Discuss the effects that each event might have on people's lives. Would you look forward to or dread each prediction coming true?

by 1996: The first human being will be successfully brought back to life after being frozen and thawed.
by 1999: Schools will be open all the year round, with pupils attending classes as often or as little as they wish.
by 2003: There will be 2,000-seat aircraft flying hourly between major cities.
by 2009: There will be controls built into your clothing to change the colours and designs of the fabric at the touch of a switch.
by 2015: Every form of cancer will be curable, if discovered soon enough.
by 2030: The average human being will live to the age of 120.
by 2030: It will be possible to grow buildings by programming crystal structures.

61

Your partner will begin by reading out an earlier extract from the same text. Then read this extract to your partner.

In the dual economy of a typical developing country, we may find fifteen per cent of the population in the modern sector, mainly confined to one or two big cities. The other eighty-five per cent exists in the rural areas and small towns. For reasons which will be discussed, most of the development effort goes into the big cities, which means that eighty-five per cent of the population are largely by-passed. What is to become of them? Simply to assume that the modern sector in the big cities will grow until it has absorbed almost the entire population – which is, of course, what has happened in many of the highly developed countries – is utterly unrealistic. Even the richest countries are groaning under the burden which such a maldistribution of population inevitably imposes.

(from *Small is Beautiful* by E. F. Schumacher)

● Discuss with your partner the points made in the two extracts you've read.

62

Your partner has the other half of these two 'cartograms'. Find out about your partner's information by asking questions. Discuss what conclusions you reach from studying the information given.

NATIONAL INCOME (the larger the area, the higher the share of total world GNP)

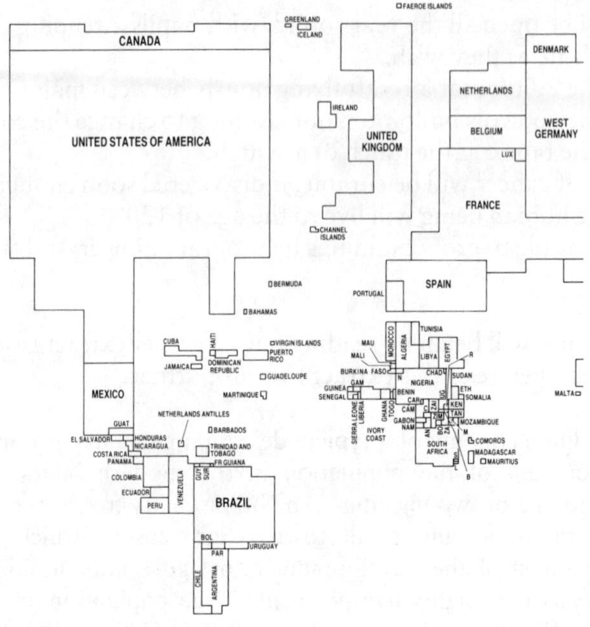

POPULATION (the larger the area, the greater the share of world population)

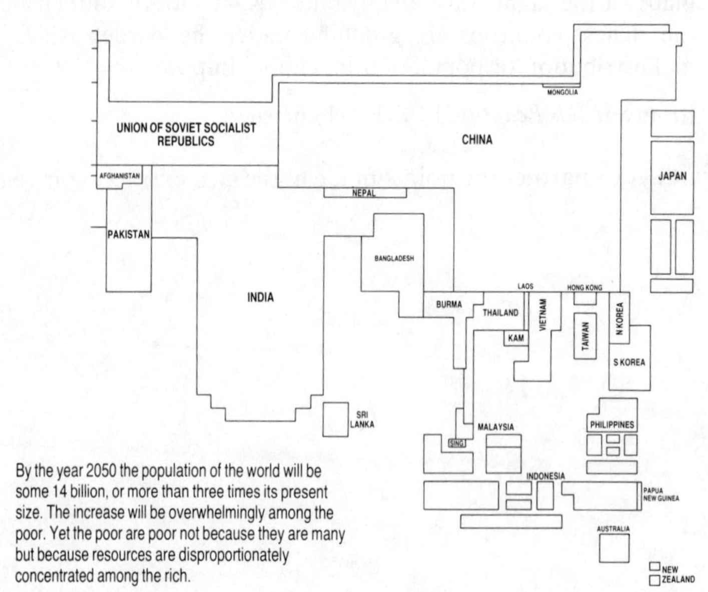

By the year 2050 the population of the world will be some 14 billion, or more than three times its present size. The increase will be overwhelmingly among the poor. Yet the poor are poor not because they are many but because resources are disproportionately concentrated among the rich.

63 THE AZTECS

Largest extent of Aztec empire (1519): whole of Central Mexico from the Caribbean to the Pacific.

Capital city: Tenochtitlan (now Mexico City) – largest city in the world with 200,000 people. Built on islands in centre of Lake Texcoco: canals as streets, pyramids, temples, palaces filled with gold and treasures.

Constantly at war with surrounding subject tribes, who were forced to supply them with food and gold. Prisoners of war always needed too, see below.

Highly developed agriculture (maize originates from this area – also chocolate).

Gold-working techniques.

They did not have writing, iron-working techniques, the wheel or gunpowder.

Worshipped gods who demanded human sacrifices: hearts torn out of living bodies. 10,000 to 50,000 prisoners of war each year died in this way.

Belief that Quetzalcoatl (a white-skinned, bearded god) would return from the east.

Last king Moctezuma II killed by Cortés in 1521. Aztec empire destroyed.

64

The chart shows how many milligrams of sodium are present in various foods. Your partners have different information. Find out what your partners know and discuss the implications of this on your own diets.

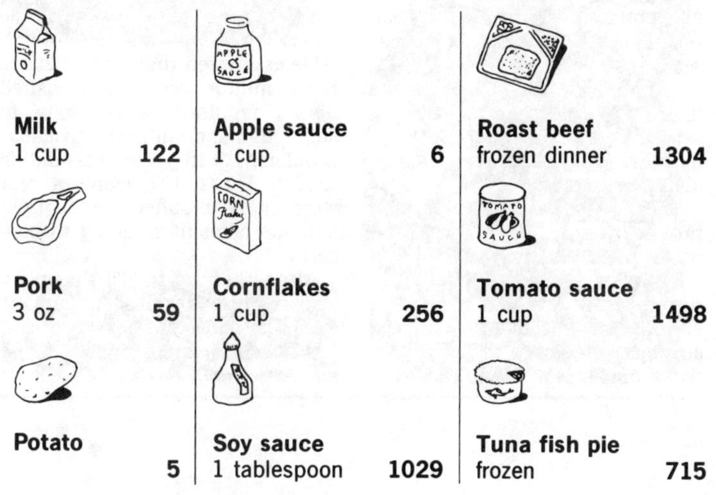

Milk
1 cup 122
Pork
3 oz 59
Potato
5
Apple sauce
1 cup 6
Cornflakes
1 cup 256
Soy sauce
1 tablespoon 1029
Roast beef
frozen dinner 1304
Tomato sauce
1 cup 1498
Tuna fish pie
frozen 715

65

Read your parts of this article out to your partners. They have the the missing paragraphs.

When you have finished, discuss your reactions to the article.

'Deafness risk' in personal hi-fi

By Andrew Veitch

1 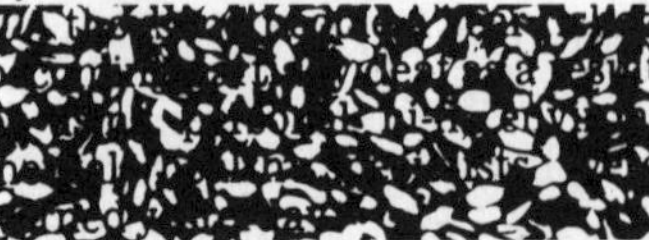

2 Headphones plugged into home stereo units and cassette players were potentially more dangerous than discos or pop concerts, Mr John Bickerdike, principal lecturer at Leeds Polytechnic, told the Institute of Environmental Health Officers' annual congress in Scarborough.

3 The widespread use of stereo

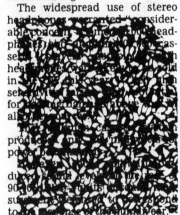

4

5

6 Levels above 100dB(A) were therefore easily obtainable. Yet the safety limit for factories was 90dB(A), and at this level, 17 per cent of workers experienced hearing loss sufficient to cause difficulty in understanding speech.

7 Makers should warn customers

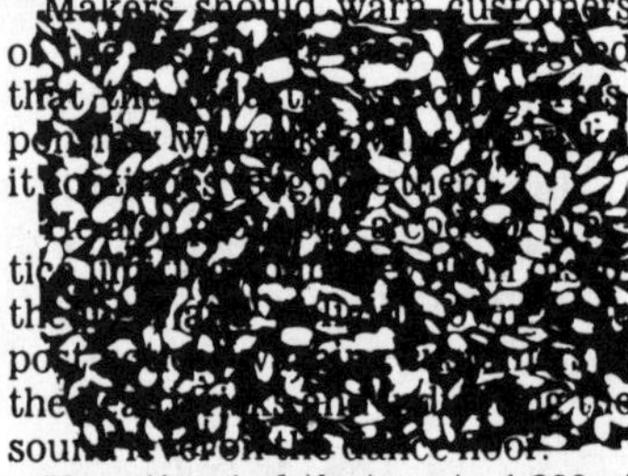

8

9 He estimated that up to 1,200 of the 6 million people who visited discos regularly were likely to suffer damage sufficient to cause problems in understanding speech. Up to 100 people a year were likely to suffer similar problems as a result of going to concerts.

10 Altogether, up to 3,000 people a

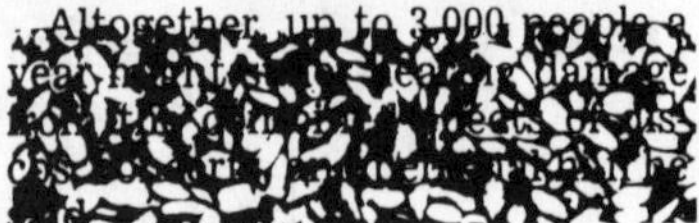

66

Answer your partner's questions about this photograph:

Ask your partner these questions about his or her photograph:

What is happening in the photograph? Describe the people there.
Where do you think it was taken?
Would you join their demonstration?
Who is their demonstration intended to influence, do you think?
What are your own views on nuclear disarmament?
What can be done to reduce the likelihood of a nuclear war breaking out?
What is your government's policy on nuclear weapons?

67

Compare the information given here with the information your partner has.

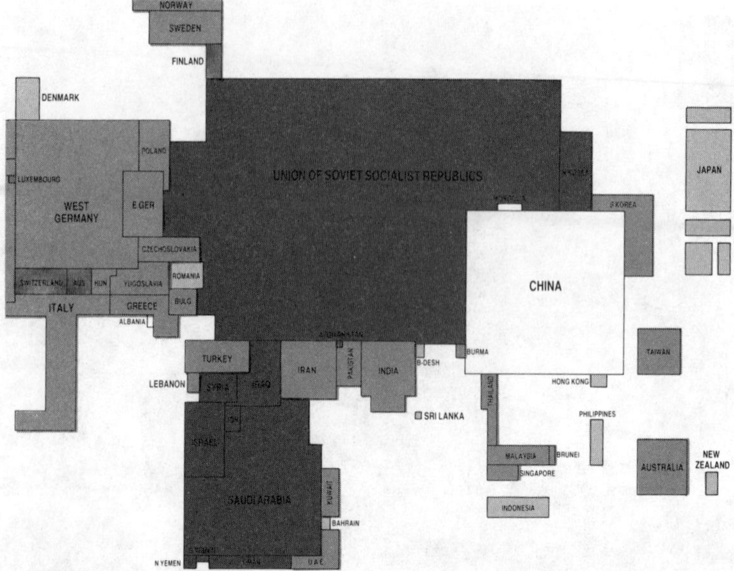

The darker the tone the higher the proportion of GNP devoted to military spending. The larger the area the greater the share of world military spending (the USA and USSR together account for over 50%).

- There are about 3,000 military bases located on foreign soil in other countries in the world (+ innumerable 'military advisers').
- Major air, sea or land bases overseas:
  USA in over 20 countries; USSR, France and UK each in about 10 countries; plus nearly 20 other countries with military bases in another country.

68

Begin by studying the information on the right. Your partner has more information on the same theme and should be able to answer these questions:

What exactly are negative ions?
What kind of people use ionisers?
Why do we feel better after a thunderstorm?
Why are some winds depressing?
How do waterfalls create negative ions?
Why is watching TV or using a computer display screen fatiguing?

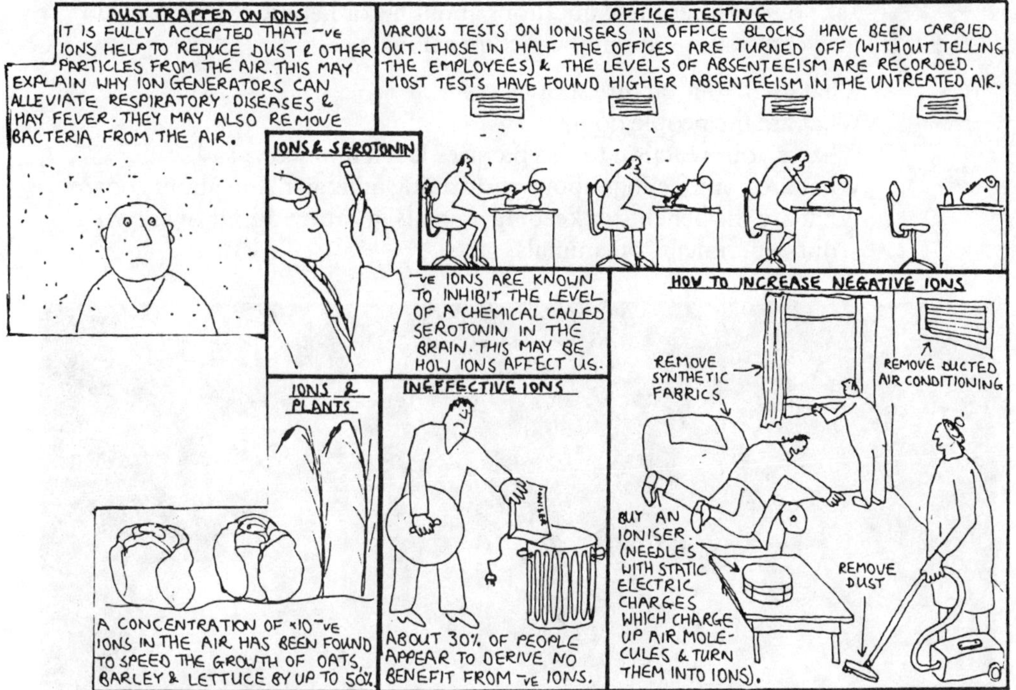

DUST TRAPPED ON IONS
IT IS FULLY ACCEPTED THAT -VE IONS HELP TO REDUCE DUST & OTHER PARTICLES FROM THE AIR. THIS MAY EXPLAIN WHY ION GENERATORS CAN ALLEVIATE RESPIRATORY DISEASES & HAY FEVER. THEY MAY ALSO REMOVE BACTERIA FROM THE AIR.
OFFICE TESTING
VARIOUS TESTS ON IONISERS IN OFFICE BLOCKS HAVE BEEN CARRIED OUT. THOSE IN HALF THE OFFICES ARE TURNED OFF (WITHOUT TELLING THE EMPLOYEES) & THE LEVELS OF ABSENTEEISM ARE RECORDED. MOST TESTS HAVE FOUND HIGHER ABSENTEEISM IN THE UNTREATED AIR.
IONS & SEROTONIN
-VE IONS ARE KNOWN TO INHIBIT THE LEVEL OF A CHEMICAL CALLED SEROTONIN IN THE BRAIN. THIS MAY BE HOW IONS AFFECT US.
HOW TO INCREASE NEGATIVE IONS
REMOVE SYNTHETIC FABRICS
REMOVE DUCTED AIR CONDITIONING
BUY AN IONISER. (NEEDLES WITH STATIC ELECTRIC CHARGES WHICH CHARGE UP AIR MOLECULES & TURN THEM INTO IONS).
REMOVE DUST
IONS & PLANTS
A CONCENTRATION OF ×10⁻VE IONS IN THE AIR HAS BEEN FOUND TO SPEED THE GROWTH OF OATS, BARLEY & LETTUCE BY UP TO 50%
INEFFECTIVE IONS
IONISER
ABOUT 30% OF PEOPLE APPEAR TO DERIVE NO BENEFIT FROM -VE IONS.

69

Tropical rain forests occupy only 6% of the world's land surface, yet they contain over half the world's plant and animal species. Here are some facts and ideas to use in a discussion with your partner. Study them *before* you start.

- Already half the world's forests have gone and the speed of destruction is accelerating. 40 hectares a minute are being irreplaceably destroyed.
- In 25 years the great forests of South America will have shrunk to a fraction of their present size.
- Plants that grow in the forests may be valuable to us as medicines and natural resources in the future.
- Tropical rain forests are self-contained ecological systems that grow on very poor soil. Most forest trees are very slow-growing.
- Desperately poor people often have no choice but to clear forests to produce food to survive.
- But governments are also to blame for their ignorance: it is not true that forests are suitable places for agriculture.
- The consumer demand for tropical timbers is also to blame.
- There is no hope of stopping the destruction if we just shrug our shoulders and do nothing.

70

Ask your partner these questions about his or her picture before you answer questions about the picture below.

What does your picture show?
What are the people doing?
What is your reaction to this picture? Is it a funny or a sad scene?
What are your feelings about performing animals? And about zoos?
What are the benefits of keeping animals in captivity? Or of carrying out experiments on animals?

71

To make it easier to read the passage, the version beneath is printed in 'breath-sized chunks' and the *catenation* is marked.
Read your description *last*.

LOOE, Cornwall

Looe has remained largely unspoiled over the centuries. East Looe and West Looe, which were first granted charters in the 14th century, stand on either side of a narrow estuary linked by an ancient bridge. The people of the area originally depended on seafaring, fishing and smuggling for their livelihood. Nowadays, however, the town welcomes holidaymakers attracted by the captivating charm and tranquillity of the place and by the sandy beach at the mouth of the river. Both the beach and the harbour are protected by a stone jetty known as the Banjo Pier because of its shape.

/luː/

Looe has remained largely unspoiled over the centuries.
East Looe and West Looe,
which were first granted charters in the 14th century,
stand on either side of a narrow estuary
linked by an ancient bridge.
The people of the area
originally depended on seafaring, fishing and smuggling for their livelihood.
Nowadays, however, the town welcomes holidaymakers
attracted by the captivating charm and tranquillity of the place
and by the sandy beach at the mouth of the river.
Both the beach and the harbour are protected by a stone jetty
known as the Banjo Pier because of its shape.

- Where do you think each text was taken from? What details of the style and content reveal the origin of the passages?

72

Begin by answering questions from your partner (the 'examiner') about this photograph:

Afterwards, ask your partner (the 'candidate') these questions about his or her photo, which shows a street scene.

What's happening in your photo?
Where and when do you think the photograph was taken?
Could it have been taken in your country? Why not?
What is your reaction to the situation shown here?
How would you feel if you met the two young men alone at night?
What is the cause of violent behaviour in society? Can it be 'cured'?

73 Look at this reproduction of a Victorian 'narrative painting'. Tell your partners what you think is the story behind this picture. Your partners' paintings show different parts of the same story. Then see if you can work out how the three scenes fit together and what must have happened in between.

Decide on suitable titles for the three paintings, and for the complete story.

74 This amusing extract comes from *Up the Garden Path* by Sue Limb. Your partners have different extracts from the same book.

After you have heard your partners' extracts, read yours out to them. Concentrate on conveying the mood of the passage, especially the hysterical despair welling up inside Izzy. The dialogue may require you to change your tone of voice to show that different characters are speaking.

8

Izzy made up a bed for Maria on the sofa. She wanted to phone Michael, but felt intimidated by Maria's grim face. Maria seemed to be evolving into a piece of furniture. She sat about, motionless, staring through the walls. Izzy, who could usually cheer people up quite easily, was utterly defeated and felt her spirits drain away out of some deep plughole of the soul, till nought remained but emptiness and scum. Once she'd made the bed up, though, she had an idea.

'Maria—let me sleep on the sofa. You have my bed.' With Maria safely stowed in the bedroom, she could manage a private phone call to Michael.

'Nonsense, Izzy. I wouldn't dream of it. I'll sleep here. This will be fine.'

'But I *want* you to sleep in my bed. I really do. Then you can lie in tomorrow and I won't disturb you.'

'I don't want to lie in tomorrow. No, really, Izzy, I'll be perfectly all right here.'

Izzy now discovered what the phrase *gnashing of teeth* meant. Actually, her whole body seemed to be gnashing slightly.

● When all three extracts have been read, discuss the connections between them. Can you guess what may have taken place between each scene described? What have you found out about the characters?

75

The chart shows how many milligrams of sodium are present in various foods. Your partners have complementary information. Find out what your partners know and discuss the implications of this on your own diets.

Steak
3 oz 55
Tomato
14
Tuna
3 oz 50
MILK
Dried milk powder
½ cup 322
Bacon
4 slices 548
POTATO CHIPS
Potato crisps
10 200
Apple pie
⅛ frozen 208
CORN
Canned corn
1 cup 384
Salt
1 teaspoon 1938

76

Look at the information given below about the advantages and disadvantages of spending a holiday in some exotic parts of the world. Use it as the starting point for a discussion with your partners, who have more information about the same places.

The Pros

● Dramatic scenery, white beaches and clear, multi-colour lagoons characterise the South Pacific, with only a few exceptions such as the main island of Tahiti. ● The people are generally very friendly, relaxed and welcome visitors with smiles and flowers. ● Western influence and tourism have brought advantages in the way of good watersports, sophisticated hotels and excellent restaurants to the main resorts, while outer islands remain relatively unspoilt.	**SOUTH PACIFIC**

The Cons

SOUTH EAST ASIA	● That excellent service doesn't automatically mean that you'll have no problems in South East Asia. English may be universal here, but language problems may occasionally annoy you. Don't let your irritation show. The people are more impressed by patience and good humour than by loud voiced confrontations. ● If you are on a comprehensive Far East tour, do make allowances for the different (often humid) climate zones you will be passing through. And remember that unbroken sunshine is something that South East Asia, like most other places on earth, does not guarantee you! ● The larger resorts and hotels cater for many groups on a year round basis – expect to to be inconvenienced a little when this happens.
SRI LANKA	

77 The rearranged version of this news item should help you to read it more fluently.

Hang-glider and eagle in Alpine air battle

Trento (AFP) – The Italian Alps were recently the scene of an eerie air battle between an eagle and an unfortunate hang-glider who had strayed into eagle territory.

Fabio Valentini, aged 30, was sailing over the Dolomites when he spotted an eagle circling above him. But before he could dodge it, the bird came for the glider slashing its wings with its beak and claws. The eagle attacked four or five times as Signor Valentini struggled to escape.

Hang-glider and eagle
in Alpine air battle

The Italian Alps
were recently the scene of an eerie air battle
between an eagle and an unfortunate hang-glider
who had strayed into eagle territory.
Fabio Valentini, aged thirty, was sailing over the Dolomites /dɒləmaɪts/
when he spotted an eagle circling above him.
But before he could dodge it,
the bird came for the glider
slashing its wings with its beak and claws.
The eagle attacked four or five times
as Signor Valentini struggled to escape.

78

Read your parts of this article out to your partners. They have the missing paragraphs.

When you have finished, discuss your reactions to the article.

'Deafness risk' in personal hi-fi

By Andrew Veitch

1 

2 in Scarborough.

3 The widespread use of stereo headphones warranted "considerable concern." Some 850,000 headphones and another 400,000 cassette players complete with headphones were likely to be sold in the UK this year. "Their high sensitivity raises their potential for hearing damage above that of all other sources."

4 The Walkman cassette system

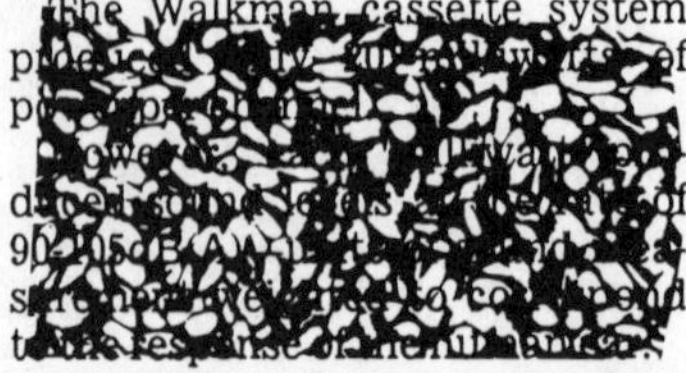

5

6 Levels

7 Makers should warn customers of the risks. "It may be argued that the industry is acting irresponsibly when, knowing the risks, it continues to ignore them."

8 He also proposed a code of prac-

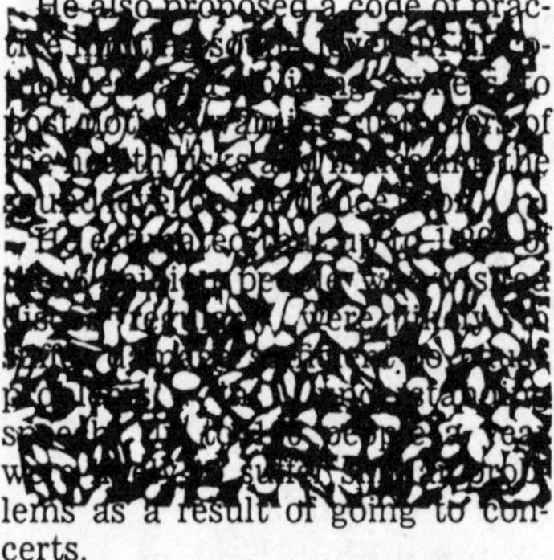

9 lems as a result of going to concerts.

10 Altogether, up to 3,000 people a year might suffer hearing damage from the combined effects of discos, concerts, and personal hi-fi he said.

79 Look at this reproduction of a Victorian 'narrative painting'. Tell your partners what you think is the story behind this picture. Your partners' paintings show different parts of the same story. Then see if you can work out how the three scenes fit together and what must have happened in between.

Decide on suitable titles for the three paintings and for the whole story.

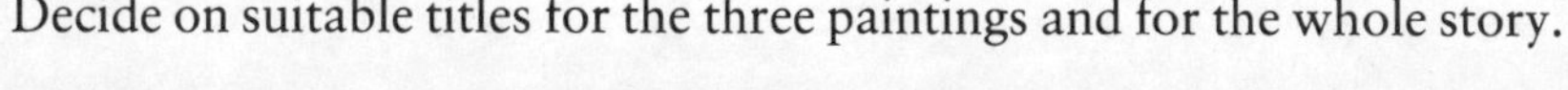

Acknowledgements

The author and publishers are grateful to the authors, publishers and others who have given permission for the use of copyright material identified in the text. It has not been possible to identify the sources of all the material used and in such cases the publishers would welcome information from copyright owners.

The Guardian and the following journalists and correspondents for their articles and letters which appeared in *The Guardian*: 4.3 Nigel Cross; 4.6 Iain Guest; 5.3 Tom Tickell; 6.2 Dennis Barker; 6.3; 6.10 and communication activities 11 and 50 Peter Chapman; 6.11 Penny Chorlton; 7.2 Christopher Reed; 9.2 Eve-Ann Prentice; 9.3 John Ezard; 9.3 Colin Brown; 9.4 Ian Aitken; 9.6 Dennis Johnson; 10.2 Stuart Wavell; 10.3 Peter David; 10.6 Jane McLoughlin; 11.4 Andrew Veitch; 11.6 Sir Clive Sinclair; 11.6 Peter Smee; 12.3; 12.6 Trish Silkin; 12.7; 13.3 Alex Brummer; 14.2 Michael O'Donnell; 14.6 Catherine Mant; 15.4 Ian Aitken; 15.6 Prof. Robert A. Hinde; 16.2 Richard Boston; 16.3 David Fairhall; 16.3; 18.2(3) Martin Wainwright; communication activities 27, 65 and 78 Andrew Veitch. 1.2 Jonathan Cape Ltd and the Estate of Peter Fleming for the extract from *Brazilian Adventure* by Peter Fleming; 1.3, 5.4, communication activities 33 and 68 reproduced by courtesy of *The Observer*, London. (*The Observer* publishes a resource pack of authentic source material for teachers of EFL. In nine monthly packs, from October to June, over 150 *Observer* articles are used, each with a specially written worksheet and exercises. Available by subscription only, further details from: The Observer EFL Service, 8 St Andrew's Hill, London EC4V 5JA); 1.4 The Rolex Watch Company Ltd; 1.6 Mitchell Beazley for the extract from *The Story of Africa* by Basil Davidson, published 1984; 2.2 Hodder & Stoughton Educational for the extract from *Language Made Plain* by Anthony Burgess; 2.3 Oxford University Press for the extract from *Stylistics and the Teaching of Literature* by Henry Widdowson; 2.3 and 3.3 Tessa Sayle Literary and Dramatic Agency and Jonathan Cape Ltd for the poems from *New Numbers* by Christopher Logue; 2.6 Penguin Books Ltd for the extract from *Stylistics* by G. W. Turner (Pelican Books 1973) copyright © G. W. Turner 1973; 3.2 Martin Secker & Warburg Ltd for the extract from *Wilt* by Tom Sharpe; 3.3 James McGibbon, the executor, and New Directions Publishing Corporation, for the poem from *The Collected Poems of Stevie Smith* (Penguin Modern Classics) copyright © 1972 by Stevie Smith; 3.4 Weidenfeld (Publishers) Ltd for the extract from *Jerusalem the Golden* by Margaret Drabble; 3.6 Penguin Books Ltd and Deborah Rogers Ltd for the extract from *Women's Rights* by Anna Coote and Tess Gill (Penguin Handbooks, third edition 1981) copyright © Anna Coote and Tess Gill 1974, 1977, 1981; 4.2 Collins Publishers and A. D. Peters & Co for the extract from *The Towers of Trebizond* by Rose Macaulay; 4.6 Reuters; 5.2 Collins Publishers for the extract from *Hollywood The Pioneers* by Kevin Brownlow; 5.6 The Prado and DACS for 'Guernica' by Picasso; BBC Publications and Alfred A. Knopf Inc for the extract from *The Shock of the New* by Robert Hughes copyright © 1980 by Robert Hughes; 5.11 *The Sunday Times* for the article which appeared on 1.7.84; 6.2 and 6.3 Associated Newspapers Group for the articles from *The Daily Mail*; 6.2 and 6.3 *The Times* for the articles which appeared on 28.6.84; 6.6 Michael Buerk for the article which appeared in *Airport* magazine; 7.3 Consumers' Association for the extract from *Which?*; 7.4 *The Times* for the article which appeared on 28.6.84; 7.6 Advertising Standards Authority; 8.2(1) William Heinemann Ltd for the extract from

Grapes of Wrath by John Steinbeck; 8.2(2) Gillon Aitken Ltd for the extract from *The Mosquito Coast* by Paul Theroux; 8.2(3) Jonathan Cape Ltd, executors of the Ernest Hemingway Estate and Charles Scribner's Sons for the extract from *A Farewell to Arms* by Ernest Hemingway copyright © 1929, copyright renewed © 1957 Ernest Hemingway; 8.3(1) Jonathan Cape Ltd, Salman Rushdie and Alfred A. Knopf Inc for the extract from *Midnght's Children* by Salman Rushdie; 8.3(2) Faber and Faber Publishers Ltd and A. P. Watt Ltd for the extract from *The Affirmation* by Christopher Priest; 8.3(3) Weidenfeld (Publishers) Ltd for the extract from *The Millstone* by Margaret Drabble; 8.6 Anthony Sheil Associates Ltd for the extract from *The French Lieutenant's Woman* by John Fowles; Jonathan Cape Ltd, William Wharton and Alfred A. Knopf Inc for the extract from *Dad* by William Wharton; 11.2 and 11.3 *The Times* for the articles which appeared on 1.5.84 and 25.6.84; 12.2 *New Internationalist*; 13.2 Laurence Pollinger Ltd, the Estate of Alan Moorehead and Harper & Row Publishers Inc for the extract from *The Fatal Impact* by Alan Moorehead copyright © 1966 by Alan Moorehead; 13.4 Times Books Ltd and Hammond Inc for the extract from *The Times Atlas of World History*; 13.6 Hamish Hamilton Ltd for the extract from *The Second World War* by A. J. P. Taylor; 14.3 *The Sunday Times*; 15.2 A. P. Watt Ltd for the extract from *Goodbye to All That* by Robert Graves; 15.3 Chatto & Windus and W. W. Norton & Co Inc for 'Futility' by Wilfred Owen reprinted from *Wilfred Owen, The Complete Poems and Fragments*, edited by John Stallworthy copyright © by the Executors of Harold Owen's Estate, 1963 and 1983; George Sassoon and Viking Penguin Inc for 'The General' by Siegfried Sassoon from *Collected Poems* copyright © 1918, 1920 by E. P. Dutton & Co, 1936, 1946, 1947, 1948 by Siegfried Sassoon, published by the Viking Press in January 1949; 15.11 Franklin D. Roosevelt Library; 16.6 Sinclair Vehicles; 17.2 Nicholas Enterprises Ltd for the extract from *Mammals of the Seas* by R. M. Martin; 17.3, 17.4 and 17.6 Collins Publishers for the extracts from *The Stationary Ark* by Gerald Durrell and from *Life on Earth* by David Attenborough; 18.2(1) Victor Gollancz Ltd and Continuum Publishing Co for the extract from *Crowds and Power* by Elias Canetti, English translation copyright © 1962, 1973 by Victor Gollancz Ltd; 18.2(2) William Heinemann Ltd for the extract from *Delight* by J. B. Priestley; 18.5 Anne Bonsall for the article which appeared in *The Times* on 22.6.84.

Communication activities: 2, 5 and 38 Longman for the extracts from *Longman Lexicon of Contemporary English*; 6 Tate Gallery for 'Past and Present No. 2' by Augustus Egg; 8, 47 and 76 Thomas Cook Holidays for extracts from the Rankin Kuhn brochure; 10, 24, 41 and 48 Reuters; 13 and 51 American Express Europe Ltd; 13 and 51 British Telecom Radiopaging; 14 and 42 United Press International; 15, 53 and 74 Tessa Sayle Literary and Dramatic Agency for the extracts from *Up the Garden Path* by Sue Limb; 18 and 57 *The Sunday Times* for the article which appeared on 23.5.82; 19 Ericsson Information Services Ltd; 21 and 61 Muller, Blond and White Ltd and Harper & Row Publishers Inc for the extracts from *Small is Beautiful* by E. F. Schumacher copyright © 1973 by E. F. Schumacher; 23 City of Manchester Art Gallery for 'Answering the Emigrant's Letter' by James Collinson; 26 Tate Gallery for 'Bank Holiday' by Strang; 32 and 43 Davis Group Ltd; 40 Oxford University Press for the extract from *Oxford Advanced Learner's Dictionary of Current English* by A. S. Hornby; 44 Parfums Givenchy Ltd; 49 Tate Gallery for 'Portsmouth Dockyard' by James Tissot; 54 Equity and Law Life Assurance Society; 70 Russell-Cotes Art Gallery and Museum, Bournemouth for 'A Tempting Bait' by Arthur J. Elsey; 73 Tate Gallery for 'Past and Present No. 1' by Augustus Egg; 77 Agence France Presse; 79 Tate Gallery for 'Past and Present No. 3' by Augustus Egg.

For permission to reproduce photographs: English Tourist Board for 1.1 and communication activities 1 and 37; London Express News and Features Services for 1.10; Charlotte Attwood, Nigel Luckhurst and Jeremy Pembrey for the photographs in 3.1; Cornwall County Council for the photographs of Looe and Fowey and Lynton Tourist Information

Centre for the photograph of Lynmouth in 4.9; Speedbird Holidays for the photograph of the hotel and Lions of Longleat and Jarrold Colour Publications for the photograph of the lion in 4.11; *The Sunday Times* for the photograph by Louise Gubb, dated 1.7.84, in 5.11; *The Guardian* for 9.6, by Denis Thorpe; *The Times* for 10.9, by Derek Cattani, dated 23.5.82; National Army Museum for 13.11; *The Guardian* for 14.6, by E. Hamilton West; Sinclair Vehicles for 16.6; London Express News and Feature Services for the photograph in communication activity 3, by Philip Dunn, which appeared in *The Daily Express*; *The Guardian* for the photographs in communication activities 16, 28, 36 (by Denis Thorpe), 59, 66 (by Don McPhee) and 72 (by Denis Thorpe); Windsor Safari Park for the photograph in communication activity 35; Nigel Luckhurst for the photograph in communication activity 42.

The cartoons are all reproduced by kind permission of *Punch*.
Artwork by Gecko Ltd, Wenham Arts, Chris Evans and Reg Piggott
Book design by Peter Ducker MSTD